# No More Kin

# Understanding Families

*Series Editors: Bert N. Adams, University of Wisconsin*
*David M. Klein, University of Notre Dame*

This book series examines a wide range of subjects relevant to studying families. Topics include parenthood, mate selection, marriage, divorce and remarriage, custody issues, culturally and ethnically based family norms, theory and conceptual design, family power dynamics, families and the law, research methods on the family, and family violence.

The series is aimed primarily at scholars working in family studies, sociology, psychology, social work, ethnic studies, gender studies, cultural studies, and related fields as they focus on the family. Volumes will also be useful for graduate and undergraduate courses in sociology of the family, family relations, family and consumer sciences, social work and the family, family psychology, family history, cultural perspectives on the family, and others.

Books appearing in **Understanding Families** are either single- or multiple- authored volumes or concisely edited books of original chapters on focused topics within the broad interdisciplinary field of marriage and family.

The books are reports of significant research, innovations in methodology, treatises on family theory, syntheses of current knowledge in a family subfield, or advanced textbooks. Each volume meets the highest academic standards and makes a substantial contribution to our understanding of marriages and families.

The National Council on Family Relations cosponsors with Sage a book award for students and new professionals. Award-winning manuscripts are published as part of the **Understanding Families** series.

*Multiracial Couples: Black and White Voices*
Paul C. Rosenblatt, Terri A. Karis, and Richard D. Powell

*Understanding Latino Families: Scholarship, Policy, and Practice*
Edited by Ruth E. Zambrana

*Current Widowhood: Myths & Realities*
Helena Znaniecka Lopata

*Family Theories: An Introduction*
David M. Klein and James M. White

*Understanding Differences Between Divorced and Intact Families*
Ronald L. Simons and Associates

*Adolescents, Work, and Family: An Intergenerational Developmental Analysis*
Jeylan T. Mortimer and Michael D. Finch

*Families and Time: Keeping Pace in a Hurried Culture*
Kerry J. Daly

*Parenting: Contemporary Issues and Challenges*
Edited by Terry Arendell

*No More Kin: Exploring Race, Class, and Gender in Family Networks*
Anne R. Roschelle

Anne R. Roschelle

# No More Kin

## Exploring Race, Class, and Gender in Family Networks

UNDERSTANDING FAMILIES

TABOR COLLEGE LIBRARY
HILLSBORO, KANSAS 67063
981025

Copyright © 1997 by Sage Publications, Inc.

All rights reserved. No part of this book may be reproduced or utilized in any form or by any means, electronic or mechanical, including photocopying, recording, or by any information storage and retrieval system, without permission in writing from the publisher.

---

*For information:*

SAGE Publications, Inc.
2455 Teller Road
Thousand Oaks, California 91320
E-mail: order@sagepub.com

SAGE Publications Ltd.
6 Bonhill Street
London EC2A 4PU
United Kingdom

SAGE Publications India Pvt. Ltd.
M-32 Market
Greater Kailash I
New Delhi 110 048 India

Printed in the United States of America

*Library of Congress Cataloging-in-Publication Data*

Roschelle, Anne R.
No more kin: Exploring race, class, and gender in family networks / Anne R. Roschelle.
p. cm.—(Understanding families; v. 8)
Includes bibliographical references (p. ) and index.
ISBN 0-7619-0158-2 (cloth: acid-free paper).—ISBN 0-7619-0159-0 (pbk.: acid-free paper)
1. Family—United States. 2. Kinship—United States. 3. Household—United States. 4. Social networks—United States. 5. Minorities—United States—Family relationships. 6. Minorities—United States—Social networks. I. Title. II. Series.
HQ536R65 1997
306.85'0973—dc21 97-4677

97 98 99 00 01 02 03 10 9 8 7 6 5 4 3 2 1

---

*Acquiring Editor:* Margaret N. Zusky
*Editorial Assistant:* Renée Piernot
*Production Editor:* Diana E. Axelsen
*Production Assistant:* Karen Wiley
*Typesetter/Designer:* Yang-hee Syn Maresca
*Indexer:* Trish Wittenstein
*Print Buyer:* Anna Chin

# Contents

# Preface

The vitriolic debate on welfare reform that is currently sweeping the nation assumes that if institutional mechanisms of social support are eliminated, impoverished families will simply rely on an extensive web of kinship networks for their survival. Because extended support networks historically have been found in minority communities, this argument reflects the belief that welfare recipients are primarily people of color. Consequently, the political discourse surrounding poverty and welfare reform has become increasingly racialized. The implementation of social policy that presupposes the availability of familial safety nets in minority communities could have disastrous consequences for individuals who do not have access to extended kin networks. Therefore, it is imperative for social scientists to determine whether or not extended social support networks traditionally found in minority communities continue to flourish.[1]

During the past 25 years, there has been much debate over the nature and extent of informal social support networks, especially among minority families. The initial discussion centered around the argument that "pathological" elements inherent in minority cultures were responsible for deviant family structures. Black families were depicted as being matriarchal, disorganized, and ultimately dysfunctional, whereas Latino families were characterized as rigidly patriarchal (Bermudez, 1955; Heller, 1966; Lewis, 1966; Moynihan, 1965; Rainwater, 1966). Extended households and elaborate social support networks among minority families were seen as deviations from the norm of the middle-class White nuclear family.

As a direct response to and rejection of the pathological approach, alternative perspectives were advanced. Some scholars suggested that extended kin networks were a reflection of positive cultural norms endemic to minority communities (Aschbrenner, 1978; Billingsley, 1968, 1992; Hill, 1972; Montiel, 1970; Nobles, 1974; Romano, 1968). Other scholars argued that extended living arrangements and informal social support networks represent survival strategies used to mitigate against the deleterious effects of poverty (Adams, 1968a, 1970; Allen, 1979; McAdoo, 1980; Stack, 1974). More recently, scholars have begun to integrate social structural and cultural perspectives by examining how the intersections of race, class, and gender affect family organization.[2]

Using an integrative framework, this book examines extended kinship networks among African American, Chicano, Puerto Rican, and non-Hispanic White[3] families in contemporary America. I have selected these four racial-ethnic[4] groups for several reasons. First and foremost, my expertise in the area of racial and ethnic minorities is on African Americans, Chicanos, and Puerto Ricans. In addition, although the National Survey of Families and Households (NSFH), from which I draw my data, includes Native Americans and Cubans, in both cases they comprise less than 1% of the sample, making comparisons problematic. Furthermore, the categories "other Hispanic" and "Asian American" consolidate distinct Latino and Asian American ethnic groups, homogenizing their unique sociohistorical experiences. Finally, the inclusion of non-Hispanic Whites in the sample is necessary because the literature on minority families claims that they are less likely to participate in extended kinship networks than are Latinos and Blacks.

An important component of participation in kin networks is extended households. Household structure is defined as extended if the household includes any nonrelatives or any relatives other than the spouse or children of the main householder. This definition requires that some individuals other than the main householder's nuclear family be present (Anderson & Allen, 1984). Extended family members may be children, or they may be adults, as long as they are not the spouse or children of the household head.

In addition to extended living arrangements, a second major component of kin networks is informal social support networks. Informal social support networks are characterized by frequent interaction, close affective bonds, and exchanges of goods and services among family and nonfamily members who typically live in close proximity to one another but *not* in the same household. The mutual aid that defines these networks can be either emotional or socioeconomic (see Litwak, 1960b; Sussman, 1965). Members of this informal social support network interact by choice and are connected to one another by means of mutual aid and social activities (Cantor, 1979; Taylor, 1986).

There are many different types of mutual aid exchanged in social support networks. Expressive aid includes offering general daily advice and providing emotional support during times of crisis or stress. The expressive function of the social support network is primarily to help solve socioemotional problems. The exchange of emotional support does not necessarily require close proximity of network members, as in the case of frequent phone contact (Aldous & Klein, 1991; Litwak & Kulis, 1987).[5]

Instrumental aid includes assistance with child care, grocery shopping, and division of household labor. Instrumental help can also include monetary exchanges; intrahousehold division of expenses; and exchanges of goods and services, such as food stamps, clothing, and furniture. Although there are no exact statistics accounting for the prevalence of extended social support networks, there is an abundance of social science research that analyzes various aspects of these networks and depicts them as common elements of minority family life. Women frequently comprise the core of the extended family network because of their role in child care and household work (e.g., see Adams, 1968b; Aschbrenner, 1973; Keefe, Padilla, & Carlos, 1979; McAdoo, 1980; Stack, 1974).

When talking about kinship networks, it is important to recognize that they customarily include both family and friends. Network members rarely differentiate between blood relatives, relatives acquired through marriage, and fictive kin. Therefore, in my discussions of social support networks, unless I specifically make a distinction between family and nonfamily network members, I am referring to both.

Because of the historical significance of extended networks in racial-ethnic communities, many scholars and political analysts assume that thriving kin and nonkin social support networks continue to characterize minority family life. However, policy recommendations based on these underlying assumptions may lead to the implementation of harmful social policy. In recent years, there has been some concern over the increasing isolation of minority groups as a result of persistent residential segregation (Massey & Denton, 1993), escalating economic deprivation, and the influx of drugs to low-income, minority communities. Some scholars speculate that a result of this social isolation is a decline in the prevalence of household extension and informal social support networks (Anderson, 1990; Collins, 1990; Jewell, 1988; Ladner & Gourdine, 1984; Wilson, 1987; Zinn, 1989). The hypothesized decline in extended kinship networks would represent the erosion of a historical safety net. Subsequently, severe cutbacks in social service programs may devastate minority families. In this book, I explore the nature and extent of informal social support networks, examine a priori assumptions about the persistence of kin networks in racial-ethnic communities, and determine whether there are racial and gender differences in the likelihood of participation in the extended kinship network. The decline in network participation among minority families alluded to in recent years is substantiated empirically by the findings of this research.

The brief discussion above reveals the importance of studying extended household living arrangements and informal social support networks. However, despite the plethora of literature on this subject, numerous gaps in our knowledge remain. Past research has focused primarily on homogeneous ethnic enclaves. Although these studies have provided rich detail about the daily lives of network members, they are rarely comparative and are not generalizable.

One contribution of this study will be to use data from the NSFH to analyze a nationally representative sample of extended kin and nonkin networks. Analysis of these data will allow me to draw more general conclusions about minority families living in the United States. The oversampling of Blacks, Chicanos, and Puerto Ricans provides me with a unique opportunity to compare and contrast minority families with one another and with non-Hispanic Whites, thus exploring diverse family forms. In addition, the effect of household composition on participation in social support networks will be examined to determine whether the presence of extended household members facilitates or hinders network participation. Another unique contribution of this research is the separate examination of Chicano and Puerto Rican families. There has been a tendency in the sociological literature to ignore the unique sociopolitical histories, migration patterns, and cultural norms of these two ethnic groups and simply lump them together for the purpose of more manageable analysis.

Finally, most of the research examining social support networks was done prior to the 1980s. Recent anecdotal evidence suggests that extended kinship networks traditionally associated with minority communities may no longer persist (Anderson, 1990; Collins, 1990; Facio, 1993; Jewell, 1988). However, there has been very little empirical research examining the availability of kin networks in recent years. In this book, I analyze network participation systematically among a national sample of minority families. The results of my research indicate that informal social support networks typically found in minority communities are not as pervasive as they were in the past.

This research also address gaps in the theoretical literature. Past theoretical approaches have attributed participation in extended kinship networks to either social structural or cultural factors. However, simplistic notions of culture versus structure have hindered the development of a broader theoretical paradigm (Wilson, 1991) from which to examine determinants of household extension and informal social support networks. This study seeks to provide an integrated theoretical framework for examining how the simultaneity of gender, race, and class oppression affects minority family organization. By framing my empirical analysis within what I call the culture-structure nexus[6] and focusing on participation in informal social support networks, I can develop new theoretical interpretations of minority family life. This is an important theoretical contribution because feminist scholarship sometimes lacks historical specificity and minimizes the interrelationships of diverse axes of oppression (Bordo, 1993). Therefore, the book examines both economic and cultural determinants of participation in extended social support networks for each racial-ethnic group while simultaneously examining the effects of gender.

Finally, a major goal of this research is to determine whether or not Black and Latino families are more familistic (i.e., attitudes, values, and beliefs that give primacy to the family over the individual) than non-Hispanic White families, or if, in fact, participation in social support networks is less prevalent than implied by both the theoretical and empirical literature. Depicting minority family structure accurately may have important implications for policymakers who sometimes assume that extended kinship networks ameliorate sufficiently the damaging effects of poverty. The book investigates determinants of participation in informal social support networks among African American, Chicano, Puerto Rican, and non-Hispanic White families. The data come from the NSFH, which was conducted in the United States from March 1987 through May 1988. Chapters 1 through 3 present the major theoretical tenets commonly used by past researchers to examine minority families, including the culture of poverty perspective, the strength resiliency perspective, and the structural or economic perspective. In addition, a more integrative approach that investigates the impact of cultural and social structural factors on family life is discussed.

The integrative approach examines how the simultaneity of race, class, and gender affects minority family organization, and it represents the theoretical framework on which my analysis of participation in support networks is predicated. In developing this theoretical framework, it becomes necessary to examine the intricate web of practices, institutions, and cultural norms that sustain positions of dominance and subordination in a particular domain (Bordo, 1993). My research aims to develop new theoretical interpretations of the multiple axes of race, gender, and class inequality by examining the complexities of mutual aid exchanged within the family domain. Essentially, this book extends the integrative perspective by applying it to a historically specific empirical case.

Implicit in the integrative perspective is the assumption that race, gender, and class represent interacting categories of oppression. Given the vast amount of research that documents racial-ethnic, gender, and class stratification (e.g., see Almaguer, 1994; Amott & Matthaei, 1991; Anderson & Collins, 1992; Chow, Wilkinson, & Zinn, 1996; Davis, 1991; Ezekiel, 1995; Glenn, 1985; Reskin & Hartmann, 1986; Rothenberg, 1995; Zinn & Dill, 1994) in American society, this research also presupposes the presence of race, gender, and class oppression and therefore does not measure it directly. Accordingly, throughout the book, I will refer to race, gender, and class as interacting hierarchies of power and domination.

These chapters also review the empirical research on household extension and informal social support networks. Chapters 1 through 3 document the historical legacy of extended kin networks that were pervasive in minority communities. The presence of both cultural norms and economic survival strategies promoting the maintenance of informal networks is made evident.

These chapters do not include a review of the literature on extended kinship networks for non-Hispanic White families. This book is an attempt to bring previously marginalized groups into the center of research and theory (Andersen, 1988) and to articulate aspects of their experiences that have been ignored (Glenn, 1985) or distorted by mainstream sociologists. The early, "classic" work on American kinship focused primarily on White ethnic families, ignoring racial and ethnic minorities. The findings from this research were frequently generalized to the American population, treating non-Hispanic Whites as the normative group by which to judge all American families. In addition, some scholars argue that non-Hispanic White families have never been characterized by extensive participation in kin and nonkin networks (Coontz, 1992; Hareven, 1978).[7] Nevertheless, non-Hispanic White respondents are included in multivariate analyses because the literature on racial-ethnic families frequently argues that Whites participate less in social support networks than do minority group members.

In Chapter 4, I describe the methods of analysis employed in the research. Chapter 5 presents the results of the descriptive statistics, which indicate that both men and women do participate in support networks, but their participation is divided along traditional gender lines. Women are responsible for child care, and men are responsible for household repairs. This gender role behavior does not differ by race, demonstrating the intractability of gender stratification. In Chapter 6, I discuss patterns of giving and receiving child care help from family and nonfamily network members for women. Surprisingly, women of color are not more likely than Anglo women to participate in child care networks. Chapter 7 presents patterns of giving and receiving household assistance from family and friends for men and also finds network participation more prevalent among non-Hispanic Whites than among men of color. Finally, Chapter 8 synthesizes empirical findings with a discussion of the erosion of informal social support networks in racial-ethnic communities. The theoretical implication of these findings is that interacting systems of race and class oppression prevent people of color from achieving their familistic identities. Minority group members are, in fact, highly familistic and want to participate actively in exchange networks.[8] However, the constraints of a hostile economic system prevent them from participating in exchange networks. Consequently, minority group members are oppressed both culturally and economically: They are unable to live by the values essential to their cultural survival because they are economically disenfranchised. Given that individuals with more education and economic resources were more likely to participate in kin and nonkin networks, it is evident that cultural norms are indeed constrained by class oppression.

## Notes

1. Participation in informal social support networks among women of color has been well documented by historians and social scientists alike. The most frequently cited work depicting extended kinship networks is Carol Stack's extraordinary book *All Our Kin,* published in 1974. I do not dispute the findings of Stack's book nor of other research that illustrated the prevalence of thriving kin and nonkin networks within minority communities. Rather, it is my contention that there has been a historical decline in the availability of extended kinship networks in the past 20 years. The title of my book, *No More Kin,* is a reflection of this decline.

2. Throughout the book, I discuss various aspects of family and household configuration. I use the terms *family* and *household organization, structure,* and *composition* synonymously to refer to the actual makeup (e.g., single-parent family, extended family, presence of children under age 5, etc.) of that family or household. The terms *household* and *family structure and organization* should *not* be confused with the structural economic perspective, which refers to socioeconomic resources and institutions at the macro level.

3. I use the terms *African American* and *Black* interchangeably to refer to Americans with either African or Caribbean heritage. The NSFH does not distinguish between Blacks of African descent and Blacks of Caribbean descent. Subsequently, the use of these terms synonymously is meant to encompass both groups. The term *Chicana/o* was adopted by Mexican Americans during the height of the Chicana/o civil rights movement to symbolize their identification with Mexico and with their Indian heritage. Although some Americans of Mexican descent prefer the term Mexican American, Chicana/o reflects a more politicized viewpoint. *Puerto Rican* refers to respondents who were born in Puerto Rico or are descendants of individuals born in Puerto Rico. Finally, *non-*

*Hispanic White* refers to individuals who are Caucasian and have European ancestry. Because these categorizations are socially constructed and not biologically determined, they are configured and reconfigured over time and across geographic location.

4. The term *racial-ethnic* denotes groups that are simultaneously racial and ethnic minorities. I use it throughout the book to refer collectively to Blacks, Puerto Ricans, and Chicanos because they share a legacy of economic disenfranchisement and racialized forms of oppression.

5. The focus of this book is solely on the exchange of instrumental aid. Although an examination of expressive assistance would be enlightening, the scope of the book was becoming too unwieldy to include yet another dimension of social support. Future research on network participation should include an analysis of expressive aid in kin and nonkin networks.

6. I would like to thank Rebecca Chiyoko King for suggesting the phrase *culture-structure nexus* to reflect my synthesis of the cultural and structural perspectives.

7. Much of the early research on American kinship debated whether extended families evolved into isolated nuclear families as a result of industrialization (Linton, 1949 as cited in Adams, 1970; Parsons, 1943), in which they were better suited to industrial capitalism than consanguineal families (Goode, 1963); became modified extended families in which kin no longer lived in intergenerational households (Litwak, 1960a, 1960b; Sussman & Burchinal, 1962); or were always predominantly nuclear (Laslett, 1977). For an excellent review of this literature, see Sussman (1965), Adams (1970), and Lee (1980).

8. Because of inadequate measures of familism (reported in Chapters 6 and 7), I was unable to test directly the importance of cultural norms among respondents in the NSFH sample. However, in a qualitative follow-up study of Puerto Rican women, the presence of familism was clearly evident (see Roschelle, 1997).

# Acknowledgments

I can never express the depth of gratitude I have for Glenna Spitze, Karyn Loscocco, and Chris Bose, all of whom have contributed to my professional development in innumerable ways. As mentors, they taught me the rigors of sociological research and how to demand excellence from my students while providing them with support and guidance. I want to especially thank my good friend Karyn, whose relentless critiques of my writing and sarcastic wit have guided me throughout my sojourn in academia. I would also like to thank my newest mentor, Jennifer Turpin, a wonderfully supportive colleague and friend who encouraged me to publish this book despite my doubts. Thanks to them and to all the other feminist scholars who preceded me and created a space within which I could thrive.

Thank you to David M. Klein and Bert N. Adams, the editors of the Sage series *Understanding Families,* for their constant encouragement throughout this project. Dave and Bert's confidence in my work and their willingness to share their wisdom with me were truly inspiring. Thanks also to Jim Nageotte, who encouraged Sage to publish my manuscript, to my editor, Margaret Zusky, for her insightful comments and tireless work, and to Reneé Piernot (Editorial Assistant) and Diana Axelsen (Production Editor) for their excellent guidance. My student assistant, Patricia Alvarez, deserves thanks for all the work she did that enabled me to finish this project.

I would also like to thank my parents, Stanley and Irma, my brothers, Steven and Richard, and my Aunt Bernice for their endless encouragement and for never saying, "So . . . what are you . . . a social worker?"

Thanks to Marcia, Ray, Sarah, Amanda, and Blaze for all those wonderful free dinners at El Loco and most especially for allowing me to be part of your remarkable family. Thank you, Lenny and Marilyn Siegel, for including me in your warmhearted Passover seders. To my extraordinary friend Pamela Cubbage, with whom I share backpacking and travel adventures beyond comparison. Thanks to Chris Nemeth, Brenda and George Grober, Wendy Furst, Maria Zementauski and Jackie Baldwin, Maya Rhinewine, Rose Lazarro, and especially James V. Miller for helping me to hold on to my sanity and for keeping me laughing. To my newest friends Karen Bouwer, Lois Lorentzen, Tracy Seeley, and Pedro Lange-Churion—thanks for making the transition to my new life a smooth yet riotous one. Without the support of my parents, my brothers, and my extended family, this book would not exist.

Finally, I would like to thank Nico, whose unconditional love keeps me warm on those raw San Francisco summer nights.

*For my dad, who taught us all*
*what a family should be*

# 1

# The Cultural Context of Care

The following chapter is an explanation of the cultural approach to the study of minority families. In the ensuing discussion, I will first examine the culture of poverty or pathological approach, followed by the cultural relativity or strength resiliency approach. After explaining each theoretical perspective, I will present the empirical literature that has been guided by these two perspectives. Both approaches attempt to explain the existence of extended living arrangements and informal social support among minority families, and each is predicated upon a particular ideological viewpoint. Although many sociologists contend that theoretical frameworks based on ideological considerations are not "scientific," I would argue that most theories contain a priori assumptions about social reality and are rarely value neutral. Similarly, Max Weber (1994) argued that "all knowledge of cultural reality, as may be seen, is always knowledge from particular points of view" (p. 257). The culture of poverty and the strength resiliency perspectives clearly represent value-laden theorizing.

## Theoretical Frameworks

### THE CULTURE OF POVERTY

#### *African Americans*

The current pathological approach to African American families can be traced to the work of E. Franklin Frazier (1932, 1939, 1949), who attempted to explain the condition of the Black family in the 1920s and 1930s. His analysis of the African American family was an attempt to refute previous research that presented the behavior of all Black families as uniformly disorganized. He was one of the first scholars to demonstrate the diversity in familial conduct in the Black community by examining the role of class differences (Gutman, 1973). Frazier vehemently rejected arguments attributing high rates of out-of-wedlock births, marital instability, and family disorganization among Blacks to innate biological deficiencies (Allen, 1979). However, despite his rejection of models predicated on biological determinism, Frazier's analysis was also problematic.

In conducting his historical analysis, Frazier (1939) observed two different types of Black family life. The more prevalent type was a matriarchal family with high rates of illegitimacy that he argued was directly influenced by the conditions of slavery and rural southern life. Frazier (1932, 1939) believed that marital instability and sexual permissiveness in the matriarchal Black family were a result of the disruptive forces of slavery, emancipation, and migration, which eroded the cultural bases for kinship and healthy family relations among Blacks (Allen, 1978). The second, less common, type of family was the two-parent, male-headed family that existed among a small group of middle-class, property-owning artisans. Because very few African Americans owned property or were skilled craftspeople, Frazier (1939) concluded that the matriarchal family was more common, and therefore it became the focus of his research (Gutman, 1973). Frazier (1939) argued that the widespread disorganization that characterized the urban Black experience in the 1920s and 1930s was a result of unstable matriarchal families that could be traced back to the conditions of slavery.

Frazier (1949) asserted that as a result of slavery, the "Negro's African cultural Heritage had practically no effect on the evolution of his family in the United States" (Mathis, 1978, p. 668). He believed that all significant African cultural traits were essentially destroyed during slavery (Dodson, 1988; Mathis, 1978). Consequently, Frazier (1939) argued that the slave household was characterized by a fatherless, matrifocal pattern that became self-sustaining over time and was transmitted intergenerationally. Similarly, Osofsky (1963) argued that "slavery initially destroyed the entire concept of family for American Negroes and the slave heritage, bulwarked by economic conditions, continued into the twentieth century to make family instability a common factor in Negro life" (as cited in Gutman, 1973, p. 470). Furthermore, it was argued that emancipation was a crisis for the Black family, which no longer had the master's authority to regulate sexual and conjugal behavior. According to Frazier (1932), "When the yoke of slavery was lifted, the drifting masses were left without any restraint upon their vagrant impulses and wild desires" (as cited in Gutman, 1973, p. 471).

It is important to note that Frazier's analysis of the Black family was not based on race per se but rather on the effects of slavery on the Black community. In fact, Frazier did recognize that the structural constraints of slavery precipitated the loss of African cultural identity. However, in his discussion of the Black family, Frazier focused primarily on cultural pathology, rendering social structure negligible. Other scholars argued that racial inferiority was the cause of family breakdown among postbellum Blacks. African Americans were consistently depicted as sexually promiscuous animals who, without the protection of their masters, were doomed to lives of total chaos. It was argued that Blacks were incapable of entering into monogamous relationships and had not developed feelings of concern that "normal" kinspeople usually share. In fact, freedmen and -women were characterized as having no marital traditions and being totally devoid of family mores. With slavery abolished, Blacks could no longer be protected from their promiscuity and depravity (Bruce, 1889; Fitzhugh, 1866; Toombs, 1871; all as cited in Gutman, 1973, 1976).

These pervasive assumptions about the negative effects of the abolition of slavery on the family led Frazier (1939) to conclude that the typical Black family in the rural and urban South between 1855 and 1880 was headed by a female. He argued that female-headed households had become a legitimized family form by women who eschewed the traditional nuclear family. Out-of-wedlock motherhood was accepted by a large number of Black women, who imparted similar values to their offspring. He contended that these matriarchal families were especially common among ex-slaves and nonskilled laborers (Gutman, 1973). Finally, he asserted that this disorganization was transmitted via family values that resulted in a self-perpetuating tradition of fragmented, pathological interaction within lower-class Black urban communities (Allen, 1979). This self-perpetuating cycle of hopelessness and destitution that was used erroneously to typify African American families subsequently has been termed the culture of poverty (Lewis, 1959). In an attempt to refute Frazier's claims that the Black family was characterized by chaos and disorder, Herbert Gutman (1976) reconstructed the household structure for the entire Black population in Buffalo, New York, between 1855 and 1875, and he sampled households in 1905 as well as in 1925. He also collected data on New York City; Troy, New York; Mobile, Alabama; Richmond, Virginia; Charleston, South Carolina; Beaufort, South Carolina; Natchez, Mississippi; and several other southern townships and counties. He also gathered historical documents from the Freedmen's Bureau in the National Archives. In all, Gutman (1976) analyzed detailed information about the composition of nearly 19,000 African American households of differing social and economic classes between 1850 and 1880. The diversity of the respondents' communities allowed a comparison of antebellum free Blacks in southern and northern cities as well as between urban and rural communities. Gutman (1976) examined whether there were, in fact, two streams of African American family life and whether the matriarchal household was as widespread as Frazier (1939) hypothesized.

Gutman (1976) found that most antebellum free Blacks in the North and South lived in two-parent households, and so did most poor rural and urban freedmen and -women. Many of the communities studied consisted of primarily urban and rural lower-income families. In addition, the fact that only 15 years after slavery ended, three out of every four Black families sampled that were headed by ex-slaves were two-parent households casts serious doubt on the proposition that class factors such as income, skill, property, and middle-class occupations determine the presence of two-parent families (Gutman, 1976). Because most of the families were headed by nonskilled workers, it seems clear that the composition of the Black household was not determined solely by income, skill, and property, as Frazier (1949) had suggested. Furthermore, the existence of two distinct types of Black family forms was not supported by Gutman (1976).

To examine the cultural mythology of Black matriarchy, Gutman (1976) created three objective measures of matriarchy as a form of household and family organization. He assessed the presence of males and of older females in the household and the earning power of women as compared to men. Percentages of two-parent families for 14 different northern and southern Black communities between 1855 and 1880 demonstrated that males (usually husbands) were found in at least 70% and as many as 90% of the households examined. Female-headed households existed but were certainly not typical. In addition, the age distribution among female-headed families illustrates that a large proportion of these families were the result of the husband's death. Therefore, Frazier's (1939) depiction of the three-generation matriarchal Black family was historically incorrect. Finally, unskilled, Black male laborers earned two to three times more per week than did female servants or washerwomen (Gutman, 1976), disputing Frazier's (1939) argument that Black men were subordinate to Black women because of their weak economic and social position in society (Allen, 1978).

More recent attempts to reconstruct the 19th-century Black family also indicate that household structure (marriage, divorce, fertility, and two-parent household rates) was similar between Blacks and Whites following the Civil War, and any differences that did exist were a result of regional variations in particular socioeconomic conditions (e.g., see Adams, 1995; Landale & Tolnay, 1991; Staples, 1988; Tolnay, 1983; Walker, 1988). This research provides compelling evidence that slavery did not destroy the Black family. In fact, anthropological research has shown that the structure of the Black family was a unique cultural form that evolved from familial and kinship patterns emanating from the conditions of slavery as well as from African cultural attributes (Herskovitz, 1941).

### *The Moynihan Report*

Despite Frazier's (1932, 1939, 1949) lack of accurate historical evidence, his argument that slavery rendered the Black family pathological gained widespread acceptance by both scholars and policymakers. The myth of the Black matriarchy reached its pinnacle with Daniel Patrick Moynihan's 1965 report for the Office of Policy Planning and Research of the U.S. Department of Labor titled *The Negro Family: A Case for National Action.* Moynihan (1965) portrayed the Black community as being characterized by female-headed households, high rates of illegitimacy, divorce, matriarchy, economic dependence, unemployment, delinquency, crime, and failure to pass armed forces entrance exams. Frequently citing Frazier (1939) to support his conclusions, Moynihan (1965) argued that the "tangle of pathology" confronting the Black community was caused by unstable Black families (Dodson, 1988; Martin & Martin, 1978; Mathis, 1978). He further argued that the precarious nature of low-income Black families was a direct result of female-dominated, and thus dysfunctional, households that commonly existed within the Black community (Allen, 1978; Martin & Martin, 1978; Moynihan, 1965; Staples, 1981). Matriarchal families were blamed for unemployment, low educational attainment, poverty, and desertion, and they were considered detrimental to the personality development of Black children and to the development of normal heterosexual roles in Black males (Martin & Martin, 1978; Rainwater, 1965).

Although Moynihan situated his analysis of the Black family within an economic framework, he attributed family disintegration to deviant cultural norms rather than to the ravages of poverty. Furthermore, proponents of the pathological approach argued that Black families have different values and cultural beliefs, and make no attempt to integrate themselves into the opportunity structure, resulting in the emergence and perpetuation of a culture of poverty (Aschbrenner, 1978; Moynihan, 1965). The main thesis of the culture of poverty perspective is that poor people have distinctive values, aspirations, and psychological characteristics that inhibit their achievement and produce behavioral deficiencies that keep them impoverished. Through socialization, these deficiencies are transmitted to their children, which results in a perpetual cycle of poverty (Zinn, 1989). Consequently, all of the social problems extant in Black ghettos were blamed solely on the breakdown of the family (see also Bernard, 1966; Liebow, 1967; Rainwater, 1970). Moynihan (1965) rejected racism as a pivotal force in the perpetuation of poverty by asserting that the tangle of pathology was "capable of perpetuating itself without assistance from the white world" (Zinn, 1989, p. 850). In addition, his major policy recommendation was for Black women to relinquish control of the Black community and restructure the family according to a White, middle-class, patriarchal model (Moynihan, 1965).

### *African American Culture of Poverty: Critique*

There are numerous flaws in the culture of poverty perspective on the Black family. A major problem is that the entire framework is predicated on the assumption of a White, middle-class, normative model. Inherent in this assumption is the denial of an African cultural heritage that uniquely characterizes the Black family. Consequently, positive Black family traits such as extended kinship networks are viewed as deviant and disorganized.

Second, referring to Black women as matriarchs is historically inaccurate (Staples, 1973). A matriarchal society is one in which most of the legal power relating to property, inheritance, marriage, and the running of the household is relegated to women. Although it is clear that Black women have had to be strong to facilitate familial survival, they have certainly not been domineering (Ladner, 1972). The cultural stereotype of the matriarchal Black woman negates the experiences of masses of Black women who have been exploited economically, sexually, and politically by the continuous onslaught of White racism.

Furthermore, the notion that Black females gained power in Black society through their economic support of the family is erroneous. As Gutman (1976) pointed out, during the 19th century, unskilled Black male laborers consistently earned more than their female counterparts. Currently, Black women who work full-time consistently earn less than White male, White female, and Black male full-time workers (Fox & Hesse-Biber, 1984; Staples, 1981; Treiman & Hartmann, 1981). Therefore, it is absurd to argue that Black women who work full-time have an economic advantage over their Black male counterparts. It is, however, true that Black male unemployment rates are persistently high. The fact that Black males suffer from the irregularity of unemployment (Wilson, 1987) is not due to any inordinate power that Black women possess. Rather, their weakened economic position is a "result of White America's racist employment barriers" (Staples, 1981, p. 341). The effect of Black males' high unemployment rates is not Black female dominance but greater economic deprivation for families deprived of their fathers' income (Staples, 1981). Portraying Black women as matriarchs allows the dominant group to blame African American women for the failure of Black children to achieve. Arguing that Black poverty is passed on intergenerationally by a pathological value system diverts attention away from the political and economic inequality affecting Black mothers and their children (Collins, 1990).

Unlike Frazier (1939), Moynihan (1965) neglected to link Black family disorganization to slavery and racial oppression. Instead, he simply blamed Black occupational and economic inequality on family instability (Allen, 1979). In addition, Moynihan's argument that the high rate of female-headed households demonstrates the breakdown in the Black family also ignores structural economic conditions. The prevalence of female-headed households among the urban poor reflects a lack of permanent well-paying jobs for Black men (Aschbrenner, 1978), not cultural pathology, as Moynihan argued. Robert Staples argues that although a majority of Black Americans are currently living in non-nuclear families, this is not a result of cultural norms that devalue the institution of marriage. His ethnographic research has led him to argue that Blacks have very traditional attitudes toward marriage, but economic conditions have limited women's choices in finding men from a restricted pool of potential partners who can successfully fulfill the normatively prescribed familial role of provider (Staples, 1989). The myth of the Black matriarch is full of false assumptions; however, White society continues to perpetuate this myth because it creates internal antagonisms in the Black community, diffusing potential attacks on the external social structure.

### *Chicanos*

As in studies of the Black family, the culture of poverty approach to Latino families is also predicated on a middle-class, normative model. Underlying this approach is an assumption of the superiority of White, middle-class culture and the devaluation of all other family forms (Staples & Mirande, 1980). However, unlike studies of the Black family, this approach to understanding Latino families focuses on male dominance and female passivity as the key to explaining Latino family disorganization. Chicano families are presented as radically different from the dominant (presumably egalitarian) Anglo American family. The primary focus of this perspective is on the debilitating effects of *machismo* (the spiritual, physical, and sexual domination of men over women). Social and economic inequality experienced by Chicanos is blamed solely on the patriarchal structure of the Chicano family (Mirande, 1985). In fact, it is argued that machismo produces maladaptive pathological responses in Chicano family members.

Bermudez (1955) argues that because Chicanos are locked into rigid conceptions of masculinity and femininity, they have difficulty fulfilling such austere gender roles and are consequently predisposed toward neurosis (Diaz-Guerrero, 1975). According to this view, marriage does not curtail the freedom of Chicano men, who are depicted as nothing more than insatiable sexual animals. Married men stay out all night; drink; fight; have complete freedom of movement; and often establish a second household, fathering numerous illegitimate children. Along with their preoccupation with sex, Chicano men are depicted by proponents of the pathological approach as being cruel, insensitive, and condescending toward women (Williams, 1990; Ybarra, 1983).

Whereas men retain much of their autonomy after marriage, women are completely constrained by their marital and familial roles (Penalosa, 1968). The Chicana is portrayed by culture of poverty theorists as self-sacrificing and submissive (Andrade, 1982; Ybarra, 1983). She is considered too morally weak to protect herself from the sexual advances of men, a serious problem "in a community filled with males stalking their prey" (Madsen, 1964, p. 22). Because women are considered less intelligent than men, their virtue must be defended by their fathers and then later by their husbands (Ybarra, 1983). Culture of poverty theorists assert that Chicanas do not question or resent their subservient positions (Ybarra, 1983). It is further argued that women who do not accept their subordinate position or who question the authority of the male are typically subject to physical punishment or abuse (Hayden, 1966). However, some theorists argue that many women welcome this punishment because it proves the profundity of their husband's love (Madsen, 1964). Moreover, culture of poverty proponents argue that the values and norms endemic to the Chicano family result in a high level of family violence. Because the authoritarian Chicano male overemphasizes strict discipline and blind obedience to authority, violence is often used as a mechanism for conflict resolution (Carroll, 1980).

According to this view, the macho patriarch demands complete deference, respect, and obedience from his children as well as from his wife. This rigid patriarchal authority structure has extremely negative consequences for the personality development of Chicano children. Chicano children fail to develop a sense of achievement orientation, independence, self-reliance, or self-worth, traits that are highly valued in American culture. Celia Heller (1966) argues that the socialization practices of Chicano families necessarily inhibit the advancement of their children.

Culture of poverty theorists argue that Chicanos overemphasize family ties, honor, masculinity, and living in the present while denigrating the Anglo values of achievement, independence, and deferred gratification. These values produce dependence, subordination, fatalism, and a present-time orientation that interferes with advancement in American society. Paradoxically, it has also been argued that Chicanos live in a perpetual "manana land" (Samora & Lamanna, 1967, as cited in Mirande, 1985). According to Rudoff (1971), the Chicano family structure is unstable because the father is withdrawn and the mother is overly nurturing. Women are depicted as overindulgent mothers whose incessant pampering of their children prevents normal psychosexual development. Alternatively, the father is portrayed as an autocrat who remains aloof from his children (Ybarra, 1983).

In sum, the Chicano male is depicted as having little concern for the future, resigning himself to his subordinate position within the larger social structure, being overly influenced by magic, viewing authority as arbitrary, and being completely alienated from Anglo culture (Mirande, 1985). For reasons different from those argued in relation to the Black family, the Chicano family is also seen as a tangle of pathology that perpetuates the subordination of women, retards individual achievement, fosters passivity and dependence, and inhibits normal personality development (Mirande, 1985).

*Chicano Culture of Poverty: Critique*

A major defect of the pathological approach to the Chicano family is that it is completely ahistorical. There is no attempt to trace sociohistorical events that have presumably shaped this behavior. Neither Spanish colonialism (1521-1821), Mexican independence (1821), the Mexican-American war (1846-1848), the Treaty of Guadalupe Hidalgo (1848), nor immigration policies are offered as possible antecedents to Chicano family disorganization. In addition, there is very little empirical evidence that supports the pathological view. There are no studies examining the roles of Chicano men and women using nationally representative data. Depictions of Chicano families tend to be based on very small samples and the perceptions of social scientists (Andrade, 1982). In fact, the pathological view of the Chicano family is so pervasive that researchers are reluctant to abandon it even when faced with contradictory evidence (Mirande, 1985). When research findings indicate that the Chicano family is less authoritarian than hypothesized, scholars either dismiss those findings or argue that they reflect Chicano family acculturation (e.g., see Hawkes & Taylor, 1975).

Another flaw in this theoretical perspective is the monolithic portrayal of the Chicano family. Chicano families have been depicted as static, homogeneous entities that can be transformed only by their assimilation to Anglo culture (Ybarra, 1983). This pathological perspective is devoid of any analysis of the complex interaction of class, ethnicity, gender, and regional history in shaping the development of Chicano family interaction. The resulting portrayal of the Chicano family has been fallacious and overly simplistic (Andrade, 1982).

Another factor contributing to the distorted portrayal of the Chicano family is the unrelenting use of the concept of machismo to explain every aspect of Chicano family life. Although the notion of machismo is not unique to the pathological perspective, it has been accepted uncritically with no attempt at verifying its prevalence in Chicano culture. As a result, there are many distortions in both the definition and usage of "machismo" and in the subsequent conceptualization of family structure. However, to argue that machismo has been overemphasized as the causal determinant of Chicano family structure is not to argue that it does not exist at all. Machismo (male domination) exists in all cultures in varying forms and in varying degrees (Ybarra, 1983). Ironically, culture of poverty theorists characterize the Anglo family as a model of egalitarianism that the Chicano family should emulate. However, there is a large body of literature that reveals that the Anglo family is, in fact, one mechanism for creating and maintaining women's oppression and is characterized by a strict division of power and gender roles (e.g., see Coverman & Sheley, 1986; Glenn, 1987; Hartmann, 1981; Hochschild, 1989; Sokoloff, 1980).

Finally, it is contradictory that culture of poverty theorists assert that African Americans must achieve a patriarchal family structure as a means of transcending their pathological conditions while simultaneously arguing that this same patriarchal structure is responsible for the impoverished conditions of the Chicano family.

### *Puerto Ricans*

Given the fact that social scientists tend to study all Latino groups as if they share the same sociohistorical experiences, it is not surprising to find the same explanations for Chicano family pathology being attributed to Puerto Rican families. Puerto Rican family disorganization is attributed to inherent flaws in Puerto Rican culture (Padilla, 1987). The family is characterized by a strict differentiation of gender roles. Puerto Rican men are presented as dictatorial and overly concerned with their machismo. Alternatively, Puerto Rican women are depicted as self-sacrificing, chaste, and dependent. Women are considered inferior to men and must defer to their authority (Torres-Matrullo, 1976).

In his much-cited study of the La Perla section of San Juan, Puerto Rico, Oscar Lewis (1966) portrayed a community characterized by uncontrolled rage, aggression, violence, extreme impulsiveness, and an unnatural preoccupation with sex. He argued that low-income Puerto Ricans were so completely obsessed with sex that that was responsible for most of the friction within the family. He contended that sex was used for procreation, pleasure, money, revenge, love, the expression of machismo, and as compensation for the utter futility of their lives (Lewis, 1966). He stated further that family solidarity, a vital element of Puerto Rican culture, was undermined by the sexual rivalry between female family members and by the threat of molestation by stepfathers. Lewis (1966) concluded his analysis of Puerto Rican sexuality by stating that Puerto Ricans' preoccupation with sex extends to male children, who are "erotically stimulated by their mothers and by other members of the family, who take pride in the child's every erection as an indication of his virility and *machismo*" (p. 26).

Although Lewis (1966) portrayed the family as patriarchal and Puerto Rican men as obsessed with machismo, he asserted that the women were actually more aggressive and violent than the men. He contended that Puerto Rican women often initiated the breakup of their marriages, denigrated men, and taught their children to distrust men. Many women had multiple spouses and preferred consensual marriages because it gave them a stronger legal claim on their children and created a more mother-centered family network. According to Lewis, however, the pattern of free unions and multiple spouses was not endemic to the "culture of poverty" because it had been a widespread pattern among wealthy rural Puerto Rican families. Ultimately, Lewis (1966) depicted a vast environment of social-psychological pathology that included cruelty, violence, deceit, human degradation, and pervasive social deviance (Cordasco, 1967). He concluded that Puerto Ricans who grow up in the culture of poverty have strong feelings of fatalism, helplessness, dependence, and inferiority; traits, he argued, that also characterize destitute Black and Mexican families.

### *Puerto Rican Culture of Poverty: Critique*

Many of the criticisms previously discussed in regard to the Chicano family also apply to the pathological perspective on the Puerto Rican family. In addition, it is contradictory to argue that the Puerto Rican family is pathological because of its extreme patriarchal structure while simultaneously arguing that women are not, in fact, subservient and actually have more power than men. The pathological perspective deals not so much with minority families as with the effects of poverty and racism on behavior. This results in an emphasis on negative attributes, which are held to be inherent qualities of minority families. For instance, the overwhelming concern with the lack of deferred gratification among low-income minority families is viewed as a sign of family disorganization rather than as a result of long-term economic and political deprivation (Aschbrenner, 1978; Billingsley, 1968). Finally, although proponents of the pathological approach to African American, Chicano, and Puerto Rican families acknowledge the prevalence of extended kinship and social support networks, they view them as inherently pathological and focus their analysis exclusively on marital disruption and female-headed households.

## CULTURAL RELATIVITY

### *African Americans*

The strength resiliency perspective arose as a response to the negative stereotypes perpetuated by culture of poverty theorists. Proponents of this perspective (Aschbrenner, 1978; Billingsley, 1968, 1992; Hill, 1972; Ladner, 1972; Nobles, 1974; Staples, 1973; Staples & Johnson, 1993; Young, 1970) argue that it is the assumptions implicit in the pathological model that reflect Black family disorganization, not problems intrinsic to the Black community itself. Consequently, the focus of the strength resiliency perspective is on positive aspects of Black family life, such as the strength of parent-child ties, informal social support networks, extended families, and shared community responsibility for child care (Aschbrenner, 1978).

A primary supposition of the adaptive approach is that the institution of the Black family did not begin with American slavery. Proponents of this perspective argue that the Black family has a historical connection to traditional African culture. Strength resiliency advocates argue that the Black family can be understood only as an institution deriving its primary attributes from its African ancestry (Herskovits, 1966; Nobles, 1974). Nobles (1974) argues that the unique relational patterns characteristic of the Black family can be traced directly to African culture. However, he insists that this sense of "Africanity" does not imply a singular, homogeneous family type.

In fact, according to Billingsley (1968, 1992), a careful reading of historical and ethnographic studies reveals a pattern of African backgrounds that is varied and highly complex. Although Nobles (1974) acknowledges that Black families are extremely diverse, he also contends that within this diversity, one is able to distinguish a "comprehensive cultural unity which has historically characterized Black families" (p. 11).

In studying similarities between African cultural patterns and African descendants living in Brazil, the West Indies, and the United States, Melville Herskovits (1966) discovered authentic African cultural patterns reflected in language, music, art, house structure, dance, traditional religion, and healing practices. He depicted family life in traditional African societies as unified, stable, and secure (Herskovits, 1938). Herskovits's research inspired proponents of the strength resiliency perspective because he raised the possibility that other aspects of "Africana" might influence the nature of the Black family in the United States (Dodson, 1978; Mathis, 1978).

In examining the American Black family, strength resiliency theorists point out that several general features of the African family can be identified. Family life in West Africa was patterned along several dimensions, such as descent, type of marriage, type of family, residential pattern, and patterns of child care and protection (Billingsley, 1968, 1992). The two most basic forms of descent in West Africa were patrilineal descent, in which kinship ties were ascribed through the father's side of the family, and matrilineal descent, in which kinship ties were ascribed through the mother's side of the family. A third pattern of descent, present in only a small part of southern West Africa, was double descent, in which kinship was identified through both parents' side of the family. The pattern of double descent, which was the only one recognized in America, was essentially unknown in the region of Africa from which American Blacks came (Billingsley, 1968).

In African ethnic culture, marriage was not just the concern of the two individuals to be wed. Marriage united two families into an elaborate system of extended kin. These kin relations had considerable influence on the married couple and were responsible for their well-being. African society included three basic forms of marriage. Monogamy, which unites one man with one woman, was the most common throughout West Africa. Polyandry, which unites one woman with two or more husbands, was extremely rare in African culture. Polygyny, which unites one man with two or more wives, was common, though not dominant, throughout the portion of West Africa from which slaves were captured (Billingsley, 1968).

There were two basic patterns of household organization in West Africa. The nuclear family configuration occurred when a man and his wife or wives and their children lived together in his house or compound. The extended family structure occurred when two or more related families lived together in the house or compound of a single household head. These two different types of family organization coexisted peacefully in many African communities (Billingsley, 1968, 1992). Furthermore, the African ethos of survival of the tribe, oneness, and mutual responsibility that were reflected in and reinforced by a strong sense of kinship enabled Africans to maintain a sense of community during slavery (Nobles, 1974).

In both extended and nuclear families, fathers played a very important role in the care and protection of children. However, in all West African societies, whether patrilineal or matrilineal, the relationship between mother and child was paramount. Until weaning at the age of 1 or 2, children were almost never separated from their mothers (Billingsley, 1968). The extraordinary bond between a mother and her child or children was a reflection of the African belief that children represent the continuity of life (Nobles, 1974).

Proponents of the strength resiliency perspective argue that neither the middle passage nor slavery totally destroyed the traditional African base of the American Black family (Blassingame, 1972; Nobles, 1974). Although the structure and function of the Black family did change dramatically under slavery, the centrality of the family never diminished. However, because marriage and family relationships were no longer under the direct control of the kinship group, new family patterns evolved that combined elements of African tribal culture with the exigencies of slavery (Staples, 1974). Whereas in Africa, the family was based on the system of kinship within the tribe, in America, the individual found his or her identity within the community of slaves. Tribal affiliation was reorganized to encompass those individuals bound together by the commonality of their servitude. Children and adults were frequently sold separately from their blood kin and were necessarily absorbed into new families (Billingsley, 1968; Staples, 1974). Consequently, a strong family orientation among Blacks is a synthesis of African heritage and the horrendous experiences of slavery, epitomized by mutual concern and characteristic of extended kin ties (Wetherall, 1981, as cited in Adams, 1995).

According to strength resiliency theorists, not only did African cultural patterns survive slavery, but new cultural patterns unique to Black Americans were created. The persistence of strong kinship ties (e.g., see Billingsley, 1968, 1992; Dubey, 1971; Hays & Mindel, 1973; Hill, 1972; Stack, 1974) among contemporary African American families is one such pattern. Most Black family structures involve a system of kinship ties that includes conjugal and blood relatives as well as nonrelated members (Mathis, 1978; Nobles, 1974).

McCray (1980) argues that Blacks' cultural heritage, historic role in society, experience of oppression, and strong religious beliefs taught them to value humanism profoundly. The origin of these humanistic values can be traced to their African cultural heritage, which placed great emphasis on marriage, kinship bonds, and responsibility to the extended family. She argues that although these values served a special function during slavery, they continue to characterize contemporary African American families (McCray, 1980). In addition, Robert Hill (1972) maintains that one of the greatest strengths of Black families is their strong kinship ties. There is a great deal of reliance on extended family for help with finances, child rearing, advice, and household help. Because of the priority given to child rearing, and as a result of economic burdens and limited resources, it is not unusual for a family member who can provide more help to raise the child of a sibling. Caring for other people's children, whether kin or not, historically has been a salient role for African American women. The willingness on the part of Black women to care for children other than their own is remarkable considering that many of them have their own children, may be employed full-time, and are not economically privileged. This strong support system among Black women often provides the backbone for both family and community survival (Hill, 1972; McCray, 1980).

*African American Cultural Relativity: Critique*

Although the strength resiliency perspective on the Black family is devoid of the racist stereotypes prevalent in the pathological model, it is not without its shortcomings. Because Black Americans came from a myriad of African societies, it is very difficult to demonstrate African cultural influences in contemporary American society (Mathis, 1978). Most American slaves were from West Africa, where the number of different cultural groups existing in the region is unknown (Elkins, 1959). Furthermore, much of the research documenting West African society, cited by proponents of this perspective, was conducted in the 20th century, long after slavery had ended. Extrapolating aspects of preslave society from contemporary data may lead to erroneous conclusions.

Another problem underlying this perspective is that it virtually ignores the effects of contemporary economic institutions on the development of family organization. The family as a cultural institution does not exist in isolation from the broader social structure and must be examined within the context of that structure. In addition, although cultures may be isolated from one another, they can still share similar marital and family customs, because these may not be entirely culturally determined. For instance, extended families frequently have been observed in a wide range of diverse cultures (Harris, 1971).

In contrast to the pathological approach, which depicts the Black woman as dominating and castrating, the adaptive approach romanticizes the Black woman as being strong and self-sufficient, ultimately responsible for the survival of the Black community (McCray, 1980). By glorifying Black motherhood, scholars refuse to acknowledge many of the obstacles facing Black women (Collins, 1990). By claiming that Black women are richly endowed with devotion, self-sacrifice, and unconditional love, proponents of this perspective inadvertently foster the controlling image of the superstrong Black mother. Although celebrating the strong Black mother represents an attempt by Black scholars to replace negative stereotypes with positive interpretations of Black women, it is still problematic. According to Collins (1990), African American women need an Afrocentric, feminist analysis of motherhood that debunks the image of both the matriarch and the superstrong Black mother and presents a more realistic depiction of the dynamics of Black motherhood.

Similarly, in an attempt to refute the negative stereotypes perpetuated by culture of poverty theorists, advocates of the strength resiliency perspective focused solely on positive aspects of Black family life. In addition, the bitter debate that surrounded the Moynihan report resulted in the hesitancy of liberal scholars to examine behavior that could be construed as unflattering or stigmatizing to racial minorities for fear of being labeled racist. Consequently, for a period of several years, well after the controversy had subsided, the growing problems of poverty concentration, joblessness, and social dislocation in the inner-city ghetto were virtually ignored by social scientists (Wilson, 1991). A more balanced approach in which scholars examine the problems confronting Black families while simultaneously extolling their strength is imperative (Nobles, 1978).

### *Chicanos*

The strength resiliency perspective on the Chicano family also emerged as a response to the negative stereotypes perpetuated by the pathological model. Critics of the pathological perspective argue that the depiction of the Chicano family as a rigid, male-dominated, authoritarian structure that breeds passivity and dependence (Mirande, 1977) is a result of the racist ideology underlying the culture of poverty theory (Mirande, 1977; Ybarra, 1983; Zinn, 1979). To refute these assertions, proponents of the strength resiliency perspective (Montiel, 1970; Romano, 1968) examine more positive aspects of the Chicano family. These revisionist scholars focus on close bonds of affection, patterns of helping behavior, and the extended network of family and friends that characterize Chicano family life (Del Castillo, 1984). In addition, this approach examines the family in the context of Aztec cultural tradition. Although it is impossible to identify one uniform Chicano family, scholars agree that it is possible to examine ideals that are characteristic of *la familia* (Del Castillo, 1984; Mirande & Enriquez, 1979).

Proponents of the strength resiliency perspective have argued that familism (the values, attitudes, and beliefs that are associated with the extended family) can be traced to pre-Colombian Mexico. Much of the information on the Aztec family and gender roles within the community comes from the Aztec codices. These historical documents were written from the perspective of the Indians and therefore are a great source of information on societal norms and prescriptions. It is important to note, however, that essentially they portray the social reality of the Aztec nobility and their alliance with the Spanish conquerors (Mirande & Enriquez, 1979). The common people relied on an oral tradition, so their vision of social reality was not as easily documented. In addition, the codices were more a codification of cultural ideals than an actual description of social interaction. Nevertheless, these codices are an invaluable source of information on the daily life of the Aztecs and provide considerable insight into the functioning of a complex and rigidly stratified society (Mirande & Enriquez, 1979).

According to the codices, marital customs were highly ritualistic and reflected traditional gender roles. Parents selected a husband for their daughter with the expectation that she obey their wishes and accept whom they chose. However, in practice, the daughter was asked to consent to the union before it was completed. Both families participated in selecting a spouse, and the bride and groom had little involvement. Marriages were always initiated by the man's family and concluded with the groom's older female relatives advising the bride on the significance of her domestic responsibilities (Mirande & Enriquez, 1979).

Marital fidelity was highly valued in Aztec society. If either the husband or wife transgressed, the family was shamed. The Aztec punishment for marital infidelity was death. The law stated that this punishment be applied uniformly by the state, not by individuals. If a husband beat his wife unjustly, she could complain to the authorities, because the law permitted divorce in such cases (Bonilla Garcia, 1959). Divorce also could be obtained if a woman proved that her husband did not provide for her survival. If the woman was sterile, did not perform her domestic duties, or abandoned the household, the husband had the right to a divorce (Bonilla Garcia, 1959).

Although fidelity and monogamy were the prevalent pattern in Aztec society, polygyny was also permitted. Because polygyny created a financial burden on the male breadwinner, it was practiced primarily by wealthy men (Bonilla Garcia, 1959). In both monogamous and polygynous families, household structure reflected the Mexica-Azteca family's emphasis on the individual's subordination to community-defined norms of behavior.

Although the Aztec family was not an extended system like the traditional Chinese family, there was a great emphasis on familism (Mirande & Enriquez, 1979). Residential clan organization in the Aztec community was based on the calpulli system, in which a parcel of land was shared by independent consanguineal nuclear families living in close proximity to each other (Sena-Rivera, 1979).

An important way in which families enlarged their ties to others in the community was through *compadrazgo*. This custom of godparenthood (which is common in contemporary Chicano families) made nonbiologically related individuals of a community members of the extended family. An important social activity among *comadres* (godmothers), especially in more isolated rural areas, was extensive visiting. Extended family members were especially important during times of crisis, when they could always be depended upon for assistance. In addition, comadres often took care of one another's children and had considerable authority over them (Del Castillo, 1984; Williams, 1990). Within this extended kinship system, the women were responsible for maintaining family cohesion and rearing the children.

According to the strength resiliency perspective, there is a historical connection between the familistic orientation of the Aztecs and the current Chicano family. However, unlike the pathological approach, which views familism as destructive to Chicano social mobility, the adaptive view suggests that familism enhances Chicano achievement by providing an extensive support network. Although proponents of this perspective agree that there is no one Chicano family type, they point to the strong emphasis on familism as one significant feature that characterizes Chicano social interaction. The Chicano family may have been modified somewhat by urbanization and acculturation, but it is still a central institution for the individual. The family is the basic source of emotional support for children, who develop lasting bonds with members of the extended network. The emphasis on familism is such that extended kinship ties assume a prominent place within the culture (Mirande, 1985). Visiting and mutual aid among extended kin are extremely common, especially in times of crisis. There is no sharp distinction between relatives and friends; consequently, both are included in the extended family structure. Because the family is fundamental to Chicano life, individuals are likely to place the needs of the family above their own (Enriquez & Mirande, 1979; Mirande, 1977, 1985; Staples & Mirande, 1980).

Central to an understanding of the contemporary Chicano family is the concept of machismo, which is defined by strength resiliency theorists in terms of family pride and respect rather than in terms of male dominance. As the ultimate authority in the family, the father is responsible for the behavior of family members. Therefore, he must exercise his familial authority to maintain family honor. However, an essential element of machismo is that a man must exercise his familial authority in an equitable manner or risk losing the respect of his family (Murillo, 1971) and the community (Mirande, 1977). Therefore, machismo is not a pathological tool for protecting male prerogatives but a mechanism for upholding family pride and integrity (Mirande, 1977, 1985; Staples & Mirande, 1980).

What was previously described as a rigid and authoritarian structure with austere gender role differentiation is redefined by strength resiliency theorists as a stable family in which the individual's place is clearly defined. The family is a nurturing institution that provides emotional security throughout one's life (Murillo, 1971). In times of trouble, one typically turns to an immediate or extended family member for assistance. Ultimately, cooperation and sharing are the cornerstones of the Chicano extended family (Mirande, 1977, 1985).

Although this approach is significantly less racist than the culture of poverty perspective, it also makes unsubstantiated generalizations about the Chicano family that minimize its internal diversity. In their attempt to contradict pejorative depictions of the Chicano family, strength resiliency advocates have discarded negative stereotypes in favor of positive ones, which ironically incorporate many of the same beliefs they sought to refute. What emerges is a romanticized caricature of the Chicano family (Mirande, 1985).

### *Chicano Cultural Relativity: Critique*

A major flaw in the strength resiliency approach is the depiction of the male as the unquestioned authority in the family. Such characterizations have focused on the formal aspects of Chicano culture, neglecting its more subtle and informal nuances. Ethnographic research has demonstrated that the father is customarily accorded much deference and respect, but he is not the all-powerful dictator of the household. Although the male officially may be the ultimate authority, he is frequently aloof or uninvolved in family matters. The father tends to be warm and affectionate when children are young, but as they enter puberty, relations between him and the children become more tenuous (Mirande, 1985; Rubel, 1966).

The depiction of women as cheerfully deferring to their husbands' authority ignores their true role in the family. Although cultural norms dictate that women subordinate their needs to those of the family, they are revered and recognized as important despite their alleged low status in the family. Aside from performing domestic tasks, they are also responsible for setting parameters on their children's behavior. Thus, although women do not have the formal prestige or status of men, they have tremendous influence in the home (Mirande, 1985). In addition, many Chicana women are beginning to challenge conventional gender role expectations. Few contemporary Chicanas are willing to accept their traditional role, and many are seeking greater equality in the public sphere (Mirande & Enriquez, 1979).

Another problem with the strength resiliency perspective is the preoccupation with familism. Although patterns of mutual aid and support are clearly established, as strength resiliency proponents argue, nuclear families are encouraged to function as relatively autonomous and independent units. One may choose to live near parents and other relatives, but the norm is that the nuclear family remains in an autonomous and separate residence (Williams, 1990).

Finally, in focusing exclusively on Aztec cultural traditions, proponents of the strength resiliency perspective disregard the influence of Spanish culture on the contemporary Chicano family. Contemporary Chicano culture is not derived solely from Aztec society but rather represents a fusion of Aztec civilization and Spanish colonial rule.

In conclusion, although the strength resiliency perspective refutes the racist stereotypes of the culture of poverty approach, it also portrays the Chicano family as being characterized by male dominance, rigid gender roles, clearly established patterns of help and mutual aid, and a strong familistic orientation in which individual needs are subordinated to the family. The basic difference between these two approaches is merely in their interpretation of these characteristics (Mirande, 1985).

*Puerto Ricans*

The strength resiliency perspective on the Puerto Rican family is also an attempt to refute the pejorative image of the family put forth by culture of poverty theorists. Critics of the pathological approach argue that many of the underlying assumptions of that model result in the depiction of the Puerto Rican family as inherently deviant. Subsequently, proponents of the strength resiliency perspective examine positive aspects of Puerto Rican family life. Close bonds of familial affection, informal social support networks, and extended family membership are the focus of the adaptive model. However, the strength resiliency perspective is less clearly defined for Puerto Ricans than it is for African American and Chicano families. In fact, there are no specific scholars who identify themselves solely with this perspective. Most of the literature on the Puerto Rican family is about Puerto Ricans on the island and is written in Spanish. The sparse literature that can be linked to an adaptive approach briefly mentions the Borinquen Indians (generally referred to as the Tainos) and the influence of Spanish culture as contributing to the development of the Puerto Rican family (Fitzpatrick, 1981). Unfortunately, these historical developments are not explained in a precisely detailed analysis. Therefore, the remainder of this section regrettably will reflect the lack of social science scholarship, from the strength resiliency perspective, on the Puerto Rican family in the United States.

A primary assumption underlying the strength resiliency perspective is that the high value placed on the extended family in Puerto Rican culture can be traced to specific historical influences. One such influence may have been the Taino Indians, who were the indigenous people who inhabited Puerto Rico before the Spanish invaded the island. The Taino Indians were believed to be a matrilineal culture in which familial descent was traced through the mother and women were not subservient to men (Fernandez-Mendez, 1972). Because of the mass bloodshed that occurred during the Spanish invasion, the

Taino were virtually wiped out. As a result of this genocide, very little is known about the impact of their culture on subsequent family life (Fitzpatrick, 1981). However, given the patriarchal structure of the Puerto Rican family, it seems implausible that the Taino had an overwhelming influence on succeeding family patterns. As a result of the insufficient historical data on Taino culture, and the fact that most Puerto Ricans identify with their Spanish ancestry, strength resiliency theorists focus primarily on the effects that Spanish colonial rule had on the development of the Puerto Rican family.

As with the Chicano family, scholars agree that it is impossible to identify a single Puerto Rican family type. However, there are certain observable patterns that are characteristic of Puerto Rican families. Proponents of the strength resiliency perspective argue that familism, the most identifiable characteristic of the Puerto Rican family, can be traced to Spanish colonial rule. As a result of the Spanish influence, Puerto Ricans defined themselves in terms of their family membership. Puerto Ricans had a deep sense of family obligation, with individual concerns often subordinated to the needs of the extended family. The extended family was often involved in the courtship of younger family members. Interaction among men and women was highly restricted and supervised. If a young man wanted to court a young woman, he had to declare his intentions to her father and get his permission. If the families disapproved, a serious relationship would almost never develop (Fitzpatrick, 1981). As with Aztec families under Spanish colonial rule, marriage among Puerto Ricans was also characterized by strict husband-wife gender role segregation.

A predominant feature of marriage in Puerto Rican culture was the patriarchal structure of the family. The husband was deemed superior and therefore had complete authority to make decisions without consulting his wife (Rogler & Santana Cooney, 1984). This patriarchal family structure reflected the cultural norm of machismo, in which the man was responsible for the honor and sustenance of the family (Comas-Diaz, 1987). Within the patriarchal family structure, both legal and consensual marriages were customary. A consensual union was a monogamous relationship between a heterosexual couple who lived together, often had children, but had not undergone a religious or civil ceremony. In addition, marriage was considered a union of two families, not merely of two individuals. Therefore, in both legal and consensual marriage, two families became consolidated, substantially widening their extended family network (Fitzpatrick, 1981).

Another consequence of the Spanish conquest on Puerto Rico was the development of an extended kinship network. Like the Chicano family, Puerto Rican families also adhered to the extended kinship system of compadrazgo. Members of this extended network included both relatives and nonrelatives, all of whom were venerated equally. All members of the kin network had a deep sense of obligation to each other for emotional and economic support. Extensive visiting patterns were common, especially among women who assisted each other with domestic responsibilities. Within this extended family network, it was ultimately the women who were responsible for maintaining family stability and for rearing the children (Fitzpatrick, 1981).

Within traditional Puerto Rican culture, child rearing was of utmost importance. The attachment between mothers and their children was considered sacred. Women were venerated for their devotion to the socialization of their progeny. Among Puerto Rican children, gender roles were rigidly defined and differentiated. In preparation for their participation in the public sector, boys were given greater freedom of movement, were allowed to be sexually assertive, and were not expected to share in the domestic or household responsibilities. In preparation for their involvement in the private sphere, girls, on the other hand, were expected to be passive, obedient, and chaste, and to participate fully in the running of the household (Comas-Diaz, 1987).

According to the strength resiliency perspective, there is a linkage between the extended kinship system prevalent in Puerto Rico during Spanish colonial rule and the familistic orientation of the contemporary Puerto Rican family. However, unlike culture of poverty theorists, who argue that familism hinders advancement, proponents of the adaptive model argue that the familistic orientation of Puerto Ricans facilitates achievement by providing an extensive support network. Although Puerto Rican families are inherently diverse, their strong emphasis on the extended family is typical. Although the structure of the family may have been altered by urbanization and back-and-forth migration, familism is still a central feature of Puerto Rican social reality (Fitzpatrick, 1981). Strength resiliency proponents depict the contemporary Puerto Rican family as a cohesive nurturing unit.

Familism is a vital tradition in Puerto Rican culture, providing norms for appropriate conduct. Proponents argue that the extended family system is embedded in the institutional structure of Puerto Rican society. Grandparents, parents, and children may live in the same household, or they may have separate households but visit frequently. Regardless of marriage (legal or consensual), the extended family is an important source of strength and support (Fitzpatrick, 1981). Unlike culture of poverty theorists, strength resiliency advocates emphasize the positive aspects of familism and demonstrate the importance of cohesion between natural and ritual relatives. Whenever possible, reciprocal assistance among all members of the extended family network is expected (Rogler & Santana Cooney, 1984). In fact, the most salient characteristic of familism is the fulfillment of reciprocal obligations (Padilla, 1987). Familism historically has played a salient role in the lives of Puerto Ricans and continues to define contemporary familial interaction (Rogler & Santana Cooney, 1984). Perhaps the centrality of familism among Puerto Ricans and Chicanos is a consequence of their shared history as a colonized people.

### *Puerto Rican Cultural Relativity: Critique*

What was previously depicted as an inherently pathological family is redefined by advocates of the adaptive approach as a functional family form. Although this approach avoids the racist stereotypes found in the culture of poverty perspective, it also makes broad generalizations about the Puerto Rican family that minimize its diversity. One important criticism is the depiction of the Puerto Rican male as the unquestioned dictator of the family. This preoccupation with machismo ignores the subtle strategies that women use to influence their husbands' decision making. As with Chicana mothers, Puerto Rican mothers are venerated and have substantial influence in the home. In addition, many Puerto Rican women are beginning to explore alternative gender roles. One alternative role to which many women aspire is that of *hembrismo* (womanhood). The concept of hembrismo connotes strength, perseverance, flexibility, and the ability to survive. Mainland Puerto Rican women may adhere to the hembrista norm as a means of preserving their cultural identity while simultaneously creating a more flexible role for themselves (Comas-

Diaz, 1987). Because many generalizations about the Chicano family are also made about the Puerto Rican family, my critique of the adaptive approach to the Chicano family (see above) also applies to an analysis of the Puerto Rican family.

In addition to the problems discussed in relation to each minority group, the adaptive approach also has some general limitations that apply to the analysis of all minority families. In their attempt to extol the strengths of minority families, strength resiliency scholars replaced negative depictions of family disorganization with a unidimensional analysis that focused exclusively on positive aspects of family organization. Ghetto families were portrayed as resilient and capable of adapting creatively to an oppressive society. These revisionist arguments shifted the focus away from discussions of consequences of racial oppression and economic exploitation to discussions of achievement. Because the focus of this scholarship is on accomplishments, little discussion was devoted to the devastating impact of economic shifts on poor minority communities and the subsequent need for economic reform (Wilson, 1987). If scholars fail to recognize the myriad social problems facing minority families and instead argue that any aspect of minority family life, no matter how deviant, serves a useful function, they will subvert any societal attempt to ameliorate these problems (Allen, 1978). The strength resiliency perspective unintentionally develops a functionalist argument, which ultimately promotes the maintenance of the prevailing social structure.

Another flaw in this perspective is the tendency among revisionist scholars to minimize social class and ethnic variations (Mirande, 1977). Although proponents of this perspective mention the existence of diversity among specific minority families, they still make generalizations that ignore salient differences in class, ethnic affiliation, religious background, migration patterns, length of residence in the United States, and so on. In addition, the strength resiliency perspective on minority families is extremely problematic because it focuses only on cultural aspects of family structure, virtually ignoring the effects of contemporary economic institutions on the development of family organization. This preoccupation with cultural ideals has meant that little attention has been given to societal conditions, which also influence family structure (Zinn, 1982a). Although it is true that many family lifestyles are differentiated by ethnicity, structural patterns differ because social and economic conditions produce and may even require diverse family arrangements. Although the family nurtures ethnic culture, families are not the product of ethnic and racial culture alone (Zinn, 1990). Therefore, a theoretical perspective on minority families that focuses solely on cultural antecedents of family structure is inadequate.

## Empirical Literature

### EXTENDED LIVING ARRANGEMENTS

The literature reviewed in this section defines a household as extended if that household includes any relatives other than the spouse or children of the main householder. This definition requires that some relatives other than the main householder's nuclear family be present (Anderson & Allen, 1984). Extended family members may be children, or they may be adult relatives, as long as they are not the spouse or children of the main householder. A more inclusive definition of extended living arrangements includes households containing at least one other relative or nonrelative of the head. Unlike the first definition of extension, this one does not require that the extended household member be related (Angel & Tienda, 1982), nor does it exclude adult children of household heads who return home after a period of absence.

The cultural explanation for extended family households tends to focus on African American families. Proponents of the cultural approach attribute racial differences in household structure to a different set of values and cultural norms that evolved out of West African traditions combined with the historical legacy of slavery and reconstruction (Anderson & Allen, 1984). The Black extended family is seen as a "cultural institution with a tradition, structure, and corresponding set of values" or cultural adaptation (Aschbrenner, 1973, as cited in Anderson & Allen, 1984, p. 146). Thus, Black families deemphasize the nuclear family and emphasize obligations to the extended family network. Some of the research on the Black family suggests that the legacy of slavery and reconstruction is strongest in the South, so reliance on extended families should be greatest among southern Black families.

In examining extended family household structure using a cultural approach, sociologists have found support for the argument that alternative family forms are characteristic of minority families. However, there is much disagreement about which minority groups are more involved in extended families. In their study of extended household structure comparing African Americans and Whites, Kristine Anderson and Walter Allen (1984) examined the nature of class differences in household structure and the utility of economic status as an explanation of differences in the likelihood of extension. They argued that although class differences do exist, social class does not account for the formation of extended households among all groups. Social class factors may predominate among certain kinds of families but may be less important among other groups. One important factor that potentially may overcome the effects of economic status is unique cultural values or norms.

Anderson and Allen's (1984) study uses data from the 15% County Group Public Use Sample of the 1970 Census of the Population. Cross-tabulations of independent variables with family structure revealed that as the educational level of the household head increased, the probability of extension decreased for both races. However, the association was stronger among Blacks than Whites. In general, lower incomes were associated with a higher incidence of extended structures, but once again, the strength of this relationship was greater among Blacks.

Log-linear analysis revealed that there were significant main effects of region, female headedness, age of household head, and race on household structure. Living in the South, having a female household head over age 45, and being Black all increase the likelihood of extended household structure. Results reveal that there is no significant main effect of income level on likelihood of extension when race, region, age, and type of headship are controlled.

It was proposed that cultural norms might be a predictor of extended families. Although the data do not fully support this argument, Anderson and Allen (1984) suggest that there is some evidence for a cultural focus. Blacks are more likely than Whites to extend at every socioeconomic level, among all age groups, and in every region of the country. Only among female-headed households did the effects of race disappear. The regional effects revealed that living in the South affects households primarily among Blacks but also among older people and those of low income, regardless of race. Thus, some support was found for the persistence of both Black and southern subcultural family patterns stressing the importance of ties to a larger kin group.

Wagner and Schaffer (1980) also used a demographic approach to understanding the cultural aspects of extended family households; however, they extend the cultural perspective by including Chicano families in their analysis. Their comparison of Mexican American, Black, and Anglo female family heads emphasized the coping strategies, patterns of formal and informal helping resources, and possible ethnic differences in the values associated with extended households. In their study of Chicano, Black, and Anglo female family heads living in a Chicano barrio in east San Jose, California, Wagner and Schaffer (1980) found that the average size of the kinship network present for the Mexican Americans was strikingly larger compared to that of other women. Chicanas were more likely to live in extended households, and a majority of the Chicanas residing in independent households lived close to their parents. Anglo and Black women were forced to rely on nonkin sources of aid to a greater extent because they lacked a comparably large kinship network. According to Wagner and Schaffer (1980), a cultural interpretation is appropriate because Mexican women were less likely to live independently as female household heads, and the Anglo and Black women did not choose to reside close to their relatives to the same extent as did the Chicanas.

Zavella's (1987) findings from her study of Chicana cannery workers in Santa Clara, California, present an interesting contradiction to Wagner and Schaffer's (1980) results. Her ethnographic research indicates that there is little evidence that familism is an overwhelmingly important factor in Chicano life. She did not find an extended kin network, and most of her respondents lived in nuclear settings. Furthermore, when respondents in her study did need help, they turned to their friends rather than family members.

One final study examining extended families from the cultural approach is Hays and Mindel's (1973) analysis of extended kinship relations in Black and White families. They examined the extent to which Blacks rely on their family and kin as well as the extent to which Blacks differ from Whites in their family patterns. They argue that extended family cohesion differs for Blacks and Whites in terms of the extensity (quantity) and intensity (frequency) of the relationship because of the higher cultural value placed on familism by African American families.

Hays and Mindel (1973) hypothesized that Black families would have more extended kin living in the same household than would White families. The data are from a subsample of a larger study conducted in a middle-size, midwestern city in 1966. The subsample consisted of 25 matched pairs of Black and White families. The pairs were matched in terms of sex, socioeconomic status, and marital status.

They found that significantly more Black families (28%) have kin other than their own children living in their household than do White families (4%). They also found that relatives who live in the extended Black families tend to be either siblings or children (grandchildren, nieces, nephews). Hays and Mindel (1973) contend that extended kin are more highly valued in Black families than they are in White families, and that the number and type of relatives who live in the household are greater and more diverse for Blacks than for Whites.

These three studies all emphasize a cultural approach to understanding extended households among minority families. Household structure is defined as extended if the household includes any relatives other than the spouse or children of the head of household. This definition does not fully uncover the breadth of the extended network because it does not include coresiding nonfamily members. Whereas Anderson and Allen (1984) use a probability sample, Hays and Mindel (1973) and Wagner and Schaffer (1980) do not. In addition to using nonprobability samples, the sample size of 25 matched pairs used by Hays and Mindel (1973) and the sample size of 38 respondents used by Wagner and Schaffer (1980) are extremely small, preventing any generalizability of their results. In addition to having a small sample size, Wagner and Schaffer's (1980) and Hays and Mindel's (1973) analyses do not employ multivariate analysis, yet they present the findings as if they can be generalized to all White and Black families.

Furthermore, Wagner and Schaffer's (1980) sample comes from a Mexican barrio in San Jose, California. To compare the few African

American and Anglo women living in that community to the Chicanas results in a biased conclusion that Mexicans are more likely to live in close proximity to their families. Perhaps a less biased approach would have been to compare Black, Chicana, and Anglo women living in similar ethnic enclaves. Finally, Hays and Mindel's (1973) analysis is based on the view that the Black family structure is informed by historical processes that have placed them in a relatively disadvantaged position. The major thrust of their argument is that Black extended families are a response to living in a hostile and racist environment. Although this may be true, I disagree with their underlying assumption that Black families are in a perpetual state of crisis.

The cultural approach alone does not fully explain the origin of extended family living arrangements. Proponents of the cultural approach argue that both African Americans and Chicanos deemphasize the nuclear family, giving primary importance to the extended kinship network. However, the proponents give no sociohistorical explanation as to why one minority group might value extended families more than another. Advocates of the cultural perspective tend to study either Latinos or African Americans in isolation from one another. As a result, Chicanos and Blacks are each defined as the most familistic minority group, with few comparisons made between them. Furthermore, there is conflicting evidence as to the actual prevalence of extended households among African American and Chicano families. Because of different measures and different types of samples, research demonstrates instances in which Blacks are more familistic than Chicanos and instances where Chicanos are more familistic than Blacks. In addition, the cultural perspective tends to ignore the salient impact of the political economy on minority families. Although research has demonstrated differences in family structure by ethnicity, patterns may differ as a result of social and economic conditions, not cultural values favoring extended family living arrangements.

## SOCIAL SUPPORT NETWORKS

In addition to extended living arrangements, a second major component of kin networks is informal social support networks. Informal social support networks are characterized by frequent interaction, close affective bonds, and exchanges of goods and services among family and nonfamily members who typically live in close proximity to one another but *not* in the same household. The mutual aid that defines these networks can be either emotional or socioeconomic (see Litwak, 1965). Members of informal social support networks interact by choice and are connected to one another by means of mutual aid and social activities (Cantor, 1979).

As with the research on extended families, there is an abundance of research on social support networks informed by the cultural perspective. Therefore, in this section, I will first present the cultural explanation for the existence of informal social support networks among African Americans, followed by a general discussion of Latinos, and concluding with a more specific discussion of Chicanos and Puerto Ricans. Next, I will present a critique of the research that compares network participation between different racial-ethnic families.

Ethnographic studies of informal social support networks tend to emphasize the cultural aspects of these networks. The cultural argument focusing on the Black family suggests that a strong legacy in both African heritage and slavery has resulted in a strong family orientation among Blacks. The devastating experience of slavery led Blacks to place great emphasis on family ties. According to this perspective, Black families tend to have an elaborate system of extended social support networks composed of relatives and nonrelatives. This model is consistent with the African concept of family and can be traced more directly to the experience during slavery of families being sold separately. In response to this breakup, children and adults were absorbed into new families (Billingsley, 1968, 1992; Staples, 1981). McCray (1980) argues that Blacks' African cultural heritage, historic role in society, experience of oppression, and strong religious beliefs resulted in strong humanistic values in which great emphasis is placed on marriage, kinship bonds, and responsibility to extended family structure.

According to Joyce Aschbrenner, family sociologists focus too much on deviations from an "ideal" family form. Based on her qualitative research, Aschbrenner (1973) identifies various types of kinship groups. She argues that the Black family is a cultural institution with a tradition, structure, and corresponding set of values. Her research in Chicago led her to believe that in most instances, the primary socializing unit was not a conjugal but an extended family, with considerable interaction taking place among households. Fictive kin were also extremely important in the Black family form. The proliferation of kin terms and relationships among Blacks underscores the strength of the extended family. According to Aschbrenner (1973), kin relationships represent more than life strategies for Black men and women: "They are matrices within which people find their identity and their purpose for living and striving" (p. 267).

Ethnographic research from the cultural perspective that focuses on Hispanics depicts the Latino family as especially familistic, with loyalty to the family as paramount over individual needs. According to De Anda (1984), informal social supports provided by primary groups are expressed within Latino culture as extended kinship networks. These networks include both family and nonfamily members who have been adopted into the nuclear or extended family. It is argued that despite generational differences in levels of acculturation, strong family relationships remain characteristic of Hispanic populations. For example, studies by Keefe et al. (1979) and by Rogler and Santana Cooney (1984) respectively found that first-, second-, and third-generation Chicanos and Puerto Ricans are equally likely to live close to kin, help with household chores, offer advice, and lend money. When examining Latino families, it is vital not to treat them as a homogeneous group devoid of distinctive historical and cultural experiences and identities. Therefore, a discussion of Chicanos followed by a discussion of Puerto Ricans will be developed.

The Chicano family is typically characterized as a large and cohesive kin group embracing both lineal and collateral relatives. Ties beyond the nuclear family are strong and extensive, and reciprocal rights and duties are connected with all relatives, including grandparents, aunts, uncles, and cousins (Madsen, 1964). Compadrazgo, or ritual coparenthood associated with choosing godparents, is described as an extension of the kinship system. Compadres take on the rights and obligations more characteristic of relatives than of friends, and they are included as members of the extended kin network.

There are two important empirical studies from the cultural perspective that examine social support networks among Latinos. Unfortunately, they make no racial comparisons. The first study examines the extent, composition, and quality of the informal support networks available to Chicana mothers of different age groups. De Anda (1984) surveyed English- and Spanish-speaking participants in Women Infant

Child (WIC) programs in the western region of Los Angeles County and the city of Long Beach. Respondents were volunteers solicited by flyers. Although this is not a representative sample, De Anda (1984) claims that because data were collected over 2 years, they are representative of a cross-section of WIC recipients. The sample consisted of 185 Hispanic women who were either currently pregnant or had delivered a child within the past year. Respondents were categorized into age groups of 12-17, 18-20, 21-29, and 30+ years. The overwhelming majority of the sample was Chicana, with 53% of the English-speaking respondents and 64% of the Spanish-speaking respondents below the poverty level.

The social support provided by mothers appeared to be the most critical for the two younger groups, and social support from husbands for the two older groups. The 18- to 20-year-old group had the broadest based network. In general, however, the respondents with the least support were the Spanish-speaking mothers. The findings indicate that despite the importance of extended family in traditional Hispanic culture, one cannot assume that emotional and physical support is available within the immediate environment. Newly arrived Spanish-speaking women may lack an available kinship support network as a result of their recent migration. Geographically isolated from their families of origin, the Spanish-speaking mothers had to rely on their husbands and were therefore more isolated and dependent upon them than earlier immigrants. Although the husbands were extremely supportive, the size of their support network was very limited.

The sample in this study is not a random probability sample, and the findings therefore cannot be generalized to the overall Chicana population. Due to the small overall *N*, sample sizes for the four age groups were extremely small. Once again, the type of analysis used to support a cultural interpretation was not very sophisticated. Use of chi-square contingency table analysis is not appropriate to test a causal model. Although De Anda (1984) espouses a cultural argument, her finding that Spanish-speaking respondents had the smallest social support networks fails to support the assertion that Latinos are more familistic and are more likely to include both kin and fictive kin in their network. This may, in fact, be a result of her sample, which consisted of newly arrived immigrants who may not have developed long-term, U.S.-based networks.

The Puerto Rican family is also depicted as placing primary importance on kin relations. According to Rogler and Santana Cooney (1984), the value system of familism emphasizes an almost sacred bond between relatives. The existence of reciprocal obligations among relatives and the duty to express concern for family is considered a highly valued cultural trait.

To determine the extent of intergenerational interdependence among Puerto Rican families in New York City, the second study (Rogler & Santana Cooney, 1984) collected case studies of 100 intergenerational families. The families in this study represent part of a recent immigrant population experiencing advantages in education, occupation, and income. The sample is also not a probability sample because getting intergenerational respondents using probability sampling methods would be extremely difficult. The sample does, however, reflect the socioeconomic diversity among New York City Puerto Ricans.

When intergenerational visiting patterns were examined, it was found that there are repeated weekly contacts between parents and their married offspring. Help exchanges are also frequent among Puerto Ricans. Reciprocal help between generations is at the core of family interaction and includes financial assistance, child care, emotional support, and advice. Among the Puerto Rican studies, 73% of the help exchanges in the parent generation and 67% in the child generation centered upon family. In comparison to their own parent generation, the Puerto Rican child generation seemed to be moving toward help exchanges with peers, neighbors, friends, and coworkers. Despite pervasive differences between the generations and little evidence of familial continuity, the Puerto Rican families were remarkably unified in a pattern of strong and viable intergenerational interdependence. No matter how the data were examined, there were no statistically important differences in intergenerational interdependence owing to differences in place of birth, educational attainment, or early socialization. The bonds of intergenerational interdependence outweigh important components of the migration experience and of socioeconomic status. According to Rogler and Santana Cooney (1984), underlying these statistical patterns are deeply rooted cultural norms in which reciprocal obligations among relatives are highly valued.

Rogler and Santana Cooney's (1984) study is one of the few examining social support networks among Puerto Rican families on the mainland and provides much-needed insight into the dynamics of Puerto Rican family life. However, because it is nonrepresentative, we cannot generalize Rogler and Santana Cooney's findings to all Puerto Ricans living in the United States. Also problematic is their use of bivariate analyses, from which they make causal inferences.

Although De Anda's (1984) and Rogler and Santana Cooney's (1984) research is enlightening, both focus on only one particular racial-ethnic group and provide no intergroup comparisons. However, there are three studies of extended social support networks in which racial-ethnic comparisons are made. In the first study, Hays and Mindel (1973) (discussed above) compare Black and White families. They hypothesized that Black families have more contact with their kin than do White families, that Black families receive more help from kin in child care and child rearing than do White families, that Black families have more frequent contact with a wider variety of kin than do White families, and that Black families perceive their extended kin as more significant than do White families.

Hays and Mindel (1973) found that the mean number of total relatives seen is higher for Black families than for White families in all categories except for parents. Blacks see other relatives more often than they see their parents, whereas White respondents see their parents more frequently than they see other relatives. In addition, they report that Black families rely more heavily on kin than do White families and have more extensive and intensive networks than do Whites. However, this finding is problematic because Hays and Mindel (1973) do not control for family size or for the number of nonrelatives seen. In the category of relatives helping with child care once a month or less, the Black families' mean number of relatives is slightly but not significantly lower (1.12) than that for White families (1.32). However, for the categories of daily, weekly, and monthly help with child care, the mean score of relatives is significantly different. Not only do more relatives help the Black families with child care, but they help more often.

Hays and Mindel (1973) also find that Black families perceive all categories of kin as more important than do White families, with the exception of parents. This finding supports their contention that extended kin are more salient for Black families than for White families. The kinship system of White families seems to be organized around the nuclear unit to a much greater degree than among Black families. Hays and Mindel (1973) conclude that even when geographic mobility, socioeconomic status, marital status, and family size are controlled, the kin interaction of Black and White families is very different.

The findings in this study tend to support the view that Black social support networks reflect a cultural phenomenon in which the extended family (both kin and nonkin) is highly valued. However, because this study is exploratory, has an extremely small sample size, is based on a nonprobability sample, and does not use multivariate analysis, we must be careful not to characterize all White and Black families according to these findings.

In contrast to Hays and Mindel's (1973) research, the second study on informal social support networks, from the cultural perspective, demonstrates that when compared to Chicanos, Blacks are not more likely to be involved in social support networks. In their examination of informal networks among Chicano, Black, and Anglo families, Wagner and Schaffer (1980) found that even when Chicana women live in independent households, they tend to live close to their parents. Their study indicates that there is a form of "resource specialization" in the kinship networks of Chicanos. During times of crisis, respondents in their study often moved in with their mothers or the mothers moved in with the respondents to help with child care, cooking, housework, and so on. They conclude their study by suggesting that their research corroborates other anthropological data that demonstrate a definite tendency among Chicanos to rely on the immediate kinship network for satisfying daily problems.

In the third study from the cultural perspective, Keefe et al. (1970) collected data on family and mental health over a 3-year period in three southern California cities and compared the family structure of Mexican Americans and Anglos and their reliance on kin for emotional support.

Their findings indicate that the kinship structure of the two ethnic groups is fundamentally different. Mexican Americans are much more likely than Anglos to have large numbers of their relatives living in the community. Anglos tend to live apart from their extended family or to have only a few relatives nearby. The difference in family structure does not, however, have much effect on the tendency to seek emotional support from relatives. Both groups rely on their families for help, but Anglos are at a disadvantage in having to go out of town to see their relatives or in having to call them long distance.

Anglos are more likely to seek help from friends, neighbors, and coworkers, and Mexican Americans' main resource is their extended kin. In contrast to the assumptions of the cultural perspective (which argues that support networks comprise kin and nonkin alike), Chicano extended family support is limited to kin; fictive kin do not often give help. Finally, there are a large number of Chicanos who think that family members should not be relied on for support because they become too intrusive. Although Keefe et al. (1979) illustrate that Mexican Americans rely greatly on familial support, there is no indication that it is a uniquely Mexican American trait. "In fact the portrait of the isolated Anglo seems dubious at best" (p. 151). Instead, Anglos appear to share and find relief from their emotional problems with all kinds of informal helping agents.

Keefe et al. (1979) argue in support of a cultural approach to understanding extended social support networks. They contend that their study supports earlier anthropological research that depicts the Latino family as more familistic than Anglo families. However, they did not control for social class and therefore cannot eliminate an economic explanation for their findings. In addition, Chicano respondents tended to limit their informal social support networks to include kin only. Anglo respondents, on the other hand, included both kin and fictive kin in their networks. Therefore, one could actually argue that in this particular study, Anglos are more familistic because they are willing to include kin and nonkin in their modified extended family network.

Overall, research on informal social support networks from the cultural perspective is problematic. Most of the studies have extremely small sample sizes and are not representative of the overall population. Many of the studies do not compare racial-ethnic groups, and the ones that do tend to make Latino-White or Black-White comparisons. Respondents in these studies also tend to be from the lower socioeconomic strata, preventing any assessment of the differential impact of class on social support networks. Finally, the cultural approach tends to be somewhat reductionist because it does not take the socioeconomic context in which people live into account. Therefore, this research will examine the effect of socioeconomic status on the likelihood of participation in social support networks. Despite the problems endemic to the cultural perspective, the bulk of the research does indicate the existence of close kin and fictive kin ties among African Americans and Latinos throughout the late 1960s until the early 1980s.

# 2

# The Structural Context of Care

The structural approach to informal social support networks and extended living arrangements argues that minority families are more likely to be familistic because of their more limited economic resources and greater susceptibility to economic deprivation. This perspective stresses economic exploitation, not differences in cultural values and norms, as a major antecedent to divergent family forms. This chapter will first present the theoretical underpinnings of the structural approach to extended kinship networks followed by a critique of research to date and a description of how this study will transcend some of the limitations of previous work. Like the cultural perspective, this framework also contains ideological presuppositions. Proponents of the structural perspective base their theorizing about participation in extended social support networks on the prevalence of economic inequality in American society.

## Theoretical Framework

Proponents of the structural approach view the family as a social institution that is inextricably bound and influenced by the larger social structure. Racial and ethnic variations in family structure are merely regarded as reflections of class divisions. Furthermore, adherents of this perspective do not prioritize social structural variables; instead, they examine particular economic antecedents of network participation. Hence, the underlying assumption of this approach is that economic rather than cultural factors are responsible for family organization (Bean & Tienda, 1987).

It follows that an important component in examining family structure is understanding the historical developments that led to concentrations of contemporary urban poverty (Wilson, 1987). Because proponents of the structural perspective virtually ignore the effects of culture on family organization, they do not explicate a separate analysis for each minority group. However, given that African Americans, Chicanos, and Puerto Ricans have different economic relationships to the larger social structure, I believe it is essential to present the unique migration histories that led to their contemporary position within that structure. Therefore, I will present a brief demographic description of each group, followed by the structural perspective on minority families in general.

### AFRICAN AMERICANS

The current concentration of African Americans in impoverished urban central cities can be traced to historical experiences of labor market discrimination. During the early 20th-century rise in industrial capitalism, employers discriminated more severely against Blacks and Asians than against White immigrants from southern, eastern, and western Europe. However, because changes in immigration policy halted Asian migration to the United States in the late 19th century, the Chinese and Japanese populations did not increase substantially. Therefore, Asians did not seem to pose as great a threat to the White workforce as Blacks did. In addition, the cessation of large-scale immigration from Asia enabled earlier migrants to solidify social support networks and to occupy particular occupational niches in small, relatively stable communities (Lieberson, 1980). Reductions in Asian immigration were quickly followed by restrictions in European immigration. However, Black migration to the urban north continued in substantial numbers for several decades. The large, continuous migration of Blacks from the South to the North, combined with the reduction of European immigrants, resulted in workers directing their antagonisms primarily toward Blacks (Lieberson, 1980; Wilson, 1987).

In addition, migration patterns made it much more difficult for Blacks to overcome the negative effects of discrimination and to find unique occupational niches. According to Lieberson (1980), only a small part of a group's total workforce can be absorbed into occupational specialties when the group's population increases rapidly or is a sizable proportion of the total population. Furthermore, the continuing influx of migrants had a deleterious effect on the urban Blacks who had migrated earlier. Large numbers of recent newcomers tend to undercut the wages and positions of other members of the community (Wilson, 1987).

The pattern of rural Black migration that began with the rise of urban industrial centers in the North has been paralleled in recent years in the South. Because of the mechanization of agriculture, there has been a large influx of rural Blacks into southern cities, which has resulted in the creation of large urban ghettos that closely resemble those in the North. The overall result is that in the last quarter of this century, many large cities have had a disproportionate concentration of low-income Blacks who are especially vulnerable to recent sectoral changes in the production economy (Wilson, 1987). In fact, in 1983, Blacks constituted approximately 23% of the population of central cities, but they comprised 43% of the poor (U.S. Bureau of the Census, 1985).

## CHICANOS

Like African Americans, Chicanos' original entry into the United States came about through conquest and subordination. Chicanos, who reside primarily in the Southwest, constituted more than 60% of the total Latino population in the United States in 1980 (Bean & Tienda, 1987). Of all Latino groups, Chicanos are the most diverse in terms of socioeconomic characteristics and migration history. This heterogeneity can be traced to U.S. westward expansion; the geographic proximity of Mexico, which has facilitated continued immigration; and the historical exploitation of Mexican workers in the U.S. economy (Bean & Tienda, 1987).

The Treaty of Guadalupe Hidalgo, which officially ended the Mexican-American War by annexing the states of California, Arizona, New Mexico, Colorado, and Texas, had profound economic ramifications for the Mexican population. Once conquered, the Southwest was opened for Anglo expansion, which resulted in the incursion of thousands of non-Hispanic Whites, who took control of the land and destroyed the social system governing the indigenous Mexican residents. The subsequent economic development of the Southwest by Anglos depended on the abundance of cheap labor often supplied by Mexicans (Bean & Tienda, 1987).

The first 30 years after the war, there was very little migration between Mexico and the United States. However, after 1880, immigration became the main avenue by which the Chicano population grew and consolidated its regional and residential segregation in the Southwest.

The increased flow of Mexican workers into the United States after 1880 coincided with the rapid expansion of commercial agriculture, mining, and railroad construction in the Southwest. In addition, massive political upheavals culminating in the Mexican Revolution drove thousands of Mexicans to the North in search of employment opportunities and political refuge. Finally, employers in the United States were eager to hire Mexicans as a cheap labor force because World War I had created labor shortages that diminished output and decreased profit margins (Bean & Tienda, 1987).

The history of Mexican immigration in the 20th century is cyclical. Between 1880 and 1929, when the U.S. economy was expanding, Mexican immigration policy was relatively unrestricted, and Mexican workers entered the United States in significant numbers. However, during the 1930s, when widespread domestic unemployment contributed to a wave of anti-Mexican sentiment, massive repatriation campaigns were implemented (Jaffe, Cullen, & Boswell, 1980). Ironically,

World War II precipitated another period of labor shortages, particularly in the agricultural industry, which had not yet been mechanized, so a contract labor system between Mexico and the United States was implemented. The *bracero* program, which lasted from 1942 to 1964, revived the tradition of regular migration to the United States (Bean & Tienda, 1987).

Pre-1930 Mexican immigration consolidated the regional and residential segregation of Mexicans into the rural economy and cemented their low status in the social hierarchy. Large numbers of Mexican immigrants created an excess labor supply during the first half of the 20th century. Capitalists used this surplus labor force to undercut wages and thwart unionization efforts, creating resentment on the part of Anglo workers. Workers' hostility, combined with opposition from small farmers who were unable to compete with large enterprises employing cheap labor, isolated Chicanos from the Anglo working class and further cut them off from potential avenues of integration into the social and economic mainstream. The divide-and-conquer strategy of employers created a set of conditions that both structured the lives of Chicanos and augmented racial and ethnic prejudice in the Southwest (Bean & Tienda, 1987).

More recently, dramatic changes have occurred in the residence patterns of Chicanos. Over the past two decades, Chicanos have become primarily an urban-based population. In 1960, more than 75% of all people of Mexican origin resided in urban areas; by 1980, the share of metropolitan dwellers had increased to about 85%. The influx of Chicanos into urban neighborhoods is the result of declining opportunities in agriculture due to the mechanization of the industry and of the expansion of the urban service and manufacturing sectors (Bean & Tienda, 1987).

## PUERTO RICANS

Compared with Chicanos, Puerto Ricans have a much shorter history in the United States, and they make up a smaller share of all Latinos. In 1980, Puerto Ricans constituted approximately 14% of the Latino population living on the mainland. Designated a U.S. territory at the culmination of the Spanish-American war in 1898, Puerto Rico became a semiautonomous commonwealth in 1952. This status eradicated economic boundaries and protective mechanisms that many Third World nations use to defend local interests and has fostered the economic dependency of the island on the United States (Bean & Tienda, 1987).

Puerto Ricans have lived in the continental United States for more than a century, but the emergence of a visible Puerto Rican community is essentially a post-World War II phenomenon. Although a small Puerto Rican population lived on the mainland before World War II, the major exodus from the island to the continental United States began in the 1940s and accelerated after 1950. Migration rates from Puerto Rico to New York more than doubled during the 1950s and then declined drastically between 1960 and 1970. This circular migration, characteristic of Puerto Ricans, is a result of the changing economic conditions in both Puerto Rico and the continental United States (Bean & Tienda, 1987).

Migration between Puerto Rico and the mainland is essentially the result of a decision to transform and develop Puerto Rico's plantation economy through a program of rapid industrialization. "Operation Bootstrap," which was in effect from 1948 to 1965, allowed unrestricted migration between the mainland and the island. Because the new industrial economy could not absorb the available workers, migration to the mainland provided a temporary solution to the acute unemployment problem. The outflow of wage laborers from Puerto Rico was so dramatic in the 1950s that it paradoxically appeared as if Puerto Rico had a booming economy with a shrinking labor force (Bean & Tienda, 1987).

Inexpensive air travel, the impact of mass communication on potential job seekers, obligatory military service, and the absence of immigration restrictions further intensified immigration from Puerto Rico to the mainland. Despite the fact that Puerto Rican immigrants were U.S. citizens, they were often relegated to the lowest level of the secondary labor market, experiencing discrimination in both housing and employment. Ironically, of the 400,000 foreign contract workers brought to the United States during World War II, few were Puerto Rican despite a 100% increase in unemployment and the fact that Puerto Ricans were serving in the military. These historical events help explain the economic conditions of contemporary Puerto Ricans. The persistent inability of many island migrants to secure steady employment on the mainland has resulted in Puerto Ricans having the lowest labor force participation rates, the lowest levels of education, the highest unemployment rates, and the highest poverty rates of all Latino groups residing in the continental United States (Bean & Tienda, 1987).

Despite the different historical circumstances experienced by African Americans, Chicanos, and Puerto Ricans, there are similarities between them that provide some insight into their current socioeconomic position. All three groups migrated in search of wage labor and were headed for unskilled blue-collar markets. African Americans, Chicanos, and Puerto Ricans landed in regional labor markets that were undergoing sectorial shifts in manufacturing and production (Zinn, 1987). All three groups have been the victims of intense discrimination and economic exploitation (Bean & Tienda, 1987).

Similarities between these three groups should not be overstated, however. Chicanos' labor market integration began largely as agricultural and has more recently evolved into urban-based work. Although African Americans and Puerto Ricans were also originally from agrarian societies, they entered into the industrial economy in larger numbers and much sooner than Chicanos. In fact, African Americans and Puerto Ricans have become almost exclusively urban based and concentrated in the manufacturing and service sectors of the Northeast. Therefore, unlike Chicanos, African Americans and Puerto Ricans have disproportionately entered into declining manufacturing industries. Consequently, on average, Black and Puerto Rican families tend to be more impoverished than Chicano families. However, since the 1970s, living conditions of Chicanos have begun to approximate Blacks and Puerto Ricans. By the 1970s, all three groups were predominantly city dwellers. Moreover, despite great ethnic diversity among these groups, they share widespread poverty due to underemployment and unemployment. In fact, African Americans, Chicanos, and Puerto Ricans lag behind Whites in every measure of well-being: jobs, income, educational attainment, housing, and health care (Zinn, 1987). In addition, the suburbanization of the production economy, combined with inadequate mass transit, has further restricted opportunities for

Blacks, Chicanos, and Puerto Ricans tied to their central city neighborhoods (Bean & Tienda, 1987).

## AFRICAN AMERICANS, CHICANOS, AND PUERTO RICANS

Now that I have outlined the unique economic experiences of African Americans, Chicanos, and Puerto Ricans, I will discuss the structural approach to extended living arrangements, informal social support networks, and female-headed households among minority families. Because the underlying assumption of this approach is that minority family organization is a direct result of economic subordination, stucturalists present their theoretical argument in a way that can be generalized to all minority families.

The structural approach to minority families contends that culture is a response to social structural constraints and opportunities (Wilson, 1987). Therefore, it is argued that family organization must be examined as a consequence of macrostructural forces, not as a result of pathological norms and values (Moynihan, 1965). Within the structural framework, the prevalence of extended households, female-headed families, and elaborate social support networks must be understood within the context of the economic structure.

A major component of the structural approach is transformations in the economy and the labor market that have harshly affected African Americans and Latinos residing in inner-city neighborhoods. Massive economic changes since the end of World War II have resulted in a major shift from a manufacturing economy to an information-processing and service economy. Although these economic shifts, which have redistributed work in national and regional economies, affect all workers, they have more serious consequences for minority workers who are concentrated in the hardest hit industries. These economic trends may appear to be race neutral, but Blacks and Latinos have been the most profoundly affected by the decline in industrial manufacturing and the growth of the service economy, as well as by the exodus of jobs from central cities to the suburbs, from the Rustbelt to the Sunbelt, and from the United States to foreign countries (Zinn, 1989). The decline in the demand for unskilled labor has been most severe in the older central cities of the North. The four largest (New

York, Chicago, Philadelphia, and Detroit), which in 1982 accounted for more than one fourth of the nation's central-city poor, lost more than one million jobs in manufacturing, wholesale, and retail between 1967 and 1976 alone at the same time that their populations were rapidly becoming minority dominant. By 1980, Blacks and Latinos accounted for virtually half of New York City's population, 57% of Chicago's, 67% of Detroit's, and 43% of Philadelphia's (Wilson, 1987).

Accompanying the transformation of major northern metropolises from goods-producing centers to centers of information processing has been a concomitant shift in educational requirements for employment. Whereas job losses in these cities have been greatest in industries with low educational requirements, job growth has been concentrated in industries with high educational requirements (Wilson, 1987; see also Kasarda, 1985). Over the past 20 years, northern cities that have experienced the greatest loss of jobs requiring less education have simultaneously experienced significant increases in minority residents. Despite increases in educational attainment since 1970, Black males over age 16 are still concentrated in educational categories in which employment opportunities declined the fastest and are least represented in educational categories where northern central city employment has most expanded. Consequently, a mismatch between the current educational distribution of minority residents in large northern cities and the changing educational requirements of their rapidly transforming industry base has occurred. This mismatch is one major reason that unemployment rates and labor force dropout rates are higher among central-city Blacks than among central-city, nonminority residents, and that Black unemployment rates have not responded well to economic recovery in many northern cities (Kasarda, 1983; Wilson, 1987; Zinn, 1989).

Rather than offering opportunities to minority residents, cities have become centers of poverty (Zinn, 1989) that require families to adopt alternative structural patterns to survive (Billingsley, 1968; Stack, 1974). According to proponents of the structural perspective, extended households may buffer the effects of labor market disadvantages (Angel & Tienda, 1982) precipitated by the changing economic structure. Economic disadvantages among low-income, minority families often prevent the establishment and maintenance of nuclear households. Consequently, extended households represent the most stable and enduring form of family organization. Extended household members cope with economic exploitation by pooling economic as well as noneconomic resources (Adams, 1968a; Aschbrenner, 1973; Gutman, 1976; Lee, 1980; Stack, 1974). Extended household members are relied on for help with finances, household work, and child care (Hill, 1972). In times of extreme economic hardship, individuals often informally adopt children of relatives or friends until the biological parents are able to raise them (Stack, 1974).

A related consequence of the profound changes in the structure of the economy and composition of the labor force over the past 40 years (Wilson, 1987) has been the rise in out-of-wedlock births among minority families. However, because opportunity structures have not declined in an identical manner and because poverty is highest in regions transformed by macrostructural economic changes, minority groups have not been affected in an equivalent manner (Zinn, 1989). For instance, in 1990, the rate of out-of-wedlock births among African Americans, Chicanos, Puerto Ricans, and non-Hispanic Whites was 67%, 33%, 56%, and 17%, respectively (U.S. National Center for Health Statistics, 1990). Structural theorists argue that as poverty and unemployment rates increase, the rates of female-headed households also increase (Bean & Tienda, 1987; Zinn, 1989). Conversely, as people experience upward mobility, reliance on extended kin and nonkin social support networks should diminish. Therefore, an economic explanation for network participation is essential.

Wilson (1987) attributes the dramatic rise in female-headed households among Blacks and Puerto Ricans to an increase in male joblessness. By devising an indicator called the "index of marriageable males," he illustrates a long-term decline in the proportion of young Black men who are in a position to support a family. He suggests that the increasing rate of joblessness (combined with high Black mortality, incarceration rates, and an unknown percentage of homosexual Black men) significantly decreases the proportion of potentially marriageable Black men. Black women are no longer marrying the fathers of their children, because these unemployable men are not able to contribute financially to the marriage and become a drain on women's already meager economic resources. Structural theorists conclude that the rise in female-headed households is an adaptive response that can be linked directly to the labor market status of Black and Latino males (Wilson, 1987; Zinn, 1989).

An alternative to maintaining an independent household, especially among younger mothers, is to live in an extended family. Because younger mothers tend to have less education, less work experience, and fewer financial resources, they are more likely to reside initially in an extended household (Bane & Ellwood, 1984). The ability to move back into households of kin during times of economic crisis is a great source of security for those living in poverty. These highly adaptive structural features of urban minority families comprise a resilient response to the social-economic conditions of poverty (Alvirez & Bean, 1976; Hoppe & Heller, 1975; Ladner, 1972; Stack, 1974).

Another adaptive response to the harsh conditions of poverty is the development of informal social support networks. These networks are characterized by ongoing systems of interaction, resource allocation, and exchange reciprocity (Stack, 1974; Zinn, 1982b). Individuals can rely on an extensive web of kin and friends for help with daily survival. Poverty creates a necessity for the exchange of goods and services because destitute families are often unable to pay for fixed expenses without help from members of their network. Because women are primarily responsible for child care and household work, ties between them often constitute the core of the extended network (Adams, 1968b; Stack, 1974). The sharing of clothing, child care, food stamps, rent money, cigarettes, food, milk, transportation, even furniture enables members of the network to cope with the hardships of daily survival. Even when young women receive welfare, they say their resources go further when they exchange goods and services daily.

The informal social support network is characterized by a system of reciprocal obligation where individuals take turns helping each other. Without the help of the network, fluctuations in the meager flow of available goods could easily destroy a family's ability to survive. Kin and close friends who fall into similar economic crises know that they may share the food, dwelling, and even the few scarce luxuries of those individuals in their network. Because of the underlying assumption of reciprocal obligation, the limited supply of material goods in a community may be redistributed perpetually among networks of kin and throughout the community. Individuals who fail to reciprocate in swapping relationships are judged harshly and usually dropped from the network. Throughout this process of exchange, people become immersed in a broad web of kinfolk and fictive kin who introduce others into the network and can be relied on for help (Stack, 1974).

Despite the ethnic diversity in the family lives of Blacks, Chicanos, and Puerto Ricans, extended family living arrangements and informal social support networks have compensated for resources withheld by the larger economic system (Zinn, 1987). Extended families pool resources, share mutual aid, and represent an attempt to cope with the tenuous necessities of survival. Clearly, advocates of the structural perspective argue that racial-ethnic group differences in the propensity to participate in kin and nonkin social support networks should disappear when controlling for socioeconomic status.

## THE STRUCTURAL APPROACH: CRITIQUE

The structural approach to extended families and informal social support networks provides an insightful analysis of the importance of economics on family structure; however, it is not without some flaws. First, although this theoretical perspective recognizes the influence of socioeconomic constraints on families, it completely disregards the influence of culture on family organization. Although family organization is certainly affected by economic forces, it is crucial to examine how culture affects the way in which different groups respond to these economic constraints. Second, the view that extended living arrangements and informal social support networks exist only among impoverished families, and are abandoned when poverty desists, is problematic. The underlying assumption of this approach is that as minority groups become solidly working class or middle class, they no longer need the extended network and therefore become individualistically oriented. Third, reducing racial-ethnic stratification to a class phenomenon is reasonable only under the assumption that controlling for socioeconomic factors will eliminate racial and ethnic differences in network participation (Bean & Tienda, 1987). In fact, there is some research that suggests that even as Black families experience upward mobility, they continue to participate in extended networks (McAdoo, 1980). Finally, much of the structural research on kin networks has been based on the findings of Carol Stack's (1974) work. However, her study has not been replicated in other large cities, limiting its generalizability. In addition, her depiction of the kin network in which everyone shares equally and no one tries to take advantage of that network may be somewhat idealized. Future research may demonstrate that there are a variety of stressors associated with participation in these social support networks.

## Empirical Literature

### EXTENDED LIVING ARRANGEMENTS

The structural explanation regarding extension and race-ethnicity is that minority families are more likely to extend than are White families because of their more limited economic resources and greater susceptibility to economic discrimination. Contemporary economic status differences are stressed, rather than differences in cultural values and norms. The structural argument has been articulated using the African American family as its focal point. According to Andrew Billingsley (1968, 1992), Black family organization must be understood within a historical context in which African Americans have been placed in a disadvantaged position. In times of economic crisis, individuals rely on family as a source of material, emotional, and social support. Therefore, elaborate kinship networks must be understood as a means of survival in the face of economic and social deprivation. Proponents of the structural perspective recently have extended Billingsley's (1968) argument to include other minority families who engage in similar survival strategies to mitigate the effects of inequality.

Proponents of the structural approach argue that scholars must study extended family living arrangements from an economic perspective for a complete understanding of why people live in alternative family forms. According to Walter Allen (1979), a problem with the cultural orientation is that when minority families don't conform to the idealized Anglo nuclear family, the tendency is to seek internal cultural, rather than external structural, causes. A major question developed in this chapter, therefore, is whether kin networks are primarily a response to economic need or whether they are characteristic of certain cultural features of racial-ethnic groups (Hofferth, 1984).

The literature on extended families from the structural perspective will now be presented. There are very few empirical studies from the structural perspective, and many of them focus on African American families. In addition, they tend to examine female headedness as a major determinant of household extension. Given the constraints of the literature, this section begins with an examination of research that compares African American and White families. Research on female-headed households that examines economic variables but does not compare racial-ethnic characteristics will follow. Next, I will present two studies that do examine racial differences among female-headed households and compare racial differences in the likelihood of extension. Following the literature on female-headed households, I will present one study that compares African American, Latino, and Anglo extended households. Finally, I will complete this section by presenting a classic ethnographic study of extended living arrangements among poor African American families.

According to Allen (1979), extended families are the result of specific structural adjustments that Black families make in response to economic deprivation that threatens their ability to provide for family members. He argues that more severe resource limitations cause low-income Black families to display higher rates of disorganization than do middle- and upper-income Black families. In his case studies of middle-class Black families, he demonstrates that the long-term economic stability of these families enhances their ability to maintain conventional patterns of organization, fulfill members' needs, and conform to societal norms. Ladner (1972), Rodman (1971), Scanzoni (1971), and Stack (1974) share this perspective by stressing the primacy of economic factors over historic, cultural factors in the determination of Black family organization. This perspective views lower-income, urban Black family departures from normative family patterns as valid, sensible adaptations to the structural circumstances of racial and economic oppression (Allen, 1979).

Data for Allen's (1979) examination of the effects of race and class on family structure are taken from the 15% sample tapes of the 1970 U.S. Census. These data are nationally representative and therefore can be generalized to the U.S. population in 1970. His log linear analysis revealed that female-headed households were more frequently extended than were husband-wife households, extended and female-headed households were more common among low-income Black families, and larger proportions of Black families were in low socioeconomic categories. Interaction effects revealed that race interacted with family composition and family structure such that not only were female-headed families more commonly Black, but they were more commonly extended as well.

Allen (1979) argues that economic deprivation must be a factor in the decisions of Black families to improvise and adopt alternatives to conventional family structure. When socioeconomic status was controlled, race differences in family structure were greatly diminished. Therefore, according to this structural perspective, it seems reasonable to expect that class will be a better predictor of family structure than will race.

Living in multigeneration households may ease some of the burdens of economic deprivation by the pooling of resources. Several scholars have hypothesized that poor Black families are especially likely to create extended households as a form of mutual aid in facing economic uncertainty (Billingsley, 1973; Stack, 1974). Scheirer (1983) tests this hypothesis by conducting a descriptive, exploratory analysis of household structure among Black and White recipients of Aid to Families with Dependent Children (AFDC). She examines the occurrence and consequences of multigeneration households among welfare families. Data were obtained from the nationally representative AFDC Recipient Characteristics Study (RCS) for 1975 and 1977 that was conducted by the Social Security Administration. In the majority of households (more than 60%), an AFDC mother was living alone with her children. In the remaining households, 14% contained a father, 10% included a grandparent, 6% included other relatives, and 9% had no mother in the household.

The distribution of AFDC households by racial-ethnic group tends to support the hypothesis that Black families are particularly likely to form extended households for mutual support when economic resources are low and unstable. Black AFDC families lived in households with grandparents in somewhat larger proportions than did White families. In this type of household, most of the mothers were never married as opposed to having moved back home after divorce, separation, or widowhood. Some differences in household structure are likely to reflect the mother's marital status, with multigenerational households more likely to occur among unmarried mothers. Life-cycle stage is examined for several age groups in relation to household structure. The only group that differs by age is women under 20, who are more likely to live with the child's grandparents. The large majority of women in every other age group live alone with their child. Ultimately, the younger a mother is, the more likely she is to live with her parents.

Scheirer (1983) examined the occurrence and consequences of multigeneration households among welfare families. Her data did not include a predefined household structure variable. However, they did list types of individuals that comprised the household in relation to the youngest child. She used this listing to create a variable indicating household type, including a mother and her children alone; a mother and father or stepfather with children; a mother and children with one or more grandparents of the youngest child; a mother and children with other adult relatives or nonrelatives; and AFDC households with no mother. In examining welfare payments, Scheirer (1983) found high negative correlations between state payments and household structure, providing strong support for the hypothesis that AFDC payment levels that are too low for a single mother and her children contribute to the formation of extended family households. According to Scheirer (1983), interpreting the high correlation coefficients as showing a causal role for the level of AFDC payments seems reasonable. States with higher levels of monthly AFDC benefits had much lower proportions of families living with the youngest child's grandparents. It appears that in low-paying states, other family members are providing the economic sustenance for many AFDC families that is lacking from welfare payments.

It is interesting to note that the overall frequency of extended households is low. A mother living alone with her children is the most common structure of poverty families regardless of race. However, lower AFDC payments do increase the proportion of three-generation household families among welfare recipients, lending credence to the structural argument.

Because the data were recorded by AFDC caseworkers, Scheirer (1983) provides very accurate information on AFDC family financial records; however, the information concerning other family characteristics is very limited. Although her bivariate analysis is nonprobabilistic and exploratory, she erroneously justifies making causal statements.

I will now present the research on economic indicators of female-headed households in which no racial or ethnic comparisons are made. In a study of shared extended living arrangements as a form of economic support for unmarried mothers, Martha Hill (1990) considers both the family and the neighborhood as determinants of the long-run economic circumstances of young mothers of out-of-wedlock children. Her major focus is on extension and direct financial kin support to noncoresidential respondents. She hypothesizes that shared housing with relatives in the years after becoming a young, unmarried mother helps the young mother avoid poverty and dependence on public assistance if the shared-housing support is of modest duration.

The data are the nationally representative Panel Study of Income Dynamics (PSID), a longitudinal data set with annual interviews tracking families and individuals since 1968. Transitions into and out of poverty, and onto and off of AFDC recipiency, are the economic outcomes of interest. The sample consists of young mothers traced over the years following the birth of their first (possibly out-of-wedlock) child.

The likelihood of living in an extended household changes during the postchildbirth period. In the years immediately following childbirth, extension is the modal situation. It is much less common by the time the child reaches age 3 and is rare after the child reaches school age. The ability of subfamily living arrangements to prevent poverty and/or break the cycle of continued welfare dependency is examined.

Findings indicate significant effects of extended living arrangements in the expected direction. Higher initial amounts of extension reduce the chances of becoming poor and of becoming an AFDC recipient while simultaneously increasing one's chances of moving out of poverty and of ceasing to be an AFDC recipient. However, the beneficial effects do not continue indefinitely. Incremental benefits decline as the level of accumulated support grows. The accumulation of more than 3.5 years of shared-housing support enhances rather than reduces chances for moving onto AFDC recipiency. The accumulation of 8 or more years of shared-housing support will raise rather than lower chances of becoming poor.

Hill (1990) concludes by suggesting that shared-housing support seems to offer improvements in the economic prospects of young, unmarried mothers. This holds for modest levels of support, but the incremental improvements diminish the longer extension is maintained. Therefore, extended living arrangements can be considered only a temporary survival strategy in the face of long-range economic deprivation.

Although Hill (1990) presents her study as a preliminary analysis, a problem with the data is the limitation on information about intrahousehold sharing of expenses and resources, which is very difficult to ascertain but also very important for quantifying the amount of support provided above and beyond extension.

In a study similar to Hill's (1990), assessing the impact of AFDC on family structure and living arrangements, Ellwood and Bane (1985) found that welfare payments have a dramatic impact on the living arrangements of young, single mothers. In low-benefit states, young mothers who are not living with a husband are very likely to live in the home of a parent. In high-benefit states, these women are much more likely to live independently.

According to Ellwood and Bane (1985), the reason that past research has missed this economic link between welfare payments and extended living arrangements is because until 1983, the Bureau of the Census (which conducts both the Census and the Current Population Survey) had a major flaw in the way "subfamilies" were coded. As a result, more than one half of all subfamilies were missed. In fact, Ellwood and Bane (1985) estimate that at least one fourth of all single mothers and more than one half of those under age 24 do not live independently. Their research indicates that the living arrangements of young mothers are strongly influenced by the level of AFDC benefits in a state. Overall, they estimate that a $100 benefit increase would cause the number of single mothers who live in subfamilies to decline by 25% to 30%.

It appears at first glance that Hill's (1990) and Ellwood and Bane's (1985) research supports a structural interpretation and demonstrates an economic basis for extended family living arrangements among AFDC recipients. However, to fully support the structural argument, this population needs to be compared to a nonpoverty population, and a racial-ethnic comparison is essential.

In contrast to Scheirer's (1983), Hill's (1990), and Ellwood and Bane's (1985) findings, some scholars argue that AFDC may, in fact, contribute to poverty by discouraging subfamily living arrangements. Approximately half of the states in the United States have AFDC rules that carry penalties for shared housing arrangements (Hutchens, Jakubson, & Schwartz, 1986, as cited in Hill, 1990). The disincentives for shared housing are built into rules governing eligibility and transfer amounts based on the income of coresidents. Exactly how AFDC rules affect the living arrangements of actual or potential AFDC recipients is, however, unclear (Hill, 1990). Whereas Ellwood and Bane (1984) find evidence of higher levels of AFDC benefits encouraging independent residence relative to subfamily membership, Hutchens, Jakubson, and Schwartz (1986, 1988, as cited in Hill, 1990) find no substantial effect (Hill, 1990).

Up to this point, the research has been problematic because some studies make no racial-ethnic comparisons, whereas others argue that Black families are more likely to have strong kinship ties, without controlling for important explanatory variables. Without these control variables, substantial comparisons between African Americans, Latinos, and Anglos cannot be made. An important difference that has not yet been controlled is the greater prevalence of female-headed households among Blacks. Whereas a number of studies have shown stronger kin ties among Blacks than among Whites (Allen, 1979; Hays & Mindel, 1973; Tienda & Angel, 1982), reasons for stronger ties have not been convincing. Some scholars argue that kinship ties are a response to economic deprivation and a survival strategy in a hostile environment. Other scholars argue that although such relationships may be economically functional, there is a greater cultural emphasis on kinship among Blacks.

Therefore, a major question of concern that still persists is whether Black and White families differ in their propensity to reside in extended households after controls for other relevant predictors are employed. Hence, I will now discuss two studies that examine racial differences among female-headed households and compare racial differences in the likelihood of extension.

The first study, Hofferth's (1984) examination of kin networks, race, and family structure, is based on the nationally representative longitudinal data from the 1979 wave of the PSID. Using log linear contingency table analysis, Hofferth (1984) found race differences in extended living arrangements: Black families are much more likely to be extended than are White families. Blacks are more likely than Whites to participate in kin networks because they are more likely to be headed by single parents, and one-parent families are more likely than two-parent families to be extended.

In sharp contrast to other studies examining female-headed families with children, there is no direct relationship between living in an extended family and race, controlling for other factors. Because Blacks are more likely to be never married, and because never-married mothers are more likely to be extended, Black female family heads appear to be more likely to live in extended family arrangements than do White female family heads. Hofferth (1984) concludes that the apparent relationship between likelihood of extension and race is entirely due to marital status differences between Blacks and Whites.

The second study that examines racial differences in the likelihood of extension among female-headed households is by Hogan, Hao, and Parish (1990). Using data from the National Longitudinal Survey of Labor Force Behavior, Youth Survey (NSLY), a nationally representative sample of young respondents ages 14 to 21 with an oversampling of Blacks, Hogan et al. (1990) attempt to build on Hofferth's (1984) work. Although their study differs in some respects from Hofferth's (1984), they also compared the propensity to live in extended families among Black and White women. Hogan et al. (1990) found that young Black mothers are much more likely to live with one or more adult kin (44%) than are Whites (11%). Adult kin coresidence is more than three times more common among single mothers than among married mothers for both races. However, the racial differences in marital status do not account fully for racial differences in coresidence. Black mothers of every marital status are nearly twice as likely to live in a household that includes an adult relative. Even though single women are more likely than married women to live with adult kin, and Blacks are more likely to be single, there is no race-marital status interaction in the effects of those variables on coresidential living. Although Blacks are more likely to live with their mothers, unlike the findings in Hofferth's (1984) study, these racial differences do not vary significantly by marital status. Given the contradictory findings of Hofferth (1984) and Hogan et al.

(1990), future research must further examine the prevalence of extension among female-headed families while controlling for other relevant predictors to determine which of these predictors has the most explanatory power.

Hogan et al. (1990) found that less than one half of the racial difference in tendency to reside with adult kin is accounted for by differences in marital status and fertility history. Taking into account their earlier ages at parenthood, higher fertility, and greater proportions of single mothers, Black women consistently are more likely to reside with kin. This Black extended family pattern is not simply a function of teenage childbearing or single motherhood, although it is increased by these factors. Rather, it may be a mechanism that reduces the costs of housing in light of low incomes. This pattern of coresidence is critical because it provides Black mothers with greater access to a child care provider and a more ready source of income support.

Although Hofferth's (1984) and Hogan et al.'s (1990) analyses are an important step in the understanding of racial-ethnic differences in the likelihood of extension among single mothers, they provide only a Black-White comparison. A more thorough analysis should compare different categories of Latinos as well, which would provide a more comprehensive understanding of the interaction between gender, race, and class. It is clear from these two studies that there is still much ambiguity as to what factors explain household extension. A major flaw in Hofferth's (1984) analysis is the absence of any examination of child care. As Hogan et al. (1990) demonstrated, a vital element in the decision of whether or not to live in an extended family arrangement is the availability of free child care. Unfortunately, neither study analyzes other types of nonfinancial assistance in which extended kin may borrow and lend important nonmonetary resources necessary for survival. Hogan and colleagues do examine financial aid; however, they do not include financial support that is less than one half of the respondent's income. It may be that they are eliminating important kin support, because many relatives may contribute small amounts of financial help to family members.

I will now present the only study on extended living arrangements, from the structural perspective, to compare African American, Latino, and non-Hispanic White families. Using a slightly different approach from Hofferth (1984) and Hogan et al. (1990), Angel and Tienda

(1982) investigated the extent to which living arrangements help buffer the effects of labor market disadvantages faced by minority household heads. They found evidence to support the argument that the extension mechanism may alleviate poverty or at least provide households with greater flexibility in allocating market and domestic roles among household members. Extended family structure was more prevalent among minority households (Blacks were 14% and Hispanics were 15% more likely than Anglos to extend) and those headed by females rather than couples. They found that variations in relative income contributions of nonnuclear members reflect differences in the labor market success of racial and ethnic groups as well as in motivation to extend. This comparative research lends strong support to the economic argument that claims that household extension is related to the desire to alleviate the low earnings of the primary breadwinner and is therefore a response to economic conditions and not a result of cultural norms that favor extension.

Angel and Tienda's (1982) study is an extremely important contribution to the literature on extended families because it is one of the few analyses to include Latino families. Furthermore, their definition of extended families includes kin as well as nonkin. Another important contribution is their finding that many minority households in their sample have incomes below the poverty level despite the supplemental income of extended members, indicating that the economic contributions of nonnuclear members do not automatically offset the economic disadvantages suffered by minority households (Angel & Tienda, 1982). Unfortunately, given the constraints of their data, they cannot determine the proportion of nonpoor families who were poor before they included nonnuclear members into their households.

Further supporting the findings of Angel and Tienda (1982) is Carol Stack (1974), who, in a seminal ethnographic study, argues that economic deficiencies among low-income Blacks militate against the establishment and maintenance of nuclear households. Her research revealed elaborate exchange networks through which extended family members shared resources, household tasks, and lodging in a system characterized by mutual obligation. Stack's (1974) anthropological study of "The Flats," the poorest section of a Black community in a midwestern city, demonstrates that the socioeconomic conditions of Black Americans have given rise to special features of family organization and extended family networks in Black communities. Stack (1974) views women as strategists, active agents who use resources to achieve goals and cope with everyday problems. She argues that households form around women because of their role in child care. Ties between women often constitute the core of the extended network. She shows that economic crises (underemployment, unemployment) contribute to constant residential shifts, bringing men, women, and children into the households of kin. Newly formed households are successive recombinations of the same domestic networks. Stack found that individuals in The Flats could draw upon a broad domestic web of kin and friends. Although households have shifting membership, they tended to maintain three generations of children and adult kin: males and females of childbearing age, a middle generation of mothers raising their own children or the children of close kin, and the parents of the middle generation. The ability to move back into the households of kin during times of economic crisis is a great source of security for those living in poverty. Because of poverty, young women with children do not perceive any choice but to live at home with their mothers or other adult relatives.

Stack's (1974) anthropological research provides a rich depiction of extended families among an impoverished community of African Americans. Her detailed account of exchange networks provides further support for a structural approach to understanding diverse family living arrangements. Because of her nonprobability sample and her participant observational research, however, it would be irresponsible to generalize her findings to all low-income Black communities. However, research cited above, as well as studies conducted by Williams (1973), Aschbrenner (1975), Hill (1971), Schneider and Smith (1973), and Gutman (1976) (all cited in Bane & Ellwood, 1985) demonstrates that Black families frequently use extended family arrangements to pool limited resources, mitigate the damaging effects of economic deprivation, and generally create more viable economic units.

Although the argument in favor of a purely structural approach is strong, it is by no means conclusive. There is substantial evidence to support the claim that extended living arrangements are a conscious strategy to help buffer the effects of poverty. However, the structural perspective presents an economically deterministic argument that completely ignores the influence of culture on these survival strategies.

Social, economic, and political forces do affect the lives of minority families, but cultural factors may determine how these families respond to these external forces. Ultimately, a more holistic approach should take into account both cultural elements and structural determinants in the decision to form extended living arrangements.

## SOCIAL SUPPORT NETWORKS

The structural perspective on social support networks asserts that sharing resources with family and nonfamily members is a deliberate strategy for survival in an attempt to ameliorate severe economic deprivation. Robert Hill (1972) contends that one of the greatest strengths of Black families is their strong kinship ties. There is a great deal of reliance on social support networks for help with finances, child rearing, advice, and household help. He argues for a structural approach to understanding extended kin networks because this network of support often provides the backbone of African American family survival.

Stack's (1974) definitive ethnographic study of The Flats demonstrated the elaborate social support networks established by impoverished African Americans as a survival strategy to mitigate against the extreme effects of economic deprivation. Respondents in Stack's study often exchanged clothing, food stamps, furniture, money, and child care with both family and nonfamily members. She argues that these strategies reflect the adaptations to survive within multiple systems of oppression and are necessary for the maintenance of the Black family. Although this study provides an in-depth analysis of the African American family, it does not allow for racial-ethnic group comparisons.

Several studies on informal support networks do attempt to provide racial-ethnic group comparisons. However, most of these studies focus primarily on Black-White comparisons. Kin network support to mothers typically involves assistance with child care and financial support. It has been found that kin support of these types is more common among single mothers than among married mothers, with Black families more frequently providing child care support and White families more often providing financial assistance. Racial differences in kin support reflect overall racial differences in patterns of exchange between kin, and the greater likelihood of single parenthood among

Blacks, rather than an extraordinary response to the challenges of single motherhood (Hofferth, 1985; Hogan et al., 1990; Parish, Hao, & Hogan, 1991). Such assistance is closely linked to physical access to kin (Angel & Tienda, 1982; Furstenberg & Crawford, 1978; Stack, 1974, as cited in Madigan & Hogan, 1990). Based on this research, investigators have concluded that informal social support networks seem to help women who head households to deal with the economic pressures and everyday responsibilities (Anderson & Allen, 1984; Angel & Tienda, 1982).

Some studies have found that Blacks and Hispanics engage in mutual support activities at higher levels than do Whites (Mindel, 1980; Mutran, 1985; Stack, 1974; Taylor, 1986, as cited in Eggebeen & Hogan, 1990). Many scholars have suggested that kin-based support networks are particularly salient for Blacks, with the strength of intergenerational ties making the higher incidence of single parenthood less problematic than it would be for Whites. Many of the studies that found strong kin ties among Black families were based on small, unrepresentative samples, and some failed to control for other differences between Black and White families that may account for differences.

Hogan et al.'s (1990) analysis of kin networks and support for young mothers using nationally representative longitudinal data for the 1980s obtained largely similar results. Black mothers have better access to income support and child care than do White mothers. Again, most of the differences are a function of the greater propensity of Black mothers to be single.

Hogan et al.'s (1990) analysis confirms that single mothers have better access to kin than do married mothers. Kin access is better among Blacks than among Whites. The effects of race and marital status operate independently (unlike in Hofferth's 1984 analysis), so that single Black mothers have the best access to kin. However, being a single mother increases the likelihood of kin access equally among both Blacks and Whites. Thus, although Blacks overall are more likely to have close access to kin, there is no unique residential response to the challenges of single motherhood. Hogan et al. (1990) conclude by stating that almost one third of the single Black mothers in the sample were not involved in support networks, and the support those not in the network received was insufficient to provide adequate access to child care.

Eggebeen and Hogan (1990) attempted to extend this analysis by comparing similarities and differences in helping behavior among diverse racial-ethnic groups. In their research, they identified four dimensions of exchange: monetary and material resources, child care, household assistance, and companionship. They found that respondents living in poverty do not have high incidences of aid. Only 17% of the possible exchanges that would bring aid to these poor families occur. Only 16% of poor families receive money, compared with 20% of those living above the poverty level. Overall, poor people are less frequently involved in exchanges of aid than are people with higher income. On average, Blacks are less involved in exchanges with their parents than are Whites, and they are less likely to receive aid. These differences are especially pronounced in the case of monetary aid, but they apply to baby-sitting, child care, advice, and household services as well. Chicanos are even less involved in exchanges of support. Only 8% of the maximum level of giving or receiving was reported for Chicano respondents.

Eggebeen and Hogan (1990) find no evidence for unique ethnic patterns of exchange. Blacks and Chicanos are less involved in exchange networks than are Whites. The consistently lower level of intergenerational support reported among Blacks in these national sample survey data is inconsistent with the ethnographic portrait of exceptionally strong family support networks among Blacks and Hispanics. People with higher levels of education are more likely to give and receive aid. People with poverty-level incomes are less involved in exchange networks, particularly child care and financial aid.

These findings may, in fact, result from their measure of social support rather than from real differences in intergenerational support. Eggebeen and Hogan (1990) examined four dimensions of exchange and then ascertained giving and receiving support for each dimension. However, rather than looking at each dimension of exchange as a separate dependent variable, they created a summary measure of intergenerational exchange by combining the four different types of support into one very broad indicator.

Ultimately, Eggebeen and Hogan (1990) do not find evidence for unique ethnic patterns of exchange. Although they recognize that past research has emphasized the greater familism of Chicanos and strong mother-daughter ties in Black families, they argue that it is a mistake to assume that strong kin ties automatically translate into kin support networks. Their research indicates that Chicanos are less involved in exchange networks primarily because of the great distances they live from their parents. Blacks are less involved than Whites in the exchange of financial assistance, household services, child care, and advice and emotional support. Even among Black single mothers with young children, the advantages in kin support claimed for Blacks do not seem to occur.

The research on informal social support networks from the structural perspective is more persuasive than the research from the cultural approach. However, there are situations in which a purely economic explanation for involvement in these networks is insufficient. It appears that both socioeconomic and cultural factors may be responsible for familistic behavior among various minority groups. Therefore, I would argue once again against a monocausal approach in favor of a more integrated one.

# 3

# The Culture-Structure Nexus

Simplistic notions of "culture" versus "social structure" have impeded the development of a broader theoretical framework (Wilson, 1991) from which to examine determinants of extended living arrangements and informal social support networks. Drawing heavily from Black and Chicana feminist thought (see Collins, 1990; hooks, 1981; Mirande & Enriquez, 1979; Smith, 1983; Zinn, 1990), I will now present a theoretical framework that begins to integrate social structural and cultural arguments by examining how the intersection of race, gender, and class affects family structure.

Analogous to the cultural perspective, the integrative approach is also informed by particular ideological underpinnings. My application of the integrative perspective views participation in extended kin and nonkin social support networks among minority families through a feminist lens. Although I use quantitative methods to understand network participation, I do not consider myself a positivist. Rather, I subscribe to the view that there is absolutely no "objective" scientific analysis of culture or social phenomena that is independent of predetermined viewpoints (Weber, 1994). This conviction does not preclude my use of the "scientific method" nor render me incapable of modifying my theoretical orientation based on research findings, nor does it mean that I would ever "massage" the data to support my position. What it does mean is that the research questions I ask, the way I ask those questions, and the analysis of my data are guided by feminist theory.

## Theoretical Framework

### THE INTERSECTION OF RACE, CLASS, AND GENDER

According to the integrative perspective, any analysis of family organization must include an examination of the impact of cultural as well as structural elements on diverse family forms. Minority families, in particular, must be examined within the context of their ethnic heritage. Racial and ethnic stratification, which is deeply embedded in American society, has a profound impact on family resources and subsequent family organization (Zinn, 1990). Therefore, when building and testing empirical models of family interaction, race-ethnicity must become the center of the analysis, not simply another variable to be examined. In addition, it is imperative to identify the association between the internal dynamics of women's family lives and economic conditions as they are bound up in broader systems of class and race inequality. The way I chose to examine this hierarchy was to assess the causal effects of cultural values and of economic indicators on informal social support networks for different racial-ethnic groups, while simultaneously examining the effects of gender. This approach enabled me to ascertain gender and racial-ethnic differences regarding individual responsibility to the kinship system and to examine the interaction effects between socioeconomic status and cultural attitudes. Studying gender, race, and class as interacting hierarchies of resources and rewards in minority families is essential for a more multidimensional depiction of minority family life (Zinn, 1990).

Black feminist scholars were the first to examine the interlocking nature of race, gender, and class oppression (Beale, 1970; Collins,

1990; Davis, 1981; Dill, 1983; hooks, 1981; Lewis, 1977). The crux of Black feminist thought is predicated on the simultaneity of oppression. Minimizing one form of oppression, although essential, may still leave Black women subjugated in other equally dehumanizing ways (Collins, 1986). Analysis of the interlocking nature of oppression shifts the investigative focus from merely explicating elements of race, gender, or class oppression to determining what the links are among these systems. Past approaches typically prioritized one form of oppression as primary, then examined remaining types of oppression as less important variables. This more integrative approach treats the interaction among multiple systems as the object of study. Instead of simply adding to existing theoretical paradigms by inserting previously excluded variables, Black feminists aspire to develop new theoretical interpretations of the interaction itself (Collins, 1986). Because other women of color are also similarly disadvantaged (Smith & Tienda, 1988), this theoretical perspective, with its focus on the linked nature of oppression (Collins, 1990), is also applicable to their experiences (see also Glenn, 1985, 1987; Mirande, 1985; Padilla, 1987).

I agree that research and theory about women of color must examine the complex interrelationship between race, gender, and class. However, scholars must be careful not to assume that minority women's experiences are interchangeable. Because of the distinct sociohistorical experiences of racial-ethnic women, scholars must examine how specific societal conditions at a particular historical moment affect these interlocking systems of oppression. A unique contribution of this work, then, is to examine a concrete empirical case and use this integrative theoretical framework to analyze it. This inductive approach allows me to contribute to theorizing about women of color by illustrating how the intersection of race, gender, and class is socially constructed within a particular sociohistorical context.

An integrative framework is particularly fruitful for examining how the simultaneity of oppression affects minority family organization. Unlike previous paradigms that examined either cultural determinants or structural determinants of family structure, this perspective combines the two for a more inclusive approach. In addition, this perspective challenges past constructs used to explain minority family interaction (Collins, 1990). Because household living arrangements and the structure of social support networks are extremely diverse, the family can no longer be depicted as a universal institution but rather as a composite of particular cultural, political, and economic contexts. For example, African American families often exhibit fluid household boundaries and are deeply embedded in a reciprocal exchange network because racial oppression has impoverished disproportionate numbers of Black families (Stack, 1974). Confronted with this economic exploitation, they invoke the Afrocentric worldview that offers alternative definitions of community and family (Sudarkasa, 1981). Similarly, informal adoption of children by nonbiological mothers, what Patricia Hill Collins (1990) terms "other mothers," represents the cultural value placed on cooperative child care traditionally found in African culture. This traditional African value has endured as a result of the adverse conditions under which so many families exist.

Similarly, it has been hypothesized that Chicano family organization is also a product of conflicts between ideological value systems and the capitalist economy (Del Castillo, 1984). Del Castillo (1984) argues for an integrative approach to studying the dynamics of Chicano family organization in which the persistent tension between cultural ideals and the social structure is examined. Extended social support networks found in Chicano and Puerto Rican communities also represent the use of ancestral values to mitigate against economic conditions. In confronting gender, race, and class oppression, maintaining community-based child care and extended social support networks represents a viable alternative to the "normative" nuclear family for African American (Collins, 1990), Chicana, and Puerto Rican women, who, because of their role in child care, often form the core of the extended family network (Stack, 1974).

However, just as we cannot assume that women's experiences are universal (Stimpson, 1980), we cannot assume that the experiences of all members of a racial-ethnic group are universal. Gender forms only one axis of a complex heterogeneous web of historically specific social interactions. Feminist scholarship must therefore analyze diverse axes of interactions (Bordo, 1990), paying particular attention to cultural differences and historical specificity (Fraser & Nicholson, 1990). It is therefore essential to examine the effects of household living arrangements on informal social support networks among different socioeconomic classes (Allen, 1995) and genders to get a more realistic depiction of the diversity of family structure within and among racial-ethnic groups.

This integrative theoretical approach to minority families illustrates that by using cultural forms where possible and creating new forms where necessary, racial-ethnics adapted their families to the larger social order (Zinn, 1990). Therefore, to understand the complexities of family organization, it is imperative to examine the interacting systems of gender, race, and class (Andrade, 1982; Collins, 1986; Dill, 1983; Glenn, 1985; Stimpson, 1980; Zinn, 1990) in contemporary American society. Subsequently, the aim of this research is to examine participation in informal social support networks among minority families and to theorize about how race, class, and gender operate within the culture-structure nexus.

The next section will present a review of the empirical literature on household living arrangements and informal social support networks based on the integrative perspective outlined above.

## Empirical Literature

### EXTENDED LIVING ARRANGEMENTS

The integrative approach to extended living arrangements examines the impact of cultural as well as structural determinants on the likelihood of extension. Although most researchers agree that the extended family system exists, what is still unknown about this issue is the extent to which cultural and/or structural factors account for household structure and whether or not extension is characteristic of African American and Latino communities. There is very little empirical research from the integrative perspective; therefore, this section will provide only a brief summary.

Hayes and Mindel (1973) demonstrated that the extended family is a more prominent structure for Black families than for Whites; however, their sample size was only 25 Black and White families. In a related study, Dubey (1971) examined the extended family using Black, White, and Puerto Rican subjects. He found that subjects with a high degree of powerlessness were significantly more likely to have an extended family than were subjects with a high degree of power.

However, McAdoo (1980) argues that extended kinship systems are not just a survival strategy for impoverished families. She found that Blacks who became middle class were not withdrawn from the extended family network.

K. Sue Jewell (1988) argues that contemporary patterns of kinship among African Americans can be explained by examining both cultural and structural factors. She contends that specific cultural experiences as well as social and economic hardships have created unique familial arrangements among Black families. In fact, Jewell (1988) argues that the systematic exclusion of Blacks from major societal institutions has had a tremendous impact on the organization of the Black family.

Similarly, Maxine Baca Zinn (1982b) articulates an integrative approach in which both culture and social structure are seen as constraining Chicano family organization. Contemporary Chicano familism represents forms of adaptation to structural conditions facing Chicanos. She does not, however, totally discount the importance of cultural symbols and meanings; rather, she gives priority to ongoing systems of interaction, resource allocation, and exchange reciprocity, and to social conditions that foster and sustain such systems. Therefore, there seems to be some evidence to support both a cultural and a structural explanation of extended households (Zinn, 1982a).

In order to assess what dimensions of familism/extension are reflections of culture and what dimensions are reflections of structure, Tienda and Angel (1982) followed up their initial study (Angel & Tienda, 1982) by examining differences in the prevalence of extended living arrangements among Black, Hispanic, and non-Hispanic White female-headed and husband-wife families. Results of logistic regression analysis indicate that greater prevalence of extended structure among Hispanics and Blacks is related to both cultural circumstances and the attempt of households to cope with economic hardships. In general, households headed by women are the most likely to have an adult extended household member. Among non-Hispanic Whites, 75% of all extended households headed by women contained one or more additional adults, compared with 64% of all extended White units headed by a married couple. Extended households headed by individuals of South/Central American origin were the most likely to contain one or more nonnuclear adults, whereas female-headed Black families were least likely of the minorities to be extended. For South/Central Americans, Chicanos, and other Spanish origin groups, the proportions of extended households containing adults did not differ significantly according to headship. Puerto Ricans exhibited a significantly lower propensity to include economically active members than did non-Hispanic Whites. Because Puerto Ricans are among the poorest minority groups, and because Chicanos, South/Central Americans, and other Spanish origin groups extend despite type of headship, this may reflect a cultural phenomenon rather than structural group differences.

This research suggests that for Latinos, headship may not be an overriding determinant of extension, even among the poorest families, pointing toward a more cultural analysis. The fact that Blacks were found to be least likely to extend among the minorities is also evidence in favor of a more cultural argument. However, although Tienda and Angel (1982) warn against an economically deterministic interpretation of household extension patterns, they emphasize economic over cultural factors in arguing that incorporation of nonnuclear members into family households encourages creative income strategies to cope with economic hardships. The historical specificity of the integrative approach provides the most effective strategy for interpreting these data. Although race-ethnicity is certainly an important indicator of extension, in this particular context, economic disenfranchisement takes priority.

The research on extended family living arrangements is inconclusive. However, some general patterns do emerge. There is evidence to support the argument that Blacks and Hispanics are more familistic than are non-Hispanic Whites. Research findings demonstrate that Blacks and Chicanos are more likely to extend than Anglos, although the research on whether Blacks or Chicanos are more likely to extend is contradictory. Furthermore, there is some question as to whether extension is a cultural or a structural phenomenon. The research from the structural perspective is clearly more robust than the research from the cultural approach. Given that women in states with lower AFDC payments are more likely to live in extended households and that initial extension does mitigate against poverty, a structural argument seems reasonable. The fact that Blacks and Chicanos are more likely to extend therefore may be a function of their lower socioeconomic status. Both Hofferth (1984) and Hogan, Hao, and Parish (1990) argue that there is some economic effect on propensity among Blacks to extend.

I would argue that the integrative perspective seems the most convincing. A dualistic argument in favor of culture or structure simplifies the complex differences that characterize racial-ethnic groups' decisions to live in extended households. The integrative approach provides a more holistic account of why people extend. The most convincing argument from the integrative perspective is Tienda and Angel's (1982) study previously mentioned. Although they find that Blacks and Hispanics are more likely than Whites to live in extended households, they argue that it may be an attempt among minority families to cope with economic hardship as well as a result of cultural differences. However, because of the lack of empirical evidence in support of this perspective, and because the bulk of this research is more than 10 years old, much more research is necessary before any final conclusions can be made.

## SOCIAL SUPPORT NETWORKS

Much of the quantitative research that attributes extended social support networks among minorities to both cultural and structural elements focuses on the elderly. This research generally agrees that the elderly in the United States are not isolated from their kinship networks but are members of modified extended families. As Litwak (1965) noted, kinship structures have evolved gradually from the traditional extended family to the modified extended family, in which a coalition of separately housed, semiautonomous nuclear families operates in a state of partial dependency with shared family functions. The modified extended family, characterized by frequent interaction, close affective bonds, and the exchange of goods and services, is composed of family members who typically live within visiting distance, interact by choice, and are connected to one another by means of mutual aid and social activities (Cantor, 1979).

Taylor (1985) examined the reported frequency of informal support that Black elderly receive from extended family members. The analyses were conducted using the National Survey of Black Americans, the first data set using a nationally representative cross section of the adult Black population living in the United States. The dependent variable was frequency of support from family members.

Elderly Blacks in this sample received some level of support from their extended family members. Most of the respondents reported fairly frequent contact with their families, and elderly Blacks indicated a high level of family affection. Multivariate analysis of frequency of support indicates that family contact and proximity of relatives were the only two family variables that had significant multivariate relationships with support. Respondents who had frequent contact with family received support more often than those who had lower levels of contact. Similarly, proximity of relatives was associated with receiving support from family.

Based on these findings, Taylor (1985) concludes that Black elderly are active participants in family networks. Elderly respondents reported significant levels of interaction with family, relatively close residential proximity to immediate family, extensive familial affective bonds, and a high degree of satisfaction derived from family life. The regional differences found suggest that the South may possess a unique set of cultural values that encourages familial assistance to the elderly. Collectively, these results are consistent with existing literature on the kinship interaction patterns and support networks of older Blacks and the general Black population (Cantor, 1979a; Jackson, 1980; Shanas, 1979; Stack, 1974; Stanford, 1978, as cited in Taylor, 1985).

One major drawback of Taylor's (1985) data is that he is unable to make comparisons between racial-ethnic groups. Although his focus on elderly Blacks provides a detailed assessment of their social support networks, it cannot assess whether Blacks are more familistic simply by virtue of their ethnic identification. Nor does he look at frequency and availability of aid. Data on types of aid would present a more rounded picture.

Cantor (1979) attempts to address the question of whether Black and Hispanic elderly are more likely than Whites to have a strong support system, solely because of their race/ethnicity. She specifically assesses whether social support networks among the elderly can be ascribed principally to ethnicity or to structural factors such as social class. Her sample includes people age 60 and over living in the inner city of New York. The majority of the sample reported frequent face-to-face and telephone contacts with their children, who gave as well as received assistance. Where children were not available, neighbors acted as substitutes for absent primary social supports.

Cantor (1979) concludes that many myths regarding minority elderly are false. One cannot assume that although minority elderly may suffer social deficits of income, health, and housing, they are in a better position than White elderly with respect to assistance from family and kin. Although Hispanic elderly are significantly more likely to have children with whom they interact more frequently and from whom they receive help, this may be short term given increasing economic hardships. Surprisingly, it is not true that Black elderly have greater potential for support from kin. Socioeconomic status and health appear to be the more powerful underlying and long-range determinants of aid from children to parents.

Middle- and upper-class White elderly receive support as well, particularly when their health deteriorates. White parents report feeling as close to their children as do Black elderly, who in turn are more likely to live in close proximity to their children. Furthermore, there is a crucial role of social class with respect to the nature and structuring of the informal system. Black, Hispanic, and other poor and working-class families are more likely to have highly developed patterns of child-parent interaction arising out of economic and social necessity than is the case among the more well-to-do elderly. As class and income rise, the spread of the social support system increases. Although these children are still involved during crisis and illness and provide parents with financial assistance, the closer, more frequent interaction characteristic of lower socioeconomic groups diminishes.

Cantor's (1979) analysis lends some support to both a cultural and a structural argument. On one hand, she finds no real difference between Blacks and Whites with respect to amount of help received from children or in the feeling of closeness of children. She suggests that measures of socioeconomic status are the more stable and overriding predictors of both the span and comprehensiveness of the social support network. However, the question of culture still exists because she finds racial differences in the flow of help from older to younger generations. Blacks assisted their adult offspring to a greater degree than did Whites (Mutran, 1985).

Cantor's (1979) study deals exclusively with low-income urban families. In addition to limiting the generalizability of the findings, the poverty of the sample may severely limit any voluntary or discretionary help that may be occurring. Whether or not the ability to help leads to a racial difference, the alternative cultural interpretation seems to be a residual explanation. If racial differences remain after socioeconomic controls are exercised, this is assumed to be a cultural effect, but the factors that produced the racial differences remain unknown. It may be that beliefs and values also influence helping behavior, and these attitudes may be held differentially across races. Furthermore, race may interact with other variables that predict family support such that a given variable may be a stronger predictor of support in one racial group vis-à-vis the other. Little attention has been given to these possible interaction effects, yet there is reason to expect they may exist (Mutran, 1985).

In a study of intergenerational family support among Blacks and Whites, Mutran (1985) explicitly looks at whether racial differences in social support networks result from socioeconomic variables or from cultural factors. The data are derived from a national survey conducted by the National Council on Aging in 1974. The dependent variables are receiving and giving help.

Results indicate that Black families do appear to be more involved in exchanges of help across generations than do White families. The slope for Blacks on both giving and receiving help is significantly higher even considering differences in sex and age composition of the group. However, once controls for socioeconomic factors are included, racial differences in the reception of help disappear. In terms of aid that flows from the younger generation to the older, socioeconomic factors, not culture, produce the observed racial difference. One could argue, however, that as racial difference persists in the behavior of the older generation, there is evidence of a cultural effect. Perhaps the younger generation of Blacks is assimilating to the dominant culture, or the racial difference in the giving of help from older to younger generations may exist because of the greater economic need of the Black middle and younger generations for continued assistance (Mutran, 1985).

Alternatively, the lack of a racial effect in receiving help after controlling for parental socioeconomic status may be due to lack of control for the ability or resources of the younger Black family members in comparison to Whites to help or assist their elderly parents. The data report only the behavior of one generation, and there is no way to assess whether there are differences in underreporting by race, so Mutran (1985) therefore cannot exclude either the cultural or socioeconomic interpretations.

The data show that socioeconomic factors eliminate some of the differences in support behavior between the two racial groups, and even among Blacks, the more educated elderly are less dependent on younger family members for help. Different factors distinguish the racial groups in producing family helping behavior, and these lend some support to the cultural argument. Most notable is the influence of attitudes on helping behavior. Elderly Blacks are significantly more likely than elderly Whites to agree that the younger generation deserves more respect. Among Whites, this variable has very little effect. Mutran (1985) concludes that it seems unwise to present the two interpretations in opposition to one another. Observed differences cannot be attributed to socioeconomic status only or cultural factors only; there is supporting evidence for both.

The integrative perspective on informal social support networks seems the most convincing. Much of the research in this section uses large probability samples and more sophisticated multivariate analysis. Causal models are presented that demonstrate the existence of both economic and cultural aspects of social support networks. There is convincing evidence that informal social support networks mitigate against the detrimental effects of poverty, as well as evidence that specific cultural values favoring familism do exist. However, the evidence is certainly not conclusive, and further research is indeed necessary.

## Conclusion

It should be clear from the above discussion that there is no conclusive evidence to support either the cultural or the structural perspective in isolation. Much of the literature, especially from the cultural perspective, tends to use extremely small, nonrepresentative samples. Despite the use of bivariate analysis, combined with the use of nonprobability samples, many of these studies are presented as if they are accurate depictions of American family life. Generalizing findings from this kind of social science research is inappropriate.

Although many scholars agree that living in close proximity to one's family is an indicator of close family ties, many erroneous conclusions have been made regarding social support networks based on past research findings. Studies examining proximity tend to look at a particular Latino enclave and argue that this demonstrates their desire to live in close proximity to their family. Researchers then compare these Latino communities to other racial-ethnic groups (particularly Anglos) not living in similar enclaves to support their contention that non-Hispanics are less familistic. To provide a more accurate assessment of the importance of proximity in kin ties, this research examines precisely how proximity affects the likelihood of participating in one's social support network.

Many of the past studies look at only one racial-ethnic group, or they tend to make Black-White or Latino-White comparisons. Also, although there is an abundance of literature on African American, Chicano, and Anglo families, there is very little literature (written in English, on the mainland) on the Puerto Rican family. In addition, there has been a tendency in the sociological literature to ignore the unique sociopolitical histories and cultures of Chicanos and Puerto Ricans and simply combine them for the purpose of more manageable analysis. A unique contribution of my research is the separate examination of Chicano and Puerto Rican families with one another and with Anglo and African American families.

Another problem with past research is the tendency to examine poverty populations in isolation. To ameliorate this inadequacy and to assess the impact of socioeconomic and cultural factors more completely, I examine socioeconomic status as a continuous variable.

In addition, it is imperative to examine geographical region to assess whether there is a cultural norm associated with kin networks that may transcend economics. Only one study included geographic region, and it did find norms in the South to be more favorable to close family ties than norms in the North.

As indicated by the literature reviewed above, very few studies examine household structure as an independent variable. An analysis of whether or not extended household members act as resources providing individuals with more flexibility to participate in their networks would be productive. Therefore, this research will operationalize household structure as a set of independent variables. Furthermore, much more in-depth analysis of the role of child care among network members is needed. Household assistance and child care variables will be included in my study as a means of identifying the specific survival strategies and exact roles of individuals involved in these networks.

Because most of the research on social support networks contends that women make up the core of the network (Stack, 1974), very few studies have addressed the role of men in these networks. This research represents the first attempt to discover the exact nature of men's participation in social support networks.

Finally, most of the research using national probability samples focuses on kin, ignoring the contributions of nonkin to the social support networks. Because the definition of familism includes the adoption of kin and fictive kin into informal networks, the role of nonkin to these networks must be examined. All of the above-stated problems with past research will be addressed in this research.

In addition, I would like to point out that there is a tendency in some of the sociological literature (particularly from the culture of poverty perspective) to view extended families, especially female-headed families, as dysfunctional. Rather than looking at family extension and elaborate social support networks as disorganized, I will be examining them as merely an alternative family. The ultimate goals of my research are to examine the nature and extent of informal social support networks (both kin and nonkin) among African Americans, Chicanos, non-Hispanic Whites, and Puerto Ricans residing in the United States and to examine the interacting effects of gender, race, and class on family organization.

By using an integrative theoretical approach, I will attempt to provide a more complete understanding of the dynamics underlying participation in informal social support networks. My strategy of examining the interconnection between culture and structure in relationship to network participation advances the literature on race, gender, and class theory. Unlike grand theories that attempt to explain all social phenomena, I argue that this perspective is contextual and is situated historically. Throughout the book, it becomes clear that race, class, and gender operate at different theoretical levels. Whereas race may be salient in one context, gender and/or class may be more salient in another. For example, women of color may have more familistic attitudes than do Anglo women, regardless of class position.

However, socioeconomic status may hinder the ability of racial-ethnic women to participate in child care networks. Framed within the culture-structure nexus, my research explores the dynamic relationship between race, class, and gender and demonstrates how that relationship is constructed socially. My strategy of using an inductive approach in which empirical observations are used to construct social theory illustrates that network participation is indeed constrained by race, class, and gender.

Because of the high level of abstraction that characterizes the theoretical framework from within which I am working, it is essential to operationalize many of the key concepts before discussing my methodological strategy. In accordance with the theoretical literature, the most appropriate way to test the tenets of the cultural perspective is to examine attitudes toward individual responsibility to the extended kinship system. The major focus of the structural perspective is that household extension and informal social support networks are used as survival strategies to mitigate against the devastating effects of economic deprivation. Therefore, within the parameters of this perspective, structure becomes defined as economic factors that reflect various aspects of a person's social position.

Feminist scholars who articulate the need for an examination of the interlocking effects of gender, race, and class on family structure have failed to ground this highly abstract theoretical perspective into concrete, empirical terms. However, the intersection of race, gender, and class is a framework for analysis, not a traditional theory with specific, testable propositions. Therefore, the operationalization of principles underlying this theoretical orientation must occur within the context of a particular research study. Subsequently, another goal of this project is to articulate how race, class, and gender operate within the culture-structure nexus.

Accordingly, the first step is to examine whether racial-ethnic differences in types of participation in social support networks are explained by cultural attitudes and structural indicators. This strategy should elucidate the different processes that determine which racial-ethnic groups engage in various types of familistic behavior; that is, are there different effects of variables on different racial-ethnic groups? In addition, gender differences in the likelihood of participation in the extended kinship network will be examined to determine whether gender differences occur within racial-ethnic categories or whether they occur independently of those categories. Economic indicators will provide insight into differences in the prevalence and types of participation in extended social support networks based on social class.

At this point in the book, readers who are unfamiliar with this theoretical approach are probably wondering why I have not put forth a series of hypotheses to be tested. Because I examine both giving and receiving help from family and friends for four categories of racial-ethnic men and women, I would have had somewhere between 30 and 50 hypotheses. I think it would absolutely bore readers and disrupt the narrative flow to list a long series of hypotheses, test them, and write the remainder of the book based on the results of each one.

More important, in contradistinction to the integrative perspective, hypothesis testing presupposes that empirical investigation is unaffected by historical context. Constructing hypotheses necessarily creates fixed categories of inquiry that ignore the fluidity of social reality (Fraser & Nicholson, 1990). This feminist perspective aims to discourage the metanarrative-like modes of theorizing that have often plagued social inquiry. By analyzing the multiple axes of race, gender, and class oppression, the integrative perspective is "more like a tapestry composed of threads of many different hues than one woven in a single color" (Fraser & Nicholson, 1990, p. 35). Accordingly, this theoretical framework gently guides analysis as a means of revealing how race, class, and gender operate at different theoretical levels and the fluid relationship between these socially constructed categories. Based on these epistemological considerations, the link between culture and structure will be examined to determine the process by which these two components affect race, gender, and class differences in the likelihood of participation in social support networks.

This epistemological approach does not, however, imply that my analyses were simply blind manipulations of data. Based on past research from both the cultural relativity and structural perspectives, I had very specific expectations about what the research results would reveal. Throughout the entire process, I was guided by a conceptual model. For instance, I expected women of color to be more familistic and participate more frequently in child care networks than non-Hispanic White women. I also speculated that economically disadvantaged women and men would participate more frequently in exchange networks than individuals with more resources. In addition, I presumed that female extended household members would be a resource promoting respondents' network participation, whereas male extended household members would be a drain, inhibiting respondents' network participation. Because these expectations went unsupported by data analyses, I was required to rethink particular components of the structural and cultural perspectives (which I articulate in later chapters of this volume) and reevaluate them in relation to the intersection of race, class, and gender.

One final point is worth noting, particularly for readers who think primarily in quantitative terms. When discussing the contextual nature of the intersection of race, gender, and class, I am not referring to multiplicative effects, interaction terms, hierarchical models, or contextual variables. Rather, I am using it as a framework for analyzing how culture and structure constrain network participation.

The next chapter will discuss the methodology that I use to examine both cultural and structural determinants of informal social support networks. Using national survey data, I assess variations in cultural values associated with participation in extended social support networks between different racial and ethnic groups by examining a series of attitudinal questions tapping the prevalence of familism. Familistic values give primary importance to the needs of the family and members of the extended network as opposed to the needs of the individual. Therefore, cultural indicators are operationalized as attitudinal questions assessing respondents' attitudes toward individual responsibility to the kinship network. The structural component will include economic indicators such as household income, educational attainment, employment status, marital status, and whether the respondent receives any government assistance. A series of models has been constructed that examines these determinants of family organization.

# 4

# Race, Class, and Gender

## *Modeling the Intersections*

This chapter will describe the data set, measures, and methods of analysis used in this research. I will begin with a description of the data from the National Survey of Families and Households (NSFH) and a brief review of relevant research using the NSFH. In addition, I will describe the survey, eligibility requirements for respondents, and sampling techniques used. The discussion of measures will begin with an explanation of the independent variables: cultural attitudes, structural or socioeconomic resources, demographic variables, and availability/proximity control variables. I will then discuss the dependent variables, including the four dimensions of social support to be examined. Finally, I will present the strategy for analysis, construction of new variables and concomitant reliability tests, strategies for dealing with potential multicollinearity, descriptive statistics, and the analytic technique used in the main analyses.

## The Data

### THE SURVEY

The National Survey of Families and Households (NSFH), which was conducted from March 1987 through May 1988, is a multistage area probability sample of U.S. households. The sample is composed of 13,017 primary respondents age 19 years and older. The purpose of the survey was to enable researchers to analyze a broad range of family-related issues, including social and economic characteristics; household composition; household history; fertility; attitudes regarding family issues; aspects of cohabiting and marital relationships; household division of labor; divorce and separation experiences; parenting; and contact with parents, children, and siblings (Sweet, Bumpass, & Call, 1988). A second wave of the survey has been completed but was not available while I was working on the current research project. Subsequently, the second wave of data will not be included in this study.

The NSFH includes a main sample of 9,643 households plus a double sampling of Blacks, Puerto Ricans, Mexican Americans, single-parent families and families with stepchildren, cohabiting couples, and recently married people. One adult per household was selected randomly as the primary respondent. Several portions of the main questionnaire were self-administered to facilitate the collection of sensitive information. The average face-to-face interview lasted 1 hour and 40 minutes. A shorter, self-administered questionnaire was given to the spouse or cohabiting partner of the primary respondent. In addition, a tertiary respondent questionnaire was filled out by the householder when the primary respondent was an adult child or other nonspouse relative of the householder. The following analyses come from the primary respondent interview and from the primary respondent self-administered questionnaire. All questionnaires were translated into Spanish, and bilingual interviewers conducted interviews in areas where there was a significant concentration of Spanish-speaking people.

## THE SAMPLE AND RELATED ISSUES

Although the NSFH is a survey of households, Sweet et al. (1988) argue that defining a household or family as the unit of observation is problematic because of the divisions and recombinations that occur within a family over time. However, with individuals as the unit of observation, researchers can clearly describe the family and household histories of the reference individual (and those of his or her partner or spouse) and his or her current circumstances, relationships, and attitudes. Subsequently, the circumstances of households, families, marriages, and adults and children in these units are analyzed from the perspective of the reference individual.

An eligible respondent in the main sample was any English- or Spanish-speaking person age 19 years or older living in a household, or connected to a particular household but living in a dorm or military barrack at the time of the interview. Individuals under 19 years of age were eligible to participate in the survey if they were married or if they resided in a household in which there was no one else over 18 years of age. The sample was created from a five-stage selection process based on equal selection probabilities that used the Institute for Social Research's Primary Sampling Unit (PSU). Based proportionally on 1985 population projections, 100 PSUs were drawn. An average of 17 secondary sampling units (SSU) that were composed of block groups or enumeration districts were drawn within each of the 100 PSUs. Within each single listing area (LA) drawn from each of the 1,700 SSUs, approximately 20 housing units were selected randomly. The approximately 34,000 resulting housing units were halved randomly into the sampling frame's main sample and oversample, and a single adult 19 years of age and older was chosen randomly from each eligible householder as the primary respondent. The NSFH had an overall response rate of 70%.

The final sample consisted of 13,017 primary respondents. The subsample used in the following analysis includes the 9,643 primary respondents and 3,374 oversampled respondents (pulled from the larger NSFH sample) who completed both the interview questionnaire and self-administered portions of the main interview. This subsample was then subdivided into four racial-ethnic groups. Weighted data adjust for oversampling and allow for subgroup comparisons with weights adjusted to avoid inflating sample size.

Because the NSFH has become available, there has been considerable research using this data set. Therefore, before discussing the measures used in my analyses, I would like to review briefly some of the relevant findings of this research. Many of the articles published using the NSFH data focus on various aspects of kinship. However, very few of the studies examine kin and nonkin network participation specifically among racial-ethnic minorities. Although race-ethnicity is central in two NSFH studies (Hatch, 1991; Raley, 1995), those studies are quite different from mine. Hatch's (1991) project examines informal patterns of exchange between older African American and older White women, focusing on the effects of paid work, religious participation, and family dynamics. Raley's (1995) work focuses specifically on kin contact and exchange among never-married adults. Other studies include race in multivariate analyses but merely as one among a series of independent variables to be examined (Eggebeen, 1992; Hogan, Eggebeen, & Clogg, 1993; White & Riedmann, 1992). Most of these studies find that minority respondents do not participate more actively in exchange networks than non-Hispanic White respondents.[1]

An important component of my research is the examination of proximity of familial network members. Only White and Riedmann (1992), Amato (1993), and Hogan et al. (1993) examine the proximity of relatives in the likelihood of network participation. Amato (1993) constructed a variable measuring the minimum distance that a respondent lived from any family members, and Hogan et al. (1993) constructed a variable that measured the distance between a parent and the nearest coresidential grandparent. In both of these cases, a series of questions measuring the distance between respondents and their siblings, adult children, and parents was collapsed, and a single new variable was constructed. In my analysis, I examine the distance between respondents and their siblings, adult children, and parents separately. Using the proximity measures, this method enables me to demonstrate that as respondents move farther away from their kin, exchange behavior diminishes (see also White & Riedmann, 1992).

In addition, most of the studies that examine various aspects of social support focus on intergenerational support among parents and their adult children. The foci of these studies include financial and household exchanges between generations (Hoyert, 1991), variations in instrumental and emotional support based on family structure

(Marks & McLanahan, 1993), family composition and well-being (Acock & Demo, 1994), the division of household labor (Spitze & Ward, 1995), differences in support given to and received from parents among never-married children (White & Peterson, 1995), and Black-White differences in kin contact and exchange among never-married adults (Raley, 1995).

Two studies that do not focus on intergenerational support examine helping behavior between adult siblings (White & Riedmann, 1992) and on urban versus rural differences in exchange networks between friends and family members (Amato, 1993). Amato's (1993) research tests three competing theoretical perspectives (social disorganization, environmental overload, and subcultural theory) used to predict the extent of helping behavior found in urban and rural communities. Amato analyzes the perceived availability of assistance (i.e., to whom respondents would turn for help in case of medical, financial, or emotional emergencies), which I do not (see also White & Riedmann, 1992). The only similarities between this project and my research are the examination of proximity in the likelihood of participation in exchange networks and the use of similar measures of instrumental social support.

The research that is the most closely related to mine is a series of studies conducted by Eggebeen and Hogan (1990), Eggebeen (1992), and Hogan et al. (1993) that examines dimensions of exchange and assistance between adult children and their elderly parents. Rather than looking at each dimension of exchange as a separate dependent variable, which is what I do, Eggebeen and Hogan (1990) created a summary measure of intergenerational exchange by combining the four different types of support into one broad indicator. Subsequently, my research provides more detail about the types of aid given and received by both family and nonfamily network members.

The remainder of these studies (Eggebeen, 1992; Hogan et al., 1993) do examine separately the same dimensions of instrumental and monetary support analyzed in my study. In addition, they include questions regarding companionship and advice not included in my study. Overall, the findings indicate that routine exchanges between generations are not all that common (Eggebeen, 1992; Eggebeen & Hogan, 1990; Hogan et al., 1993). Using latent structure analysis, these studies also revealed that patterns of support between aging parents and their adult children vary by marital status, the number of adult children, and the presence or absence of stepchildren (Eggebeen, 1992). In addition, Hogan et al. (1993) found that intergenerational assistance is affected by family structure and the needs and resources of each generation. They also found that there are higher levels of giving and receiving aid among women because of their greater involvement in exchange networks. Although my research uses similar measures of social support because I do not focus on intergenerational exchange and include fictive kin in my analyses, it is clearly different from the work of Eggebeen and Hogan (1990), Eggebeen (1992), and Hogan et al. (1993).

In addition, although these projects also examine various types of mutual aid between parents and their adult children (except Acock and Demo), only two of them (Amato, 1993; Hoyert, 1991) include fictive kin so central to informal network participation. Furthermore, Spitze and Ward (1995) and White and Peterson (1995) do not include an analysis of race-ethnicity, and only Eggebeen and Hogan (1990) go beyond making Black-White comparisons. Because I examine help that is given and received by family and friends for African American, Chicano, Puerto Rican, and non-Hispanic White respondents, my research is unique. In addition, my use of the culture-structure nexus to frame my analysis is atypical.

## Measures

### INDEPENDENT VARIABLES

#### *Cultural Attitudes*

Attitudinal questions about individual responsibility to the extended kinship system are used to determine whether different racial-ethnic groups do, in fact, value familism more highly than others. For the purpose of this study, familism will be defined as values that give importance to the family and the needs of the collectivity as opposed to individual and personal needs (Bean & Tienda, 1987). Attitudinal measures presumably reflect values regarding the importance of kin networks that may be held differentially across racial-ethnic groups.

Four statements with identical scales were used to tap these cultural attitudes: (a) Parents ought to provide financial help to their adult children when the children are having financial difficulty; (b) children ought to provide financial help to aging parents when their parents are having financial difficulty; (c) children ought to let aging parents live with them when the parents can no longer live by themselves; (d) parents ought to let their adult children live with them when the children are having problems. Values range from 1 = *strongly agree* to 5 = *strongly disagree.* Low values on each variable represent strong feelings of familism.

Factor analysis was used to determine whether index measures could be developed from these variables. I anticipated that the financial questions would be related to one another and that questions measuring household extension also would be related to one another. Therefore, I intended to construct two new variables assessing cultural attitudes toward financial help and toward household composition. However, the variables did not cluster together in the way I expected. Only one factor was extracted from the principal components analysis with all four variables clustering together (factor loading ranged from .64 to .71). Therefore, these four variables were combined to create one new variable assessing overall attitudes toward extension. A reliability test subsequently was performed to ensure accurate scaling. Although the alpha for the newly created attitudinal variable was only .59, the alpha remained fairly constant when any one of the variables used to create the scale was removed. Therefore, I felt confident that this newly created variable was indeed assessing respondents' overall attitudes toward giving and receiving help from within the kinship system.

Unfortunately, the attitudinal questions on the NSFH are not ideal cultural indicators of responsibility to the extended kinship network. The financial questions have a middle-class bias because individuals who are willing to share food, clothing, or shelter may not have extra money and might answer attitudinal questions in accordance with their actual financial situation. In addition, there are many more dimensions to familism than merely providing financial support or allowing a parent, adult child, or other relative to coreside with a respondent. Attitudinal questions about sharing furniture, food, clothing, transportation, and household labor would reflect more accurately the theoretical literature on the reciprocal nature of the extended kin network. Attitudinal questions relating to child care and the informal adoption of nonbiologically related children would provide much more insight into familistic values. Also, a series of attitudinal questions about the importance of family and nonfamily members in an individual's life and the importance of living in close proximity to those individuals would be ideal.[2]

However, despite these methodological constraints, I will at least be able to examine cultural attitudes toward household extension and financial help. Furthermore, this is the first study that attempts to identify the impact of both cultural norms and structural indicators on participation in social support networks among African Americans, Chicanos, Puerto Ricans, and non-Hispanic Whites. Because this is a new area of analysis, attitudinal measures are still in the process of being developed. However, because few researchers have attempted to identify the particular attitudes associated with familism and merely used race-ethnicity as a proxy for cultural attitudes, this research represents an important first step.

### *Socioeconomic Resources*

The structural perspective argues that extended family living arrangements and informal social support networks are survival strategies used to mitigate against the deleterious effects of poverty (Billingsley, 1968; Stack, 1974). Within the parameters of this perspective, structure becomes defined as economic factors that reflect the various aspects of a person's social position. Therefore, economic indicators will represent the structural component of the model. A respondent's employment situation will be assessed by examining his or her total employment time, which will be measured by the number of hours per week he or she usually works in a main job and a second job.

The variable for a respondent's education represents the highest grade or degree level obtained from a college, university, or professional school. Educational values range from 00 = *no formal education* to 20 = *doctorate or professional degree.*

In a series of descriptive and multivariate analyses (not reported here), I investigated the possibility of using several measures of socioeconomic status. A respondent's income was measured by total dollar income (excluding earnings from interest, dividends, and other investments) in 1986. I also evaluated a measure of a respondent's income from public assistance and from other government programs.

To determine the economic status of the marital or cohabiting dyad, a measure of the couple's total income (excluding income from interest, dividends, and other investments) in 1986 was also included, as was the couple's income from public assistance and other government programs.

To determine whether or not extended households have more total income because of the inclusion of nonnuclear members, the combined total income of the household was measured (excluding earnings from interest, dividends, and other investments), as was the household's income from public assistance and other government programs. To determine whether poverty households are more likely to include extended members, a measure of the poverty level of the household was also included.

After examining a correlation matrix and some initial regression analyses, it became clear that many of these socioeconomic indicators were multicollinear and were essentially redundant.[3] Therefore, I omitted several of these initial variables and combined the household's total income from government assistance and total income from employment with income from other government programs to create an overall measure of household income. This newly created income variable accounts for all family, nonfamily, and extended household members.

Finally, so as not to lose the substantial number of cases that did not report income, I created an "income missing" variable that was coded 1 for respondents who did not answer the income question. Respondents who did not answer the household income question were coded as having "0" income. This variable alerts us to any bias that may occur because of respondents' refusal to answer the income question.

Homeownership is included as the final indicator of a respondent's own socioeconomic resources and consists of individuals who are either paying off a mortgage or own their home outright.

These variables will provide much insight into various structural determinants of participation in extended social support networks.

*Demographic Variables*

Demographic variables included in the model are consistent with those used in past research. Because women make up the core of the extended network (Adams, 1986b; McAdoo, 1978; Stack, 1974) and are more likely to provide social support to family members (Eggebeen & Hogan, 1990; Logan & Spitze, 1996), gender is an important variable to be examined. Therefore, respondent's gender was initially dummy coded as 0 = male, 1 = female. However, based on the results of the bivariate analysis, gender was also examined for different dependent variables in separate equations.

Respondents' age may influence their attitudes toward individual responsibility to the kinship network and therefore was measured in number of years as reported by the respondent.

The race-ethnicity of the respondent was analyzed in two ways. In the initial descriptive analysis, four separate categories of race[4] were used to examine mean differences on particular indicators of social support, and gender differences within each racial-ethnic group were also analyzed. Because there were very few significant racial differences on these indicators of social support, race-ethnicity was coded as four dummy variables representing Black, Chicano, Puerto Rican, and non-Hispanic White, where White is the reference category, for later multivariate analyses. Although minority scholars justly criticize the routine use of Whites as the comparison category in the analysis of race, it is appropriate in this study because the research literature (see earlier chapters) argues consistently that Whites are less familistic than African Americans, Chicanos, or Puerto Ricans.[5]

A question about where the respondent lived immediately after his or her birth was recoded into a dichotomous variable assessing whether or not the respondent was born in the United States. This variable is an approximate gauge of migration experience. Migration experience is especially relevant in the analysis of Latino family life because immigrants may retain more cultural attitudes regarding familism than Latinos who were born in the United States. In addition, Latino respondents who have resided in the United States their entire lives may live in closer proximity to family members than would more recent immigrants and therefore may be more involved in social support networks.

Similarly, much of the work on Black families suggests that the legacy of slavery and reconstruction is strongest in the South, so it may be that reliance on the extended kinship system is greatest among southern Black families (Billingsley, 1968; Martin & Martin, 1978). Therefore, one would expect that Black-White differences in family proximity would be greatest in the South and less apparent in the North. However, others have argued (Aschbrenner, 1973; McAdoo, 1978) that familistic cultural values and norms are so ingrained and independent of external conditions that they persist in the North as well as the South (Anderson & Allen, 1984).

In addition, researchers have argued that extended social support networks among Black and Latino families are more likely to flourish in small, rural communities (Del Castillo, 1984). Therefore, the respondent's current state of residence, the size of the residence area, metropolitan status of residence, and current region of the country in which the respondent lives were also ascertained to determine whether familistic behavior is determined by region and/or urbanicity. A comparison of mean differences in proximity to relatives by region of residence failed to demonstrate any salient regional patterns. Similarly, initial regression analyses (in which each racial-ethnic group was examined separately and as a dummy variable) failed to illustrate significant differences between region of residence and whether or not respondents participate in various aspects of social support networks. These same regression results failed to reveal any significant findings regarding the size of a residence area, the metropolitan status of a residence, or whether respondents from rural or urban settings were more familistic. Therefore, state of residence, size of residence area, metropolitan status of residence, and region of residence were dropped from the final model.

### *Availability/Proximity Control Variables*

The marital status of the respondent was originally included as a socioeconomic indicator because past research has demonstrated that married couples are financially more stable than single household heads. In addition, separated, divorced, widowed, and never-married men tend to be more financially secure than separated, divorced, widowed, and never-married women. However, as the final model began to emerge, I decided that in this research design, it was more appropriate to examine marital status as one measure of social support available to respondents rather than as an economic indicator. This decision was guided by my desire to determine whether the presence of a spouse acts as a resource providing respondents with greater flexibility to participate in their networks.

To gain a fuller representation of the availability of support group members to respondents, an examination of their household structure is imperative. Much of the past literature examines extended living arrangements as a dependent variable; however, this research analyzes presence of extended household members as an independent variable because the more resources available to a respondent, the more likely he or she will be able to participate in a social support network. Conversely, the lack of resources (the presence of young children or limited extended household members) may prevent a respondent from participating in these networks. Therefore, the following variables are essential components of the model: whether respondents have a child under 5 years old, a child between 6 and 12 years old, or a child between 13 and 18 years old living in their home. In addition, whether the respondent has a daughter between the ages of 13 and 18, a son between the ages of 13 and 18, an adult female nonspouse/partner (19 or older), or an adult male nonspouse/partner (19 or older) living in the home was also examined. These variables were constructed by combining pertinent items on the household roster filled out by each respondent. Because teenagers and adult extended household members often perform tasks based on traditional gender roles, and because the literature suggests that women are more involved in support networks, it is important to compare rates of participation between men and women in these networks.

Another essential component related to participation in social support networks is the proximity of members to one another. Therefore, a series of variables examining distance between respondents and their siblings, adult children, and parents is included. The number of siblings that a respondent has living within 2 miles, between 2 and 25 miles, between 25 and 300 miles, and more than 300 miles was computed to include both biological and half or stepsiblings. A question asking how far in miles a respondent lives from his or her mother or father was recoded to how far in miles the respondent lives from at least one parent. This was recoded again to match the categories of the sibling mileage variables and to ascertain whether the respondent has at least one parent who lives within 2 miles, between 2 and 25 miles, between 25 and 300 miles, or more than 300 miles. Stepparents were not included in this variable because they made up such a small percentage of the overall sample (only 11% of respondents reported ever living with a stepparent), which is a function of the average age of the respondents participating in the survey (the majority of NSFH respondents are over 35 years of age). Finally, a series of variables determining whether the respondent has an adult child who lives within 2 miles, between 2 and 25 miles, between 25 and 300 miles, or more than 300 miles was also computed from the household roster.[6] All three of these variables were recoded so that the mileage categories are mutually exclusive. These control variables should prove to be important indicators of network participation; however, they are not directly derived from the exigencies of the culture-structure nexus.

## DEPENDENT VARIABLES

The aim of this study is to determine whether there are racial and/or gender differences in participation in social support networks and whether these differences are a consequence of cultural attitudes, economic resources, or some combination of the two.

Based on the theoretical literature, which stresses the importance of reciprocal obligations within the extended kinship system, I examined help that respondents both give and receive from parents, adult children, other family members, and nonfamily members. The three dimensions of participation in social support networks are (a) monetary resources, (b) child care help, and (c) household assistance. The questions on the NSFH ask whether the respondent's parent, spouse's parent, respondent's brother or sister, spouse's brother or sister, respondent's grandparents, spouse's grandparents, respondent's children, other relatives, and nonrelatives (a) gave the respondent a gift worth more than $200 during the past 5 years, (b) loaned the respondent more than $200 during the past 5 years, (c) received a gift from the respondent of more than $200 in the past 5 years, or (d) received a loan from the respondent of more than $200 in the past 5 years.[7]

The child care help and household assistance dimensions of social support included in the NSFH ascertain whether or not the respondent has given or received help with baby-sitting or child care, transportation, repairs to home or car, and other kinds of work around the house during the past month from any of the following: friends, neighbors, coworkers, sons or daughters, parents, brothers/sisters, or other relatives. I found significant gender differences in the types of help given and received by men and women. Women of all races were significantly more likely than men to give and receive child care help, and men of all races were significantly more likely than women to give and receive help with repairs to home and car and other work around the house.

Giving and receiving transportation help was not associated more with one gender than another. Women were more likely than men to give transportation help to children, parents, siblings, and other relatives, whereas men were more likely than women to give transportation help to friends, neighbors, and coworkers. This bivariate difference may represent traditional gender differences in participation in the public and private spheres. Men are probably carpooling to work (public sphere), and women are probably driving family members to activities/events (private sphere).

In addition, mean differences in participation between original categories of donors and recipients of help were minimal, so they were combined into family and nonfamily network members. Based on the results of these *t* tests (to be discussed more fully in Chapter 5), I also combined repairs to home and car with other work around the house to construct a variable tapping household help, dropped transportation help from the analysis, and kept help with baby-sitting or child care in its initial form. In preparation for later multivariate analysis, I disaggregated the sample by gender and examined racial differences in types of help within each category of gender (to be discussed more fully in Chapter 5). Because I was particularly interested in looking at differences between African American, Chicano, non-Hispanic White, and Puerto Rican respondents, this separate analysis by gender allowed me to examine these differences without having to use complex, difficult-to-interpret interaction terms.

Therefore, my final dependent variables are help with baby-sitting or child care for women only (Chapter 6) and household assistance for men only (Chapter 7). These variables will provide some insight into various dimensions of household extension and participation in extended social support networks. However, they will not provide a complete picture of familistic behavior. Questions about the prevalence of sharing food, public assistance, household labor, clothing, meals, furniture, child care, and so on would be more consistent with the theoretical literature on multiple indicators of the extended kinship network. In addition, because the response categories on child care help and household assistance are dichotomous, the frequency of help is not discernible. Furthermore, there is no way to determine how many people are included in each response category. The inability to determine network size is problematic because the more network members an individual has, the more help he or she can presumably give or receive. Finally, because the measures of helping behavior cover only the previous month, they limit the amount of variance as well as the depth of information provided.

## Methods of Analysis

The primary purpose of the analysis is to examine the partial effects of cultural attitudes and of structural resources on informal social support networks for different categories of racial-ethnic groups. In addition, I will examine whether or not differing household living arrangements contribute to participation in these informal networks.

Sample weights will be used in all of the initial and primary analyses of the data to correct for the oversampling of specific populations. Using the sample weights will allow me to generalize my findings to the U.S. population while simultaneously correcting for sample bias.

Before proceeding with the main analysis, preliminary investigation was conducted to ascertain whether constructed measures were appropriate. Factor analysis and reliability tests were performed on the attitudinal measures, which tap into respondents' cultural values, to determine whether index measures could be developed from these variables (see above). Reliability tests were also performed on all newly constructed variables to ensure that they produced consistent results.

Descriptive statistics were run for all of the variables to determine how they differed by race and gender. *T* tests (which provide information on the difference of means between dichotomous variables) were used to determine whether racial and gender differences in the dependent variables were statistically significant. In addition, correlations among all the independent variables were analyzed to assess whether or not there are problems of multicollinearity.[8] If there were very high correlations between variables that were of less theoretical importance to the model, all except one variable was dropped. If there was multicollinearity between variables that are essential to the theoretical framework, they were combined into new variables if factor analysis demonstrated that they tapped the same underlying construct (see Chapter 5).

In accordance with the integrative theoretical perspective, the main part of the analysis will include a series of models that assesses the contributions of cultural and structural indicators on the dependent variables while addressing gender and racial differences. I am primarily interested in whether or not racial and gender differences in participation in social support networks can be explained by different aspects of culture and structure. This strategy does not assume that cultural differences vary across racial groups; rather, it seeks to measure whether they do, in fact, exist and to what extent. Because my dependent variables are all dichotomous, I will be using logistic regression for all the main analyses.

A series of analyses will examine the effects of independent variables on indicators of social support for women and men. I will first regress participation in social support networks on race to observe the subsequent effects of different independent variables on race. I will then add a series of variables. The first variables represent the respondent's own demographic resources or needs (marital status; presence of children, teenagers, or extended household members) to the model and examine the effects that they have on helping behavior. These variables reflect household composition and the availabilty of social support within the home. Presumably, the more resources available to a respondent (e.g., the presence of adult extended household members), the more he or she is expected to provide help for network members outside the home. Alternatively, respondents who lack resources (e.g., absence of adult extended household members) may not have the time to participate in social support networks outside the household.

Next, I will add the socioeconomic indicators to the model. The structural indicators are entered next because household structure may represent certain aspects of a respondent's socioeconomic status. For instance, the presence of adults in the home may add to the household income, or they may be a drain on resources. By entering socioeconomic resources after a respondent's own demographic resources, I can examine how economic indicators affect the relationship between the respondent's household structure and participation in social support networks. Given the propensity of the literature to attribute participation in social support networks to economic causes, these variables are expected to have a significant effect on the dependent variables.

Extended family characteristics/resources representing the availability and proximity of help will be entered into the equation in the third stage because I am interested in how the effects of variables entered earlier in the steps change as the availability of family members is included in the analysis. I anticipate that the proximity of relatives will be significantly related to giving and receiving help with both child care and household repairs.

Finally, individual attitudes toward extension will be entered. This variable is entered into the equation last to see if it changes the relationships between socioeconomic indicators and the dependent variable. If cultural norms regarding extension cancel previous significant relationships, one can argue that they may take precedence over structural indicators or mediate socioeconomic differences.[9]

The first model will examine giving help with child care to family and to nonfamily members and receiving help with child care from family and from nonfamily members for women only. The second model will examine giving help with household repairs to family and to nonfamily members and receiving help with household repairs from family and from nonfamily members for men only. By examining categories of gender separately, I can analyze racial differences that may occur between men and racial differences that may occur between women on specific elements of social support.

# Notes

1. These findings are similar to mine, which is not surprising given that the same data and many of the same measures of social support were used. However, the focus of my work is specifically on racial-ethnic minorities, and these studies examine race as just another variable to be examined in the model. In addition, I do not confine my examination of social support to family members and do not focus on intergenerational support between aging parents and their children.

2. Upon the completion of this research project, I conducted a follow-up qualitative study of social support networks among women in a Puerto Rican community in upstate New York. The purpose of the qualitative component was to address some of the questions left unanswered by the quantitative analyses. Using a snowball sample, I interviewed 20 women over a 15-month period. I was particularly interested in (a) the presence or absence of familistic values among Puerto Rican women in this community; (b) whether or not community members perceived a decline in network participation, and whether this decline was a result of economic transformation; (c) the impact of circular migration patterns on network participation; and (d) whether informal social support networks have been replaced by more institutional means of social support. Throughout the remainder of the book, I will report relevant research findings. (See Roschelle, 1997.)

3. The correlation coefficient for each measure of socioeconomic status excluded from the final model was above .65.

4. Although Puerto Ricans and Chicanos are not members of a racial category per se, much of the political and economic disenfranchisement they've experienced has been racialized. Subsequently, I sometimes use the term *race* when referring to all four racial-ethnic groups in the sample.

5. As stated previously, the sample sizes of Native Americans ($n$ = 49), Cubans ($n$ = 44), and Asian Americans ($n$ = 127) were too small to make meaningful comparisons with other racial-ethnic groups and were therefore omitted from the analysis.

6. The proximity variables in my model include only parents, siblings, and adult children still living. I did not run any analyses to see how these relationships might be affected by the death of particular family members. Only .08% of the respondents reported having deceased step- or half-siblings (with whom they grew up), and only 3.26% of the respondents reported that they had deceased siblings (with whom they grew up). Although the percentages were higher for respondents with deceased mothers and fathers (34.58% and 47.53%, respectively), there was no concomitant survey question asking about adult children. Because the percentages of deceased siblings were so small, and because of the absence of a comparative measure for respondents with deceased adult children, I did not examine the impact that death might have on network participation. However, the number of living relatives that a respondent has would most likely have an impact on the types of exchanges transacted as well as on the breadth of his or her kin network (e.g., see Aldous & Klein, 1991).

7. In my analysis of monetary assistance, I intended to combine these four survey questions and construct two new variables that would determine whether a respondent gave a gift or loan of more than $200 and/or whether the respondent received a gift or loan of more than $200 in the past 5 years.

NSFH categories of potential donors and recipients were to be recoded into "respondent's parents," "respondent's adult children," "respondent's other family members," and "respondent's non-family members." This recoding scheme would have kept the response categories consistent with the dependent variables assessing household assistance and child care. This reclassification scheme would have resulted in eight dependent variables that were also to be coded as dichotomous, with response categories of 0 = no, 1 = yes. However, an examination of percentages (based on means) of respondents giving and receiving monetary help revealed that involvement in this type of social support was minimal.

Initially, there were no salient gender or race differences regardless of who was giving or receiving financial help. In fact, percentages of giving and receiving financial help for African Americans, Chicanos, Whites, and Puerto Ricans were rarely higher than 5%. The only noticeable pattern was that respondents were more likely to receive a gift or loan worth more than $200 from their parents than from other family and nonfamily members, and respondents were more likely to give a gift or loan worth more than $200 to their children than to other family or nonfamily members.

This pattern persisted when I examined giving a gift, giving a loan, receiving a gift, or receiving a loan as separate, disaggregated categories. However, when I compared all men and women in the sample and compared men and women of each race using these disaggregated categories, racial differences in parent-to-child financial help emerged. Non-Hispanic White respondents had higher percentages of giving monetary assistance to their children and higher percentages of receiving monetary help from their parents than did African Americans, Puerto Ricans, and Chicanos. No discernible patterns emerged among the remaining three racial-ethnic groups. Not surprisingly, socioeconomic status was positively related to giving monetary help, indicating that people with more financial resources are more likely to give or lend money regardless of race-ethnicity. Although these percentages seem to indicate that monetary help primarily flows from parents to children, and that non-Hispanic White families have higher percentages of giving and receiving this type of help, the percentages only ranged from 1% to 15%, indicating that monetary assistance is actually rare among all racial-ethnic groups. Therefore, this dependent variable was subsequently dropped from further analysis.

Although these findings are descriptive, they do indicate that monetary help is not an essential component of participation in kinship networks.

8. The variable assessing whether or not the respondent had a teenage child between 13 and 18 years old living in the home was highly correlated with the variable tapping whether the respondent had a teenage daughter ($r$ = .7268) or a teenage son ($r$ = .7349) living in the home. I omitted the variable Teenage Child from the model because I was interested in gender differences in teenage household help.

The relationship between whether a respondent was born in the United States and the age at which he or she first moved to the United States was also multicollinear ($r$ = .8676). Subsequently, I included only U.S. born in the model.

The final logistic regression models were unconstrained by multicollinearity. All of the associations among continuous independent variables were less than .40, and the majority of correlation coefficients were less than 1.0.

9. During the initial data analysis, I also entered the variables into the equation in different sequential order. I wanted to see if measures entered earlier in the regression analysis were more likely to affect the dependent variables. Many of the relationships found using the final model remained regardless of the order in which the variables were entered. Therefore, the final model was chosen because it made the most theoretical sense.

# 5

# A New Context Emerges

The aim of this chapter is to determine whether there are differences in participation in social support networks between particular family and nonfamily members and whether there are racial and/or gender differences in the types of help given and received. Based on the theoretical literature, which stresses the importance of reciprocal obligations within the extended kinship system, I examine help that respondents both give and receive. As stated in Chapter 4, the child care help and household assistance dimensions of social support were examined to ascertain whether or not the respondent has given or received help with baby-sitting or child care, transportation, repairs to home or car, and other kinds of work around the house during the past month from various categories of people.

In order to identify relevant patterns in the data, the first step in the analysis was to obtain mean differences in giving and receiving particular types of help and to examine whether these differences were statistically significant. A series of $t$ tests was run on the social support variables to determine whether racial or gender differences in the dependent variables were, in fact, statistically significant. The initial *t* tests examined giving and receiving help with baby-sitting or child care, transportation help, repairs to home or car, and other kinds of work around the house.

The categories of donors and recipients of help represent various kin and nonkin members of the informal social support network. Possible network members include friends, neighbors, coworkers, sons or daughters, parents, brothers or sisters, and other relatives. The first step was to examine the pooled sample to determine whether African Americans, non-Hispanic Whites, Chicanos, or Puerto Ricans differed from each other in terms of giving help and in terms of receiving help. Next, I compared all men and women to one another, and then I compared men and women of each racial-ethnic group on patterns of giving and receiving help.

The final section of this chapter is based on the findings of these initial *t* tests. Guided by these results, I combined categories of donors and recipients into family and nonfamily members and reexamined the same types of helping behavior. These *t* tests reveal some interesting findings; however, I would like to stress that these findings are inconclusive. I use these descriptive statistics to identify patterns in the data and provide a framework for further multivariate analysis. In Chapters 6 and 7, I will employ statistical controls that are absent with the use of *t* tests.

## Comparisons of Giving and Receiving Help Based on *t* Tests

### COMPARISONS OF AFRICAN AMERICAN, CHICANO, NON-HISPANIC WHITE, AND PUERTO RICAN RESPONDENTS

The first step was to ascertain whether there are statistically significant mean differences in giving and receiving particular types of help for all racial-ethnic groups. Although multiple comparison procedures would have been a more appropriate tool to examine mean differences by race, because the dependent variables are dichotomous, I was unable to employ analysis of variance, which can be used only when the variables in question are interval-level variables. Therefore, I ran a series of *t* tests comparing each racial-ethnic group to all others; that is, I compared Blacks to Whites, Blacks to Puerto Ricans, Blacks to Chicanos, Puerto Ricans to Whites, Puerto Ricans to Chicanos, and Chicanos to Whites.

As Table 5.1A illustrates, there are significant racial differences in giving child care help to particular individuals. Non-Hispanic Whites are significantly more likely to give child care help to friends, neighbors, and coworkers than are Puerto Ricans, and Blacks are significantly more likely than Chicanos to give child care help to friends. Similarly, non-Hispanic Whites are significantly more likely to give child care help to sons or daughters than are African Americans and Puerto Ricans. However, African American respondents are significantly more likely to provide help with child care to other relatives than are non-Hispanic White and Puerto Rican respondents.

In examining giving transportation help, Table 5.1A demonstrates that non-Hispanic White respondents provide more transportation help to friends, neighbors, coworkers, and to sons or daughters than do African American and Puerto Rican respondents. In addition, Whites are also more likely to give transportation help to parents than are Blacks. As with child care help, African Americans give more help with transportation to other relatives than do Whites.

When examining repairs to home and car, a similar pattern emerges. Non-Hispanic White respondents are significantly more likely than African American and Puerto Rican respondents to provide help with repairs to friends, neighbors, coworkers, sons or daughters, and parents. Although there were no significant racial differences in giving child care or transportation help to siblings, the data illustrate that Chicanos are more likely to provide repair help to siblings than are African Americans.

Non-Hispanic Whites are more likely than African Americans and Puerto Ricans to provide other kinds of work around the house to friends and to children, and African Americans are significantly more likely to provide work around the house to friends than are Chicanos. However, Chicanos are more likely to help children with household work than are Puerto Ricans. Finally, as with the other three types of help, non-Hispanic White respondents give more help with household

**TABLE 5.1A** Proportions of Giving Household Help by Racial-Ethnic Groups Based on *t* Tests: Means (Standard Deviations)

| *Household Help Item* | *Black* | *White* | *Chicano* | *Puerto Rican* |
|---|---|---|---|---|
| *Baby-sitting or child care* | | | | |
| 1. Friends, neighbors, coworkers | .17[c] (.37) | .19[d] (.39) | .11[a] (.31) | .10[b] (.30) |
| 2. Sons or daughters | .09[b] (.29) | .13[a,d] (.33) | .10 (.30) | .06[b] (.23) |
| 3. Parents | .02 (.15) | .02 (.12) | .01 (.12) | .02 (.15) |
| 4. Brothers or sisters | .11 (.31) | .10 (.30) | .14 (.35) | .07 (.27) |
| 5. Other relatives | .09[b,d] (.28) | .06[a] (.24) | .08 (.28) | .04[a] (.19) |
| *Transportation help* | | | | |
| 1. Friends, neighbors, coworkers | .30[b] (.46) | .38[a,d] (.49) | .27 (.45) | .23[b] (.42) |
| 2. Sons or daughters | .07[b] (.25) | .11[a,d] (.32) | .06 (.24) | .04[b] (.20) |
| 3. Parents | .08[b] (.26) | .11[a] (.31) | .09 (.29) | .06 (.23) |
| 4. Brothers or sisters | .10 (.30) | .09 (.29) | .12 (.32) | .06 (.24) |
| 5. Other relatives | .08[b] (.28) | .07[a] (.25) | .08 (.27) | .04 (.19) |
| *Repairs to home or car* | | | | |
| 1. Friends, neighbors, coworkers | .15[b] (.36) | .20[a,d] (.40) | .16 (.36) | .11[b] (.31) |
| 2. Sons or daughters | .03[b] (.17) | .07[a,d] (.26) | .04 (.18) | .02[b] (.12) |
| 3. Parents | .06[b] (.24) | .11[a,d] (.31) | .08 (.27) | .03[b] (.17) |
| 4. Brothers or sisters | .05[c] (.22) | .06 (.24) | .09[a] (.29) | .06 (.23) |
| 5. Other relatives | .04 (.20) | .04 (.20) | .06 (.24) | .06 (.22) |

TABLE 5.1A Continued

| *Household Help Item* | *Black* | *White* | *Chicano* | *Puerto Rican* |
|---|---|---|---|---|
| *Other kinds of work around the house* | | | | |
| 1. Friends, neighbors, coworkers | .15[b,c] | .18[a,d] | .10[a] | .09[b] |
| | (.36) | (.39) | (.30) | (.29) |
| 2. Sons or daughters | .05[b] | .07[a,d] | .07[d] | .01[b,c] |
| | (.21) | (.26) | (.25) | (.12) |
| 3. Parents | .14[b] | .18[a] | .16 | .13 |
| | (.35) | (.38) | (.37) | (.34) |
| 4. Brothers or sisters | .07 | .06 | .09 | .09 |
| | (.25) | (.24) | (.29) | (.29) |
| 5. Other relatives | .07[b] | .05[a] | .07 | .06 |
| | (.25) | (.22) | (.26) | (.24) |

a. Significantly different from Black ≤ .05.
b. Significantly different from White ≤ .05.
c. Significantly different from Chicano ≤ .05.
d. Significantly different from Puerto Rican ≤ .05.

work to parents than do African American respondents, but African American respondents are more likely than non-Hispanic Whites to give help with household work to other relatives.

The results of Table 5.1A are surprising given the theoretical and empirical literature, which argues that minority families are more involved in social support networks than are nonminority families. These results suggest that in this sample, non-Hispanic White respondents are significantly more likely to participate in informal social support networks than are the other three racial-ethnic groups. The only exception to this finding is that African Americans demonstrate a pattern of helping other relatives more than do non-Hispanic Whites. This is an interesting result because the literature suggests that members of the kin network may be nonbiologically related or distant relatives. It may be that other relatives represent cousins, aunts, uncles, and so on who are more incorporated into the support networks of African Americans than of non-Hispanic Whites. Perhaps the support network of non-Hispanic Whites is more likely to include nuclear family members and friends rather than more distant relatives.

Another interesting finding is that in all cases where there are statistically significant differences between racial-ethnic groups, Puerto Ricans are the least likely to participate in the network. Given the fact that Puerto Ricans are currently among the most impoverished racial-ethnic groups (see Eitzen & Zinn, 1992), it may be that they do not have the resources necessary to provide help within the social support network. Statistical controls for socioeconomic status should provide further insight into this phenomenon. Another possible explanation is related to the migration status of Puerto Ricans. Because a majority of Puerto Ricans were born in Puerto Rico as opposed to the mainland (Bean & Tienda, 1987), they may not have been able to cultivate ties/networks that are as well developed as those of other groups.

Interestingly, there are only four instances where Chicanos have significant mean differences on giving help, three of which are between them and African Americans. Chicanos are less likely to give help with child care to friends and less likely to give help with work around the house to friends than are African Americans, but they are more likely to give help with home and car repairs to siblings than are African Americans. In addition, Chicanos are more likely to give help with other kinds of work around the house to children than are Puerto Ricans. These results indicate that there are some significant differences between Chicanos and African Americans and Puerto Ricans, but no definitive pattern emerges.

The findings for receipt of help are somewhat different than those for giving help. As Table 5.1B indicates, non-Hispanic Whites receive more child care help from friends than do African Americans, and they are more likely to receive help from parents than are African Americans and Puerto Ricans. However, Puerto Ricans are more likely to receive child care help from children than are non-Hispanic Whites. In addition, African American respondents are also significantly more likely than non-Hispanic White respondents to receive help from children as well as from siblings and other relatives.

Non-Hispanic White respondents are significantly more likely to receive transportation help from parents, but Chicanos are more likely to receive it from siblings. African Americans receive more transportation help from other relatives than do non-Hispanic White respondents. In addition, Puerto Ricans receive more transportation help

**TABLE 5.1B** Proportions of Receiving Household Help by Racial-Ethnic Groups Based on *t* Tests: Means (Standard Deviations)

| *Household Help Item* | *Black* | *White* | *Chicano* | *Puerto Rican* |
|---|---|---|---|---|
| *Baby-sitting or child care* | | | | |
| 1. Friends, neighbors, coworkers | .09[b] (.29) | .11[a] (.31) | .09 (.29) | .10 (.30) |
| 2. Sons or daughters | .02[b] (.14) | .01[a,d] (.11) | .03 (.18) | .04[b] (.20) |
| 3. Parents | .07[b] (.26) | .09[a,d] (.29) | .08 (.27) | .04[b] (.20) |
| 4. Brothers or sisters | .07[b] (.25) | .05[a] (.21) | .08 (.27) | .05 (.21) |
| 5. Other relatives | .05[b] (.21) | .03[a] (.18) | .05 (.22) | .01 (.12) |
| *Transportation help* | | | | |
| 1. Friends, neighbors, coworkers | .22 (.42) | .22 (.42) | .20 (.40) | .24 (.43) |
| 2. Sons or daughters | .06 (.24) | .06 (.23) | .06 (.25) | .07 (.26) |
| 3. Parents | .07[b] (.25) | .08[a] (.27) | .07 (.25) | .05 (.21) |
| 4. Brothers or sisters | .08[b] (.27) | .05[a,d] (.23) | .07 (.27) | .13[b] (.33) |
| 5. Other relatives | .07[b,c] (.25) | .04[a] (.19) | .04[a] (.19) | .04 (.21) |
| *Repairs to home or car* | | | | |
| 1. Friends, neighbors, coworkers | .13 (.34) | .14 (.35) | .14 (.35) | .08 (.35) |
| 2. Sons or daughters | .03[b] (.17) | .05[a] (.22) | .04 (.20) | .03 (.18) |
| 3. Parents | .04[b,c] (.20) | .06[a] (.23) | .06[a,d] (.24) | .02[c] (.12) |
| 4. Brothers or sisters | .03[c] (.18) | .04 (.19) | .06[a] (.24) | .03 (.16) |
| 5. Other relatives | .04 (.19) | .03 (.17) | .04 (.19) | .02 (.14) |

(continued)

**TABLE 5.1B** Continued

| *Household Help Item* | *Black* | *White* | *Chicano* | *Puerto Rican* |
|---|---|---|---|---|
| *Other kinds of work around the house* | | | | |
| 1. Friends, neighbors, coworkers | .12[c] | .13 | .08[a] | .07 |
| | (.32) | (.34) | (.27) | (.26) |
| 2. Sons or daughters | .08 | .09 | .08 | .09 |
| | (.27) | (.30) | (.27) | (.28) |
| 3. Parents | .05 | .06 | .06 | .06 |
| | (.22) | (.24) | (.24) | (.24) |
| 4. Brothers or sisters | .07[b] | .04[a,d] | .05 | .08[b] |
| | (.25) | (.20) | (.21) | (.28) |
| 5. Other relatives | .06[b] | .04[a] | .05 | .04 |
| | (.23) | (.20) | (.22) | (.21) |

a. Significantly different from Black ≤ .05.
b. Significantly different from White ≤ .05.
c. Significantly different from Chicano ≤ .05.
d. Significantly different from Puerto Rican ≤ .05.

than do non-Hispanic Whites from siblings, and African Americans receive significantly more transportation help from other relatives than do Chicanos.

African American respondents are less likely to receive home or car repairs from children and parents than are non-Hispanic Whites, and they are less likely than Chicanos to receive this type of help from siblings and parents. In addition, Chicano respondents are significantly more likely than Puerto Ricans to receive help from parents with home and car repairs. The data on receiving help with other kinds of work around the house reveal that African Americans receive less help from friends, neighbors, coworkers, siblings, and other relatives than do non-Hispanic Whites. In addition, Chicanos receive more help with household work from siblings than do non-Hispanic Whites.

These data reveal that non-Hispanic Whites are not the most likely to participate in social support networks. There seems to be a salient difference between giving and receiving help. Perhaps non-Hispanic White respondents can purchase some of the services provided to minority families by support group members. Among the three minority groups, Puerto Ricans tended to be the least likely to receive particular types of help. This finding is intriguing and will be analyzed further in the next two chapters. Overall, it is difficult to say from these results that one racial-ethnic group is more familistic than another. In terms of giving help, non-Hispanic White respondents do participate more in the support network. However, they do not receive help more than other racial-ethnic groups. Ultimately, these *t* tests reveal that there are many racial differences in the types of help people give and receive. It is clear from the data that scholars should not simply argue that a particular minority group is more familistic than another. Rather, it would be more informative to discuss the particular types of helping behavior in which individuals participate.

One point worth mentioning is the lack of noticeable patterns regarding who is giving and receiving help from whom. There do not appear to be any important patterns regarding donors and recipients of help other than the fact that in several cases, African Americans are more likely to give help to and receive help from other relatives than are non-Hispanic Whites. If this lack of a pattern continues, collapsing these categories into "family" and "nonfamily" will be useful.

## COMPARISON OF WOMEN AND MEN FOR ALL RACIAL-ETHNIC GROUPS COMBINED

The results of the *t* tests (Tables 5.2A and 5.2B) comparing men and women confirm the findings of earlier analyses that I conducted. Women consistently give and receive more help with child care than do men. In fact, women are significantly more likely than men to give and receive child care help with every member of the social support network except one. There are no significant differences between men and women for receiving child care help from other relatives. This bivariate result demonstrates the virtual lack of participation in child care by male respondents.

Similarly, men are more likely than women to give help with repairs to home or car to every possible recipient. In addition, men are more likely than women to receive this type of help from friends, neighbors, and coworkers, and women are more likely than men to receive repair help from sons or daughters. Unfortunately, the coding of the data is such that help given by sons and daughters cannot be disaggregated. I would speculate that receipt of repair help is primarily from sons

**TABLE 5.2A** Proportions of Giving Household Help by Gender Based on *t* Tests: Means (Standard Deviations)

| *Household Help Item* | *Men* | *Women* | *Difference Between Means* |
|---|---|---|---|
| *Baby-sitting or child care* | | | |
| 1. Friends, neighbors, coworkers | .13<br>(.33) | .24<br>(.43) | –.11** |
| 2. Sons or daughters | .10<br>(.30) | .14<br>(.34) | –.04** |
| 3. Parents | .01<br>(.11) | .02<br>(.14) | –.01** |
| 4. Brothers or sisters | .08<br>(.26) | .12<br>(.33) | –.04** |
| 5. Other relatives | .05<br>(.22) | .07<br>(.26) | –.02** |
| *Transportation help* | | | |
| 1. Friends, neighbors, coworkers | .38<br>(.48) | .35<br>(.48) | .03** |
| 2. Sons or daughters | .10<br>(.30) | .10<br>(.30) | .00 |
| 3. Parents | .09<br>(.29) | .11<br>(.32) | –.02** |
| 4. Brothers or sisters | .09<br>(.29) | .09<br>(.29) | .00 |
| 5. Other relatives | .07<br>(.26) | .07<br>(.25) | .00 |
| *Repairs to home or car* | | | |
| 1. Friends, neighbors, coworkers | .29<br>(.46) | .10<br>(.30) | .19** |
| 2. Sons or daughters | .09<br>(.28) | .04<br>(.21) | .05** |
| 3. Parents | .13<br>(.34) | .07<br>(.25) | .06** |
| 4. Brothers or sisters | .09<br>(.28) | .03<br>(.18) | .06** |
| 5. Other relatives | .06<br>(.24) | .02<br>(.15) | .04** |

**TABLE 5.2A** Continued

| *Household Help Item* | *Men* | *Women* | *Difference Between Means* |
|---|---|---|---|
| *Other kinds of work around the house* | | | |
| 1. Friends, neighbors, coworkers | .21 (.41) | .14 (.35) | .07** |
| 2. Sons or daughters | .06 (.25) | .07 (.26) | –.01 |
| 3. Parents | .18 (.38) | .16 (.37) | .02* |
| 4. Brothers or sisters | .08 (.26) | .06 (.23) | .02** |
| 5. Other relatives | .06 (.24) | .05 (.22) | .01** |

*$p \leq .05$; **$p \leq .01$.

rather than daughters. Regardless, it appears that men are significantly more involved than women in giving home and car repairs, which demonstrates that traditional gender roles are pervasive in contemporary American society.

A parallel finding is that men provide more help than women with other kinds of work around the house to friends, parents, siblings, and other relatives. This finding indicates that respondents did not perceive this category as "housework" per se, but rather as work that men often do around the house such as building decks, laying carpet, and general maintenance. Given the vast research on the division of household labor (Coverman & Shelley, 1986; Hartmann, 1981; Hochschild, 1989), which argues convincingly that women are primarily responsible for doing the majority of housework, it seems very doubtful that men would be providing more help with housework than women would.

Transportation help did not reveal any insightful results other than that men give more transportation help to friends, neighbors, and coworkers than do women. Women are more likely to give and receive transportation help from parents and receive transportation help from

**TABLE 5.2B** Proportions of Receiving Household Help by Gender Based on *t* Tests: Means (Standard Deviations)

| *Household Help Item* | *Men* | *Women* | *Difference Between Means* |
|---|---|---|---|
| *Baby-sitting or child care* | | | |
| 1. Friends, neighbors, coworkers | .09<br>(.29) | .12<br>(.32) | –.03** |
| 2. Sons or daughters | .01<br>(.08) | .02<br>(.14) | –.01** |
| 3. Parents | .07<br>(.25) | .11<br>(.31) | –.04** |
| 4. Brothers or sisters | .04<br>(.19) | .06<br>(.25) | –.02** |
| 5. Other relatives | .03<br>(.18) | .04<br>(.19) | –.01 |
| *Transportation help* | | | |
| 1. Friends, neighbors, coworkers | .22<br>(.41) | .22<br>(.42) | .00 |
| 2. Sons or daughters | .03<br>(.18) | .08<br>(.27) | –.05** |
| 3. Parents | .06<br>(.24) | .08<br>(.28) | –.02** |
| 4. Brothers or sisters | .06<br>(.23) | .06<br>(.24) | .00 |
| 5. Other relatives | .04<br>(.19) | .04<br>(.20) | .00 |
| *Repairs to home or car* | | | |
| 1. Friends, neighbors, coworkers | .16<br>(.37) | .11<br>(.32) | .05** |
| 2. Sons or daughters | .04<br>(.20) | .05<br>(.22) | –.01* |
| 3. Parents | .05<br>(.22) | .05<br>(.23) | .00 |
| 4. Brothers or sisters | .04<br>(.19) | .04<br>(.19) | .00 |
| 5. Other relatives | .03<br>(.17) | .03<br>(.17) | .00 |
| *Other kinds of work around the house* | | | |
| 1. Friends, neighbors, coworkers | .14<br>(.35) | .11<br>(.31) | .03** |
| 2. Sons or daughters | .07<br>(.25) | .11<br>(.31) | –.04** |
| 3. Parents | .06<br>(.23) | .06<br>(.24) | .00 |
| 4. Brothers or sisters | .04<br>(.20) | .05<br>(.21) | –.01 |
| 5. Other relatives | .04<br>(.19) | .05<br>(.21) | –.01 |

children. However, this pattern is not the same when I examine racial-ethnic groups separately.

## COMPARISON OF AFRICAN AMERICAN WOMEN AND MEN

Among African American respondents, similar patterns to the pooled sample confirm the existence of significant gender differences in the types of help that men and women give. Tables 5.3A and 5.3B illustrate that African American women are more likely than African American men to provide baby-sitting or child care help to friends, neighbors, coworkers, sons or daughters, brothers or sisters, and other relatives. The only category where there are no significant gender differences on giving child care help is to parents. This result may be a reflection of the fact that because a majority of respondents in this sample are over 30, their parents probably do not have young children in need of care. Similarly, African American women are significantly more likely than African American men to receive help with child care from all network members except other relatives.

African American men are also significantly more likely than African American women to give help with home and car repairs to friends, parents, siblings, and other relatives. As with the pooled sample, African American men are more likely than African American women to receive help from friends, but African American women are more likely than African American men to receive repair work from children.

African American men are also more likely than African American women to give help with other kinds of work around the house to friends, and African American women are more likely to receive help around the house from children.

African American men give more transportation help to friends than do African American women, but African American women receive more transportation help than African American men from children and parents.

## COMPARISON OF NON-HISPANIC WHITE WOMEN AND MEN

Tables 5.4A and 5.4B reveal that for giving and receiving child care help, the results for non-Hispanic White respondents are exactly the same as for African American respondents. Non-Hispanic White women are significantly more likely than non-Hispanic White men to

*(text continues on p. 122)*

**TABLE 5.3A** Proportions of Giving Household Help by Race-Ethnicity and Gender Based on $t$ Tests: Means (Standard Deviations)

| *Household Help Item* | *Black* Men | *Black* Women | *Difference Between Means* |
|---|---|---|---|
| *Baby-sitting or child care* | | | |
| 1. Friends, neighbors, coworkers | .11 (.32) | .21 (.41) | –.10** |
| 2. Sons or daughters | .06 (.24) | .12 (.32) | –.06** |
| 3. Parents | .02 (.13) | .03 (.17) | –.01 |
| 4. Brothers or sisters | .07 (.25) | .14 (.35) | –.07** |
| 5. Other relatives | .06 (.24) | .11 (.31) | –.05** |
| *Transportation help* | | | |
| 1. Friends, neighbors, coworkers | .33 (.47) | .26 (.44) | .07** |
| 2. Sons or daughters | .07 (.25) | .06 (.25) | .01 |
| 3. Parents | .06 (.25) | .08 (.28) | –.02 |
| 4. Brothers or sisters | .09 (.29) | .10 (.31) | –.01 |
| 5. Other relatives | .08 (.27) | .09 (.28) | –.01 |
| *Repairs to home or car* | | | |
| 1. Friends, neighbors, coworkers | .26 (.44) | .06 (.24) | .20** |
| 2. Sons or daughters | .04 (.19) | .02 (.14) | .02 |
| 3. Parents | .08 (.27) | .05 (.21) | .03** |
| 4. Brothers or sisters | .08 (.27) | .03 (.16) | .05** |
| 5. Other relatives | .07 (.26) | .01 (.12) | .06** |
| *Other kinds of work around the house* | | | |
| 1. Friends, neighbors, coworkers | .19 (.39) | .12 (.33) | .07** |
| 2. Sons or daughters | .04 (.20) | .05 (.22) | –.01 |
| 3. Parents | .13 (.34) | .15 (.36) | –.02 |
| 4. Brothers or sisters | .07 (.25) | .07 (.25) | .00 |
| 5. Other relatives | .07 (.26) | .07 (.25) | .00 |

*$p \leq .05$; **$p \leq .01$.

**TABLE 5.3B** Proportions of Receiving Household Help by Race-Ethnicity and Gender Based on *t* Tests: Means (Standard Deviations)

| | *Black* | | |
|---|---|---|---|
| *Household Help Item* | *Men* | *Women* | *Difference Between Means* |
| *Baby-sitting or child care* | | | |
| 1. Friends, neighbors, coworkers | .06 (.24) | .11 (.31) | –.05** |
| 2. Sons or daughters | .01 (.10) | .03 (.16) | –.02* |
| 3. Parents | .05 (.21) | .09 (.29) | –.04** |
| 4. Brothers or sisters | .03 (.18) | .10 (.29) | –.07** |
| 5. Other relatives | .04 (.19) | .06 (.23) | –.02 |
| *Transportation help* | | | |
| 1. Friends, neighbors, coworkers | .23 (.42) | .22 (.41) | .01 |
| 2. Sons or daughters | .03 (.17) | .09 (.29) | –.06** |
| 3. Parents | .05 (.22) | .08 (.27) | –.03* |
| 4. Brothers or sisters | .07 (.26) | .09 (.29) | –.02 |
| 5. Other relatives | .06 (.23) | .07 (.26) | –.01 |
| *Repairs to home or car* | | | |
| 1. Friends, neighbors, coworkers | .16 (.37) | .11 (.31) | .05** |
| 2. Sons or daughters | .01 (.10) | .05 (.21) | –.04** |
| 3. Parents | .04 (.19) | .04 (.21) | .00 |
| 4. Brothers or sisters | .04 (.19) | .03 (.17) | .01 |
| 5. Other relatives | .04 (.20) | .03 (.18) | .01 |
| *Other kinds of work around the house* | | | |
| 1. Friends, neighbors, coworkers | .13 (.34) | .11 (.31) | .02 |
| 2. Sons or daughters | .04 (.20) | .11 (.31) | –.07** |
| 3. Parents | .03 (.21) | .06 (.24) | –.03 |
| 4. Brothers or sisters | .06 (.23) | .08 (.27) | –.02 |
| 5. Other relatives | .05 (.22) | .06 (.24) | –.01 |

$^{*}p \leq .05$; $^{**}p \leq .01$.

**TABLE 5.4A** Proportions of Giving Household Help by Race-Ethnicity and Gender Based on *t* Tests: Means (Standard Deviations)

| *Household Help Item* | *White* Men | *White* Women | *Difference Between Means* |
|---|---|---|---|
| *Baby-sitting or child care* | | | |
| 1. Friends, neighbors, coworkers | .14 (.34) | .24 (.43) | –.10** |
| 2. Sons or daughters | .11 (.31) | .14 (.35) | –.03** |
| 3. Parents | .01 (.11) | .02 (.13) | –.01 |
| 4. Brothers or sisters | .08 (.27) | .12 (.32) | –.04** |
| 5. Other relatives | .05 (.22) | .07 (.25) | –.02** |
| *Transportation help* | | | |
| 1. Friends, neighbors, coworkers | .39 (.49) | .37 (.48) | .02 |
| 2. Sons or daughters | .11 (.31) | .11 (.32) | .00 |
| 3. Parents | .10 (.30) | .12 (.32) | –.02** |
| 4. Brothers or sisters | .09 (.29) | .09 (.29) | .00 |
| 5. Other relatives | .07 (.25) | .07 (.26) | .00 |
| *Repairs to home or car* | | | |
| 1. Friends, neighbors, coworkers | .30 (.46) | .11 (.31) | .19** |
| 2. Sons or daughters | .10 (.30) | .05 (.22) | .05** |
| 3. Parents | .14 (.35) | .07 (.26) | .07** |
| 4. Brothers or sisters | .09 (.28) | .03 (.18) | .06** |
| 5. Other relatives | .06 (.24) | .03 (.16) | .03** |
| *Other kinds of work around the house* | | | |
| 1. Friends, neighbors, coworkers | .22 (.42) | .15 (.35) | .07** |
| 2. Sons or daughters | .07 (.26) | .07 (.26) | .00 |
| 3. Parents | .19 (.39) | .16 (.37) | .03** |
| 4. Brothers or sisters | .08 (.26) | .05 (.22) | .03** |
| 5. Other relatives | .06 (.23) | .05 (.21) | .01 |

$^{*}p \leq .05$; $^{**}p \leq .01$.

**TABLE 5.4B** Proportions of Receiving Household Help by Race-Ethnicity and Gender Based on *t* Tests: Means (Standard Deviations)

| *Household Help Item* | *White* | | *Difference Between Means* |
|---|---|---|---|
| | *Men* | *Women* | |
| *Baby-sitting or child care* | | | |
| 1. Friends, neighbors, coworkers | .10 (.29) | .12 (.32) | –.02** |
| 2. Sons or daughters | .00 (.07) | .02 (.13) | –.02** |
| 3. Parents | .07 (.26) | .11 (.32) | –.04** |
| 4. Brothers or sisters | .04 (.19) | .06 (.24) | –.01** |
| 5. Other relatives | .03 (.18) | .03 (.18) | .00 |
| *Transportation help* | | | |
| 1. Friends, neighbors, coworkers | .22 (.41) | .22 (.42) | .00 |
| 2. Sons or daughters | .04 (.19) | .08 (.27) | –.04** |
| 3. Parents | .07 (.25) | .09 (.28) | –.02** |
| 4. Brothers or sisters | .05 (.22) | .06 (.23) | –.01 |
| 5. Other relatives | .04 (.19) | .03 (.18) | .01 |
| *Repairs to home or car* | | | |
| 1. Friends, neighbors, coworkers | .16 (.37) | .12 (.32) | .04** |
| 2. Sons or daughters | .05 (.21) | .05 (.22) | .00 |
| 3. Parents | .05 (.22) | .06 (.23) | –.01 |
| 4. Brothers or sisters | .03 (.18) | .04 (.19) | –.01 |
| 5. Other relatives | .03 (.17) | .03 (.17) | .00 |
| *Other kinds of work around the house* | | | |
| 1. Friends, neighbors, coworkers | .15 (.35) | .11 (.32) | .04** |
| 2. Sons or daughters | .08 (.27) | .11 (.31) | –.03** |
| 3. Parents | .06 (.24) | .06 (.25) | .00 |
| 4. Brothers or sisters | .04 (.20) | .04 (.20) | .00 |
| 5. Other relatives | .04 (.19) | .04 (.20) | .00 |

*$p \le .05$; **$p \le .01$.

give child care help to friends, children, siblings, and other relatives. In addition, White women are more likely than White men to receive child care help from all network members except other relatives.

Further demonstrating that there are salient gender differences in the types of activities that men and women do is the finding in Table 5.4A that White men are significantly more likely than White women to give help with home and car repairs to every category of recipient of help. As with African American men, White men are more likely than White women to receive repair work from friends, neighbors, and coworkers. This finding demonstrates that men are working together on these tasks with friends and neighbors as part of their leisure activity, whereas women are receiving this type of help from family members because they are not as adept at this traditionally "male" work.

White men give significantly more help with other types of work around the house to friends, parents, and siblings than do White women. Interestingly, the same pattern for receipt of household work is evident for Whites as was found for African Americans. White men receive more help with household work from friends than do White women, but White women are more likely to receive this type of help from children. Help with other kinds of work around the house is clearly emerging as help in which men are primarily engaged.

The only significant gender difference in transportation help is that non-Hispanic White women provide it to parents more than do men and receive it from children and parents more than do non-Hispanic White men.

## COMPARISON OF CHICANO WOMEN AND MEN

Among Chicano respondents (Tables 5.5A and 5.5B), the general pattern of gender differences for child care help and help with home and car repairs continues to occur but for fewer categories than for Whites and African Americans. Chicanas are significantly more likely to give child care help to friends, children, and siblings than are Chicano men, and they are more likely than Chicano men to receive child care help from children and siblings. It would be fruitful if the category of brothers or sisters could be disaggregated to determine gender differences in which sibling is providing which type of help. It seems reasonable to assume that it is the sisters in all racial-ethnic groups who are doing the bulk of the child care work.

**TABLE 5.5A** Proportions of Giving Household Help by Race-Ethnicity and Gender Based on *t* Tests: Means (Standard Deviations)

| | *Chicano* | | |
|---|---|---|---|
| *Household Help Item* | *Men* | *Women* | *Difference Between Means* |
| *Baby-sitting or child care* | | | |
| 1. Friends, neighbors, coworkers | .07 (.27) | .14 (.35) | –.07* |
| 2. Sons or daughters | .06 (.25) | .13 (.34) | –.07** |
| 3. Parents | .01 (.10) | .02 (.14) | –.01 |
| 4. Brothers or sisters | .10 (.30) | .18 (.38) | –.08* |
| 5. Other relatives | .07 (.25) | .10 (.30) | –.03 |
| *Transportation help* | | | |
| 1. Friends, neighbors, coworkers | .34 (.47) | .21 (.41) | .13** |
| 2. Sons or daughters | .04 (.19) | .08 (.28) | –.04* |
| 3. Parents | .05 (.22) | .14 (.35) | –.09** |
| 4. Brothers or sisters | .10 (.30) | .13 (.34) | –.03 |
| 5. Other relatives | .11 (.31) | .05 (.22) | .06* |
| *Repairs to home or car* | | | |
| 1. Friends, neighbors, coworkers | .27 (.44) | .04 (.20) | .23** |
| 2. Sons or daughters | .05 (.21) | .02 (.15) | .03 |
| 3. Parents | .08 (.28) | .07 (.26) | .01 |
| 4. Brothers or sisters | .13 (.34) | .05 (.22) | .08** |
| 5. Other relatives | .09 (.29) | .03 (.17) | .06** |
| *Other kinds of work around the house* | | | |
| 1. Friends, neighbors, coworkers | .09 (.29) | .10 (.30) | –.01 |
| 2. Sons or daughters | .03 (.16) | .11 (.31) | –.08** |
| 3. Parents | .13 (.34) | .19 (.39) | –.06 |
| 4. Brothers or sisters | .10 (.31) | .07 (.26) | .03 |
| 5. Other relatives | .09 (.29) | .05 (.21) | .04* |

$^{*}p \leq .05$; $^{**}p \leq .01$.

**TABLE 5.5B** Proportions of Receiving Household Help by Race-Ethnicity and Gender Based on *t* Tests: Means (Standard Deviations)

| | *Chicano* | | |
|---|---|---|---|
| *Household Help Item* | *Men* | *Women* | *Difference Between Means* |
| *Baby-sitting or child care* | | | |
| 1. Friends, neighbors, coworkers | .08<br>(.28) | .11<br>(.31) | –.03 |
| 2. Sons or daughters | .01<br>(.09) | .06<br>(.23) | –.05** |
| 3. Parents | .06<br>(.23) | .10<br>(.30) | –.04 |
| 4. Brothers or sisters | .05<br>(.23) | .10<br>(.30) | –.05* |
| 5. Other relatives | .03<br>(.18) | .06<br>(.25) | –.03 |
| *Transportation help* | | | |
| 1. Friends, neighbors, coworkers | .21<br>(.41) | .18<br>(.39) | –.03 |
| 2. Sons or daughters | .03<br>(.17) | .10<br>(.30) | –.07** |
| 3. Parents | .07<br>(.25) | .07<br>(.25) | .00 |
| 4. Brothers or sisters | .07<br>(.25) | .09<br>(.28) | –.02 |
| 5. Other relatives | .01<br>(.12) | .06<br>(.24) | –.05** |
| *Repairs to home or car* | | | |
| 1. Friends, neighbors, coworkers | .17<br>(.38) | .11<br>(.31) | .06* |
| 2. Sons or daughters | .04<br>(.19) | .05<br>(.22) | –.01 |
| 3. Parents | .05<br>(.21) | .08<br>(.27) | –.03 |
| 4. Brothers or sisters | .07<br>(.26) | .04<br>(.21) | .03 |
| 5. Other relatives | .04<br>(.19) | .03<br>(.18) | .01 |
| *Other kinds of work around the house* | | | |
| 1. Friends, neighbors, coworkers | .10<br>(.30) | .06<br>(.24) | .04 |
| 2. Sons or daughters | .03<br>(.18) | .13<br>(.34) | –.10** |
| 3. Parents | .06<br>(.24) | .06<br>(.24) | .00 |
| 4. Brothers or sisters | .04<br>(.19) | .06<br>(.24) | –.02 |
| 5. Other relatives | .05<br>(.22) | .05<br>(.22) | .00 |

$^*p \leq .05$; $^{**}p \leq .01$.

Tables 5.5A and 5.5B reveal that Chicano men are more likely than Chicanas to give repair help to friends, siblings, and other relatives and to receive help from friends, neighbors, and coworkers.

Chicanas are significantly more likely than Chicano men to both give help to and receive help from children with other work around the house, and Chicano men are significantly more likely than Chicanas to provide this help to other relatives.

Chicanas give more transportation help to children and other relatives than do Chicano men. Chicano men are more likely to receive transportation help from other relatives, but Chicanas are more likely to receive help from children.

## COMPARISONS OF PUERTO RICAN WOMEN AND MEN

Among Puerto Rican respondents, there are very few significant gender differences found in the data. Tables 5.6A and 5.6B reveal that there are no significant gender differences among Puerto Ricans in giving or receiving transportation help, giving help with household work, receiving help with child care, or receiving repairs to home or car.

Puerto Rican women are significantly more likely than Puerto Rican men to provide child care to friends, neighbors, and coworkers. Maintaining the gender division in home and car repairs, Puerto Rican men give more repair help than Puerto Rican women to friends, parents, siblings, and other relatives. Finally, Puerto Rican women are more likely to receive household help from parents than are Puerto Rican men. The lack of significant gender differences between Puerto Rican men and women has several possible explanations: (a) Strict gender roles among Puerto Ricans are nonexistent; (b) Puerto Rican men and women are simply not participating in informal social support networks; (c) because a large percentage of Puerto Rican families are female headed, they are too overburdened to participate in support networks; or (d) perhaps the sample size is too small ($N$ = 147) to ascertain significant differences.

These data reveal several interesting patterns. Although past research purports that women make up the core of the extended social support network (Adams, 1968b; Stack, 1974), it is clear from the descriptive analyses that men also participate in network activities.

**TABLE 5.6A** Proportions of Giving Household Help by Race-Ethnicity and Gender Based on *t* Tests: Means (Standard Deviations)

| | Puerto Rican | | |
|---|---|---|---|
| *Household Help Item* | *Men* | *Women* | *Difference Between Means* |
| *Baby-sitting or child care* | | | |
| 1. Friends, neighbors, coworkers | .00 (.00) | .16 (.37) | –.16** |
| 2. Sons or daughters | .03 (.18) | .07 (.26) | –.04 |
| 3. Parents | .01 (.12) | .03 (.17) | –.02 |
| 4. Brothers or sisters | .04 (.20) | .10 (.30) | –.06 |
| 5. Other relatives | .00 (.00) | .06 (.24) | –.06 |
| *Transportation help* | | | |
| 1. Friends, neighbors, coworkers | .28 (.45) | .20 (.40) | .08 |
| 2. Sons or daughters | .03 (.17) | .05 (.22) | –.02 |
| 3. Parents | .04 (.20) | .07 (.25) | –.03 |
| 4. Brothers or sisters | .04 (.20) | .08 (.27) | –.04 |
| 5. Other relatives | .07 (.25) | .01 (.12) | .06 |
| *Repairs to home or car* | | | |
| 1. Friends, neighbors, coworkers | .21 (.41) | .04 (.20) | .17** |
| 2. Sons or daughters | .00 (.00) | .02 (.15) | –.02 |
| 3. Parents | .07 (.25) | .00 (.06) | .07* |
| 4. Brothers or sisters | .11 (.32) | .02 (.14) | .09* |
| 5. Other relatives | .11 (.32) | .01 (.08) | .10** |
| *Other kinds of work around the house* | | | |
| 1. Friends, neighbors, coworkers | .13 (.35) | .06 (.25) | .07 |
| 2. Sons or daughters | .00 (.00) | .02 (.15) | .02 |
| 3. Parents | .11 (.32) | .15 (.34) | –.04 |
| 4. Brothers or sisters | .09 (.29) | .09 (.29) | .00 |
| 5. Other relatives | .09 (.29) | .04 (.20) | .05 |

*$p \leq .05$; **$p \leq .01$.

**TABLE 5.6B** Proportions of Receiving Household Help by Race-Ethnicity and Gender Based on *t* Tests: Means (Standard Deviations)

| | *Puerto Rican* | | |
|---|---|---|---|
| *Household Help Item* | *Men* | *Women* | *Difference Between Means* |
| *Baby-sitting or child care* | | | |
| 1. Friends, neighbors, coworkers | .06<br>(.24) | .12<br>(.33) | –.06 |
| 2. Sons or daughters | .06<br>(.24) | .03<br>(.16) | .03 |
| 3. Parents | .02<br>(.12) | .06<br>(.24) | –.04 |
| 4. Brothers or sisters | .03<br>(.17) | .06<br>(.24) | –.03 |
| 5. Other relatives | .00<br>(.00) | .02<br>(.15) | –.02 |
| *Transportation help* | | | |
| 1. Friends, neighbors, coworkers | .22<br>(.42) | .25<br>(.44) | –.03 |
| 2. Sons or daughters | .05<br>(.23) | .08<br>(.28) | –.03 |
| 3. Parents | .00<br>(.00) | .08<br>(.27) | –.08 |
| 4. Brothers or sisters | .19<br>(.40) | .08<br>(.28) | .11 |
| 5. Other relatives | .08<br>(.27) | .02<br>(.16) | .06 |
| *Repairs to home or car* | | | |
| 1. Friends, neighbors, coworkers | .12<br>(.33) | .06<br>(.24) | .06 |
| 2. Sons or daughters | .05<br>(.21) | .02<br>(.15) | .03 |
| 3. Parents | .03<br>(.16) | .01<br>(.09) | .02 |
| 4. Brothers or sisters | .04<br>(.19) | .02<br>(.15) | .02 |
| 5. Other relatives | .00<br>(.00) | .03<br>(.18) | –.03 |
| *Other kinds of work around the house* | | | |
| 1. Friends, neighbors, coworkers | .09<br>(.28) | .06<br>(.24) | .03 |
| 2. Sons or daughters | .07<br>(.26) | .10<br>(.30) | –.03 |
| 3. Parents | .00<br>(.00) | .10<br>(.31) | –.10* |
| 4. Brothers or sisters | .06<br>(.25) | .09<br>(.29) | –.03 |
| 5. Other relatives | .08<br>(.27) | .02<br>(.15) | .06 |

$^*p \leq .05$; $^{**}p$

However, because there are no frequency measures in the data, it is difficult to determine which group is participating more often. But there are significant gender differences in the types of behavior in which men and women engage. Women are clearly more involved in both giving and receiving child care help, and men are more involved in behaviors that include repairing cars and homes and other kinds of household work. Given the fact that child care is a daily activity and repair work is not, I would argue that women do, in fact, participate more frequently in their social support networks than do men. No salient patterns emerged regarding transportation help, although in some cases, men were more likely to provide transportation to friends, neighbors, and coworkers than were women.

Racial differences were a bit more difficult to discern from the data. It appears that non-Hispanic White respondents are giving more types of help to more people than are other minority groups and that Puerto Ricans are the least likely to give help. The lack of involvement in social support networks among Puerto Ricans may be a result of their severe economic deprivation. Because Puerto Ricans are currently one of the most economically disadvantaged minority groups in America (Eitzen & Zinn, 1992) and have experienced a substantially greater increase in female-headed families than have other racial-ethnic groups (Cherlin, 1996; Santana Cooney & Colon, 1980), they may not have the resources necessary to fulfill the reciprocal obligations required for participation in support networks. Similarly, because non-Hispanic White families are among the least impoverished groups, they may have more time and resources available to share. Perhaps these results indicate the need to reformulate the causal link between economic factors and participation in social support networks proposed by structural theorists. In addition, Puerto Ricans have a history of back-and-forth migration between Puerto Rico and the mainland, which may prevent them from cultivating tightly knit support networks. Circular migration patterns, the rise in female-headed families, and the increasing poverty rates among Puerto Ricans may all impede their ability to participate in exchange networks. Further multivariate analyses will help determine the dynamics underlying the lack of participation among Puerto Rican respondents.

Finally, the data do not reveal any salient differences in who is giving help to respondents or receiving help from them. No family members stand out as consistently more likely to be involved in the social support networks. In addition, friends, neighbors, and coworkers do appear to be important members of these networks. Therefore, in the next set of bivariate analyses, sons or daughters, parents, brothers or sisters, and other relatives were combined and recoded to create a new variable representing family support group members. Friends, neighbors, and coworkers remained the same and are now referred to as nonfamily support group members.

## Comparisons of Giving and Receiving Help for Family and Nonfamily Based on *t* Tests

### COMPARISONS OF AFRICAN AMERICAN, CHICANO, NON-HISPANIC WHITE, AND PUERTO RICAN RESPONDENTS

The next step in the analysis was to rerun the t tests examining the same four categories of help among family and nonfamily members. The results of these descriptive statistics further supported earlier findings and determined the models to be used in the multivariate analyses. Therefore, rather than discuss the findings in detail, I will summarize them briefly and discuss any new patterns in the data. The complete results are presented in Tables A1.A-A6.B, in the appendix to this volume, pp. 203-214.

Two salient racial patterns emerge that confirm earlier findings. Non-Hispanic White respondents are significantly more likely to provide particular types of help to network members than are African Americans, Chicanos, and Puerto Ricans. In addition, Puerto Ricans are significantly less likely to give or receive particular types of help than are the other three racial-ethnic groups. As before, no identifiable racial patterns regarding receipt of help are evident except that of all three racial-ethnic groups, Puerto Ricans are the least likely to receive help.

Proponents of the cultural perspective often argue that familism is intrinsically valued by Latinos. The descriptive analysis does not support the contention that there is a common culture endemic to all Latinos. In fact, there are many differences in exchange behavior between Chicanos and Puerto Ricans. Further multivariate analyses of Puerto Rican and Chicano helping behavior will be a first step in dispelling erroneous assumptions made by past researchers.

In addition, there are still no distinctive patterns in terms of family versus nonfamily help.

## COMPARISON OF AFRICAN AMERICAN, CHICANO, NON-HISPANIC WHITE, AND PUERTO RICAN WOMEN AND MEN

Consistent with previous findings, women of all races are significantly more likely than men to give and receive help with baby-sitting or child care from both kin and nonkin network members. Similarly, men of all races give more help with home and car repairs to family and nonfamily than do women, and they are more likely than women to receive this type of help from nonfamily members. In addition, men participate in household work more frequently with more people than do women.

These findings confirm initial gender differences. Men participate in traditionally male work, and women participate in work associated with child care. In addition, men participate in household work (e.g., building things, laying carpet, general maintenance) more frequently with more people than do women.

## COMPARISON OF AFRICAN AMERICAN WOMEN AND MEN

Patterns for African American respondents continue to parallel earlier findings and demonstrate gender differences in types of help that social support members both give and receive. African American women are more likely than African American men to participate in child care help. Alternatively, African American men give more home and car repairs to family and friends and receive more home and car repairs from friends than do African American women.

Similarly, African American men are more apt than African American women to give help with other kinds of work around the house to nonfamily members. However, African American women are more likely to receive this type of help from family than are their male counterparts.

## COMPARISON OF NON-HISPANIC WHITE WOMEN AND MEN

As with African American respondents, non-Hispanic White women give and receive more help with child care from family and friends than do non-Hispanic White men. In addition, Anglo men participate in repair work more frequently and with more people than do Anglo women.

Non-Hispanic White men are also more likely to give help with other kinds of work around the house to family and nonfamily network members than are non-Hispanic White women, but women are more likely than men to receive household help from family members. The data indicate that Anglo men give more help with household work than do Anglo women, but that Anglo women receive more help with household work than do Anglo men. Overall, it appears that men are involved in this type of help more often than women, which further confirms my assertion that this variable was not perceived by respondents to measure traditional housework but rather male-typed tinkering, building, and fixing.

### COMPARISON OF CHICANO WOMEN AND MEN

Gender differences found for African American and non-Hispanic White respondents also hold true for Chicano respondents. Chicanas participate more often than Chicano men in network behavior associated with child care. Chicano men participate more frequently and with more people than do Chicanas in home and car repairs and household work.

### COMPARISON OF PUERTO RICAN WOMEN AND MEN

There are fewer significant gender differences between Puerto Rican respondents than expected. Puerto Rican women provide more child care help to family and friends than do Puerto Rican men, and Puerto Rican men receive more home and car repairs from family and nonfamily than do Puerto Rican women. No other significant gender differences occurred. These results do strengthen the argument that child care is primarily women's responsibility and that repair work is primarily men's responsibility. In terms of the other variables, it may be that Puerto Rican respondents do not adhere to such strict gender roles or that they are not participating as frequently as the other racial-ethnic groups in informal social support networks.

## Conclusion

These results indicate that both women and men are members in social support networks. It appears, however, that social support networks are gender specific with very little interconnection between men and women. The types of helping behavior in which men and women participate reflect traditional gender roles. This gender norm behavior does not differ tremendously by race, illustrating the pervasive nature of gender stratification. Racial differences in participation in the social support network exist, but they are not a function of gender.

Because the data do not include measures of the frequency of helping behavior, I cannot test the argument made by past researchers that women make up the core of the extended social support network (Adams, 1968b; Stack, 1974). However, repairs to home and car and household assistance are sporadic activities and, in some cases, may be considered leisure activity. In contrast, child care is an ongoing activity that requires daily preparation and attention. Therefore, it is reasonable to speculate that women's network behavior is more constant and necessary for the daily maintenance of the family.

Based on these results, I decided to examine two types of helping behavior in the multivariate analysis. Child care help, which is clearly women's domain, will be examined for women, and other kinds of work around the house and repairs to home and car will be combined to construct a new variable measuring household assistance for men only. Chapter 6 will present the results of logistic regression for women's participation in child care, and Chapter 7 will present the results of logistic regression for men's participation in household assistance. In both sets of analyses, racial differences in these two types of help will also be examined.

# 6

# Takin' Care

## *The Role of Women*

The purpose of this chapter is to determine whether there are significant racial differences in participation in social support networks and whether these differences can be attributed to cultural norms, socioeconomic factors, or a combination of the two. Based on the theoretical literature, which stresses the importance of reciprocal obligations between kin and nonkin, I examine help that respondents both give to and receive from family and nonfamily members. Because the descriptive analyses indicated that women of all racial-ethnic groups hold primary responsibility for child care, this chapter will examine the determinants of giving and receiving child care help from family and nonfamily members for women only.

### Results

#### DESCRIPTION OF THE MODELS

Before discussing the final logistic regression results, it is essential to mention why the variable representing cultural attitudes is absent from the analysis. In all of the models examining giving and receiving child care help (as well as household assistance for men), the variable measuring cultural attitudes was not significant. Regardless of the sequence in which the attitude variable was entered into the equation, it remained nonsignificant. Perhaps cultural attitudes do not play a significant role in the decision to participate in social support networks. Respondents may participate in support networks despite their lack of familistic values simply because a network member needs help. It is also possible that the variable was not measuring what it was intended to measure. As stated previously, the attitudinal variable estimated the respondent's attitude toward the exchange of financial support and coresidence with family members. The lack of significance of this variable may be due to the fact that there are dimensions of familism not being measured by this variable. Attitudinal questions about sharing items necessary for daily survival and about the importance of living in close proximity to family and nonfamily network members would reflect more accurately the theoretical literature on the reciprocal nature of the extended social support network. Based on these considerations, the attitudinal variable was subsequently dropped from the final models.[1]

Each logistic regression equation has four steps. The order in which the variables were entered into the equation was based on the following theoretical and practical considerations: The first set of variables entered into the equation represents race-ethnicity. Race was entered first so I could observe how relationships between race and child care help changed as I added each additional set of control variables.

The second set of variables entered included the respondent's own demographic characteristics, such as age, marital status, or type of people-related resources (e.g., the presence of young children, teenagers, or adult extended household members). It is important to note that help that respondents give to and receive from family or nonfamily members does *not* include people living in their household. The variables measuring household living arrangements are viewed as representing the availability of support from within the household to respondents. Theoretically, the more resources available to a respondent (presence of adult extended household members), the more time she is expected to devote to support members outside her household. Alternatively, respondents who lack resources (presence of young children, absence of a spouse) may be overburdened and therefore unable to participate actively in external social support networks.

Based on the theoretical perspective that involvement in social support networks mitigates against the destructive effects of poverty, the respondent's own socioeconomic characteristics/resources represent the structural component of the model. This set of control variables was entered third because household structure may reflect certain aspects of socioeconomic status. For instance, extended adult members may add to the household income if they contribute, or they may be a financial burden if they do not contribute economically (unless they provide child care, which increases the ability of single mothers to work). The presence of numerous children also may be a financial burden on some households. Respondents who work long hours may provide financial resources to the household but may be too busy to participate actively in their support networks. Educational attainment and homeownership should also provide insight into the relationship between socioeconomic status and household structure. Based on past research, I would expect that respondents with more education and respondents who are homeowners would be less likely to have extended household members present (other than adult children who return home). Therefore, socioeconomic resources were entered next as control variables to examine how they affected the relationship between respondent's household structure and participation in social support networks.

Finally, the variables representing the respondent's extended family characteristics/resources were entered into the equation. These variables include whether the respondent was born in the United States and the proximity of the respondent's nuclear relatives. As stated previously, proximity of relatives was included only in the regression equations examining familial help. I was particularly interested in how the effects of variables entered in earlier steps changed as availability of family members was included in the analysis. I especially wanted to see if the effects of the socioeconomic variables changed as the proximity of relatives was accounted for. If relationships between economic variables and the likelihood of participation were eliminated by the inclusion of these variables, perhaps they are less central in predicting involvement in support networks than the theoretical literature suggests. In addition, I would argue that an essential component of familial participation in social support networks is the proximity of its members to one another.

## GIVING CHILD CARE HELP TO FAMILY AND NONFAMILY

Tables 6.1 and 6.2 present logistic regression coefficients for giving child care help to family and to nonfamily members. I will begin my discussion of the results of the logistic regression equations by presenting racial-ethnic differences in giving child care help to family members (Table 6.1, Model 1) and to nonfamily members (Table 6.2, Model 1). Then I will present the relationship between a respondent's own demographic resources and giving child care help to family (Table 6.1, Model 2) and to nonfamily (Table 6.2, Model 2). Similarly, I will discuss the relationship between a respondent's socioeconomic resources and giving child care help to family (Table 6.1, Model 3) and to nonfamily (Table 6.2, Model 3). Finally, I will present the relationship between a respondent's extended family characteristics and giving child care help to family (Table 6.1, Model 4) and to nonfamily (Tablc 6.2, Model 4). Presenting the results of the multivariate analysis in this way will allow me to describe similarities and differences in the effects of particular sets of variables on giving child care help to family versus giving child care help to nonfamily network members.

Model 1 in Table 6.1 reveals that African Americans and Chicanas are significantly more likely than non-Hispanic Whites to give child care help to family. Yet once statistical controls are entered into the equation, significant racial differences in giving child care help to family members disappear. The initial racial differences in giving child care help to family are composed of the effects of the respondent's own demographic resources for Chicanas and extended family characteristics for African Americans.

As indicated by Table 6.2, the results for giving child care help to nonfamily members among minority groups are very different. African Americans and Chicanas are significantly less likely than non-Hispanic Whites to provide help with child care to nonfamily members, despite the introduction of control variables. At first glance, this finding seems to contradict much of the past theoretical and empirical literature. However, Joyce Ladner and Ruby Morton Gourdine (1984), William Julius Wilson (1987), K. Sue Jewell (1988), and Patricia Hill Collins

**TABLE 6.1** Logistic Coefficients for Regression of Giving Child Care Help to Family Members for Women on Selected Independent Variables

| *Independent Variables* | *Model 1* | *Model 2* | *Model 3* | *Model 4* |
|---|---|---|---|---|
| Black | .17* | .28** | .28** | .02 |
| | (.08) | (.08) | (.08) | (.09) |
| Puerto Rican | –.29 | –.25 | –.30 | –.06 |
| | (.26) | (.26) | (.27) | (.29) |
| Chicano | .26* | .24 | .13 | .11 |
| | (.13) | (.14) | (.14) | (.15) |
| Children Under 5 | | .03 | .02 | .06 |
| | | (.05) | (.05) | (.05) |
| Children Between 6-12 | | –.07 | –.08 | –.03 |
| | | (.04) | (.05) | (.05) |
| Female Children Between 13-18 | | –.07 | –.09 | –.03 |
| | | (.07) | (.07) | (.07) |
| Male Children Between 13-18 | | –.26** | –.28** | –.27** |
| | | (.07) | (.07) | (.07) |
| Adult Female 19 and Over | | .02 | .02 | .01 |
| | | (.05) | (.06) | (.06) |
| Adult Male 19 and Over | | .04 | .05 | .02 |
| | | (.06) | (.06) | (.06) |
| Age | | –.01** | –.02** | –.02** |
| | | (.00) | (.00) | (.00) |
| Divorced, Widowed, Separated | | –.32** | –.26** | –.23** |
| | | (.07) | (.08) | (.08) |
| Single | | –.61** | –.49** | –.42** |
| | | (.09) | (.10) | (.11) |
| Education | | | –.05** | .01 |
| | | | (.01) | (.01) |
| Household Income | | | 6.2 | 1.1 |
| | | | (7.6) | (7.7) |
| Missing Income (1 = missing) | | | –.05 | –.05 |
| | | | (.07) | (.07) |
| Homeownership (1 = yes, 0 = no) | | | .23** | .15* |
| | | | (.07) | (.07) |
| Work Hours | | | –.00 | –.00 |
| | | | (.00) | (.00) |
| Born in the U.S. (1 = yes, 0 = no) | | | | .64** |
| | | | | (.13) |
| Siblings Within 2 Miles | | | | .29** |
| | | | | (.03) |
| Siblings Between 2-25 Miles | | | | .23** |
| | | | | (.02) |
| Siblings Between 25-300 Miles | | | | .05* |
| | | | | (.02) |

*(continued)*

**TABLE 6.1 Continued**

| *Independent Variables* | *Model 1* | *Model 2* | *Model 3* | *Model 4* |
|---|---|---|---|---|
| Siblings More Than 300 Miles | | | | .01 |
| | | | | (.02) |
| Adult Children Within 2 Miles | | | | .49** |
| | | | | (.05) |
| Adult Children Between 2-25 Miles | | | | .42** |
| | | | | (.04) |
| Adult Children Between 25-300 Miles | | | | .12* |
| | | | | (.05) |
| Adult Children More Than 300 Miles | | | | .03 |
| | | | | (.04) |
| Constant | –.84** | –.17 | .45 | –1.18** |
| -2 log-likelihood | 8239.080 | 8130.670 | 8103.088 | 7548.556 |
| Model chi-square | 9.041 | 108.411 | 27.581 | 554.533 |

NOTE: Numbers in parentheses are standard errors.
$*p \leq .05$; $**p \leq .01$.

(1990) have speculated recently that because of the increasing social isolation, severe economic deprivation, and the influx of drugs into minority communities (Anderson, 1990), extended support networks historically found in these communities may not be as prevalent as in the past. This hypothesis is strengthened by the findings on socioeconomic indicators reported below.

Table 6.2 reveals another extremely interesting result. Puerto Ricans are significantly less likely than non-Hispanic White respondents to provide friends with child care help net of all control variables except origin of birth. When the variable measuring whether or not the respondent was born in the United States is introduced into the equation (Model 4), the logistic regression coefficient decreases slightly, and the relationship is no longer significant. This is an extremely salient finding, because past research attributes Puerto Ricans' lack of involvement in extended family structures or support networks to cultural values that devalue these networks. These studies have not considered the back-and-forth migration patterns of Puerto Ricans, which may inhibit their ability to develop strong network ties. Puerto Ricans who frequently migrate between Puerto Rico and the mainland may not be accepted into nonkin social support networks because their constant movement may be perceived as preventing

**TABLE 6.2** Logistic Coefficients for Regression of Giving Child Care Help to Nonfamily Members for Women on Selected Independent Variables

| *Independent Variables* | *Model 1* | *Model 2* | *Model 3* | *Model 4* |
|---|---|---|---|---|
| Black | –.18* | –.49** | –.43** | –.44** |
| | (.10) | (.11) | (.11) | (.11) |
| Puerto Rican | –.52 | –.93** | –.74* | –.60 |
| | (.31) | (.33) | (.33) | (.34) |
| Chicano | –.55** | –1.19** | –.95** | –.88** |
| | (.18) | (.19) | (.20) | (.20) |
| Children Under 5 | | .37** | .35** | .36** |
| | | (.05) | (.05) | (.05) |
| Children Between 6-12 | | .39** | .38** | .39** |
| | | (.04) | (.05) | (.05) |
| Female Children Between 13-18 | | .29** | .30** | .30** |
| | | (.07) | (.07) | (.07) |
| Male Children Between 13-18 | | .08 | .09 | .09 |
| | | (.07) | (.07) | (.07) |
| Adult Female 19 and Older | | –.10 | –.06 | –.05 |
| | | (.07) | (.07) | (.07) |
| Adult Male 19 and Older | | –.05 | .03 | .04 |
| | | (.07) | (.08) | (.08) |
| Age | | –.05** | –.05** | –.05** |
| | | (.00) | (.00) | (.00) |
| Divorced, Widowed, Separated | | .10 | .20* | .19* |
| | | (.09) | (.10) | (.10) |
| Single | | .00 | .09 | .09 |
| | | (.10) | (.11) | (.11) |
| Education | | | .08** | .08** |
| | | | (.01) | (.01) |
| Household Income | | | 2.0 | -2.3 |
| | | | (8.5) | (8.5) |
| Missing Income (1 = missing) | | | –.21* | –.21* |
| | | | (.09) | (.09) |
| Homeownership (1 = yes, 0 = no) | | | .11 | .10 |
| | | | (.08) | (.08) |
| Work Hours | | | –.00* | –.00 |
| | | | (.00) | (.00) |
| Born in the U.S. (1 = yes, 0 = no) | | | | .31** |
| | | | | (.27) |
| Constant | –1.22** | .53** | –.43 | –.43 |
| -2 log likelihood | 7049.917 | 6049.049 | 6004.476 | 5998.708 |
| Model chi-square | 16.336 | 1000.868 | 44.573 | 5.768 |

NOTE: Numbers in parentheses are standard errors.
$*p \leq .05$; $**p \leq .01$.

them from reciprocating help. Because Chicanas do not have circular migration patterns, they may have less difficulty than Puerto Ricans establishing friendship networks after they have resided in the United States for several years.

Table 6.2 also reveals that an important predictor of giving child care help to nonfamily members is the presence of young children. Respondents with children under 5 years of age and with children between the ages of 6 and 12 have a significant positive effect on providing child care help to nonfamily. This is an especially interesting finding given the fact that the presence of young children has no effect on the likelihood of providing child care to family members. Because young children are often a drain on resources, this finding may seem unusual. However, there appears to be a reciprocal exchange in which respondents help friends and neighbors who may live in the same neighborhood and whose children often play together.

Model 2 in Tables 6.1 and 6.2 reveals that the presence of teenage boys has a negative effect on giving child care help to family, and the presence of teenage girls has a positive effect on giving child care help to nonfamily. This finding may indicate that teenage sons do not contribute to the maintenance of the household and therefore hinder the respondent's ability to participate in support networks. Alternatively, teenage daughters are a resource allowing respondents to participate more freely in their nonkin network. These results suggest that traditional gender norms persist among teenagers: Girls are expected to help with housework and take care of younger siblings. Recent research suggests that this gendered division of household labor continues into adulthood and persists among intergenerational household members (Logan & Spitze, 1996; Spitze & Ward, 1995).

Tables 6.1 and 6.2 illustrate that the presence of adult extended household members has no effect on the likelihood of providing child care help to family or friends. This is somewhat surprising. I would have expected the presence of adult extended household members, particularly women, to act as a resource enabling respondents to participate more actively in their network. However, perhaps when respondents live with adult extended household members, they no longer need to participate in informal social support networks because they give and receive help from members of their household. Alternatively, the presence of adult household members may prevent respondents from participating in their external networks because extra household members drain resources that respondents usually reserve for members of their network. Given the nonsignificance of these variables, it is difficult to determine whether or not either interpretation is accurate. Table 6.1 also reveals that respondents who are divorced, widowed, or separated, or who are single, are significantly less likely to give family members help with baby-sitting than are married respondents. The presence of a spouse functions as a resource, providing married respondents with more flexibility and enabling them to participate more actively in their network, regardless of economic and extended family situation.

The results for marital status on giving child care help to nonfamily are somewhat different. As Models 3 and 4 in Table 6.2 illustrate, nonmarried respondents are significantly more likely than married respondents to provide child care help to friends. I speculate that divorced respondents are helping friends and neighbors who may be part of a community in which help is given freely.

The older a respondent is, the less likely she will be to help both family members (Table 6.1) and nonfamily members (Table 6.2) with child care. Perhaps older women, who have already raised children, would prefer to participate in leisure activities with members of their own peer group. In addition, older respondents probably have fewer young grandchildren and friends with small children in need of child care.

Introduction of socioeconomic variables into the equation indicates that there is a positive relationship between economic resources and network participation. A respondent's education is positively related to giving child care help to nonfamily network members and persists net of the proximity control variables (Table 6.2). Similarly, homeownership is positively associated with giving child care to family (Table 6.1) but has no significant effect on giving child care help to nonfamily (Table 6.2).

These results suggest that, contrary to the structural theoretical perspective, respondents do not engage in giving child care help primarily out of economic necessity. In fact, it seems that as people increase their socioeconomic standing, they increase their participation in the support network. Although this finding contradicts the literature presented in earlier chapters, it corroborates the results of a 10-year research project conducted by Cochran, Larner, Riley, Gunnarson, and Henderson (1990), who found that contrary to popular belief, networks are more highly developed among white-collar families than among those in the lower socioeconomic strata. The assertion that, as a result of social dislocation among minority families, their network participation is eroding is further substantiated.

Finally, Model 4 demonstrates the importance of extended family characteristics. Table 6.1 illustrates that the proximity of relatives is an important predictor of giving child care help to family members. Logistic regression coefficients reveal that the likelihood of giving child care help decreases the farther away siblings and adult children live from the respondent. The proximity of respondents' parents was omitted from this particular model because their parents are primarily middle aged and are not likely to have young children. Similarly, I did not examine the proximity of relatives when analyzing the exchange of child care help between respondents and nonfamily network members. It seems reasonable to assume that geographic location of relatives is unrelated to whether or not a respondent participates in her nonfamily social support network. However, this set of variables is an essential component in understanding the dynamics of participation in extended social support networks among families.

Respondents born in the United States are significantly more likely to give help with child care to family and nonfamily members than are those born elsewhere (Table 6.1). Perhaps respondents born outside of the United States have difficulty in establishing friendship networks because of their limited English language skills. In addition, recent immigrants may have left their relatives behind, temporarily severing familial network ties. An examination of migration patterns is especially important because much of the past research has failed to measure the importance of minority group geographical mobility.

These results do not support many of the theoretical arguments presented earlier. It appears that accessibility of support group members and the presence of available resources is more important than economic need and cultural attitudes in predicting network participation. Nor did I find that giving child care help is more prominent among minority families. In fact, non-Hispanic White families with more economic resources are more involved with giving social support than are Chicanas or African Americans. Similarly, respondents who have more resources available (e.g., spouses, teenage daughters) are also more involved in the network.

A more obvious result is the consistent finding that the closer a respondent lives to her relatives, the more likely she is to give child care help. Participation in kin networks is facilitated by having relatives live close by. As family members move farther away, they become increasingly less likely to participate in their support networks, although they may still offer emotional support (e.g., see Aldous & Klein, 1991).

## RECEIVING CHILD CARE HELP FROM FAMILY AND NONFAMILY

As before, I will begin my discussion of the results of the logistic regression equations by presenting racial differences in receipt of child care help from family members (Table 6.3, Model 1) and from nonfamily members (Table 6.4, Model 1). Then I will present the relationship between a respondent's own demographic resources and receipt of child care help from family (Table 6.3, Model 2) and from nonfamily (Table 6.4, Model 2) network members. Similarly, I will discuss the relationship between a respondent's socioeconomic resources and receipt of child care help from family (Table 6.3, Model 3) and from nonfamily (Table 6.4, Model 3). Finally, I will present the relationship between a respondent's extended family characteristics and receipt of child care help from family (Table 6.3, Model 4) and from nonfamily (Table 6.4, Model 4).

Model 1 in Table 6.3 illustrates that the only racial-ethnic group different from non-Hispanic Whites is African Americans. Black women are significantly less likely than White women to receive child care help from family, but once the economic variables are entered in the equation (Model 3), the relationship is no longer significant. Therefore, when class is controlled, there are no longer differences in the receipt of child care help from family between African American and non-Hispanic White respondents. However, when the proximity variables are entered into the equation (Model 4), African Americans are again significantly less likely than non-Hispanic Whites to receive child care help from family. This finding may indicate an interaction effect between socioeconomic status and family proximity that is being masked when only the economic variables are entered. Another

**TABLE 6.3** Logistic Coefficients for Regression of Receiving Child Care Help From Family Members for Women on Selected Independent Variables

| *Independent Variables* | *Model 1* | *Model 2* | *Model 3* | *Model 4* |
|---|---|---|---|---|
| Black | –.34** | –.28* | –.24 | –.43** |
| | (.12) | (.14) | (.14) | (.15) |
| Puerto Rican | –.77 | –.75 | –.48 | –.44 |
| | (.41) | (.43) | (.43) | (.48) |
| Chicano | –.27 | –.22 | –.01 | .05 |
| | (.18) | (.19) | (.20) | (.22) |
| Children Under 5 | | .18** | .19** | .21** |
| | | (.06) | (.07) | (.07) |
| Children Between 6-12 | | –.02 | .01 | –.01 |
| | | (.06) | (.06) | (.06) |
| Female Children Between 13-18 | | –.30** | –.27** | –.34** |
| | | (.10) | (.11) | (.11) |
| Male Children Between 13-18 | | –.37** | –.34** | –.40** |
| | | (.10) | (.10) | (.11) |
| Adult Female 19 and Over | | .27* | .32* | .43** |
| | | (.13) | (.13) | (.14) |
| Adult Male 19 and Over | | –.18 | –.05 | .09 |
| | | (.15) | (.16) | (.17) |
| Age | | –.04** | –.06** | –.03** |
| | | (.01) | (.01) | (.01) |
| Divorced, Widowed, Separated | | –.08 | .12 | –.06 |
| | | (.13) | (.14) | (.15) |
| Single | | –.38* | –.15 | –.30 |
| | | (.18) | (.18) | (.19) |
| Education | | | .03 | .07** |
| | | | (.02) | (.02) |
| Household Income | | | 2.1 | 2.4 |
| | | | (1.2) | (1.2) |
| Missing Income (1 = missing) | | | –.19 | –.16 |
| | | | (.14) | (.14) |
| Homeownership (1 = yes, 0 = no) | | | .40** | .28* |
| | | | (.11) | (.12) |
| Work Hours | | | .00* | .00* |
| | | | (.00) | (.00) |
| Born in the U.S. (1 = yes, 0 = no) | | | | .37* |
| | | | | (.05) |
| Siblings Within 2 Miles | | | | .18** |
| | | | | (.05) |
| Siblings Between 2-25 Miles | | | | .04 |
| | | | | (.04) |
| Siblings Between 25-300 Miles | | | | .03 |
| | | | | (.04) |
| Siblings More Than 300 Miles | | | | –.01 |
| | | | | (.04) |

**TABLE 6.3 Continued**

| *Independent Variables* | *Model 1* | *Model 2* | *Model 3* | *Model 4* |
|---|---|---|---|---|
| Parents Within 2 Miles | | | | .90** |
| | | | | (.18) |
| Parents Between 2-25 Miles | | | | .86** |
| | | | | (.17) |
| Parents Between 25-300 Miles | | | | .03 |
| | | | | (.19) |
| Parents More Than 300 Miles | | | | –.37 |
| | | | | (.20) |
| Constant | –.05 | 1.21** | .86* | –1.07* |
| -2 log-likelihood | 2946.688 | 2807.795 | 2769.537 | 2602.424 |
| Model chi-square | 12.392 | 138.893 | 38.258 | 167.112 |

NOTE: Numbers in parentheses are standard errors.
$*p \leq .05$; $**p \leq .01$.

possible explanation is that the relationship is being suppressed by a variable not present in the model.

Table 6.4 reveals an interesting racial-ethnic pattern in receipt of help from nonfamily members. African Americans are significantly less likely than non-Hispanic Whites to receive child care help from nonfamily. This relationship remains despite the introduction of control variables. Chicanas are also less likely than non-Hispanic White women to receive child care help from friends despite the introduction of respondents' demographic or economic resources. However, when migration status is entered into the equation (Model 4), the relationship decreases and becomes nonsignificant. Therefore, there are no significant differences between Chicana and non-Hispanic White women when controlling for origin of birth. The data demonstrate the importance of examining migration status in the study of involvement in social support networks. Paradoxically, Chicanas who are not born in the United States, and who therefore may need considerable help from friends, are unable to cultivate extended support networks.[2] An interesting avenue for further inquiry would be to determine the level of English proficiency obtained by Chicanas born outside the United States. Perhaps language barriers prevent Chicanas from developing network ties with English-speaking women in their communities.

Tables 6.3 and 6.4 reveal significant effects for presence of children on receiving child care help from both family and friends. Children

**TABLE 6.4** Logistic Coefficients for Regression of Receiving Child Care Help From Nonfamily Members for Women on Selected Independent Variables

| *Independent Variables* | *Model 1* | *Model 2* | *Model 3* | *Model 4* |
|---|---|---|---|---|
| Black | –.65** | –.61** | –.62** | –.64** |
| | (.14) | (.16) | (.16) | (.16) |
| Puerto Rican | –.57 | –.57 | –.14 | .10 |
| | (.44) | (.45) | (.46) | (.47) |
| Chicano | –1.0** | –.96** | –.58* | –.47 |
| | (.24) | (.24) | (.25) | (.26) |
| Children Under 5 | | .19** | .19** | .20** |
| | | (.07) | (.07) | (.07) |
| Children Between 6-12 | | .15* | .22** | .23** |
| | | (.06) | (.06) | (.06) |
| Female Children Between 13-18 | | –.66** | –.58** | –.60** |
| | | (.12) | (.13) | (.13) |
| Male Children Between 13-18 | | –.48** | –.37** | –.39** |
| | | (.12) | (.12) | (.12) |
| Adult Female 19 and Over | | –.13 | –.04 | –.03 |
| | | (.15) | (.15) | (.15) |
| Adult Male 19 and Over | | –.17 | .00 | .02 |
| | | (.17) | (.18) | (.18) |
| Age | | .01 | –.01 | –.01 |
| | | (.01) | (.01) | (.01) |
| Divorced, Widowed, Separated | | .23 | .37* | .34* |
| | | (.14) | (.15) | (.15) |
| Single | | .02 | .20 | .21 |
| | | (.19) | (.20) | (.20) |
| Education | | | .18** | .18** |
| | | | (.02) | (.02) |
| Household Income | | | 7.3 | 6.2 |
| | | | (1.1) | (1.1) |
| Missing Income (1 = missing) | | | –.29* | –.27 |
| | | | (.15) | (.07) |
| Homeownership (1 = yes, 0 = no) | | | –.00 | –.00 |
| | | | (.12) | (.12) |
| Work Hours | | | .00 | .00 |
| | | | (.00) | (.00) |
| Born in the U.S. (1 = yes, 0 = no) | | | | .52* |
| | | | | (.20) |
| Constant | –.60** | –1.09** | –2.86** | –3.43** |
| -2 log-likelihood | 2647.050 | 2571.417 | 2500.250 | 2493.256 |
| Model chi-square | 41.988 | 75.633 | 71.167 | 6.994 |

NOTE: Numbers in parentheses are standard errors.
*$p \leq .05$; **$p \leq .01$.

under 5 years of age often require a tremendous amount of attention, and the data indicate that women are receiving the support they need from relatives and friends with this often time-consuming task. Alternatively, teenagers are often self-sufficient and less likely to require an enormous amount of parental supervision; they may, in fact, be helping their parents with some child care. Model 2 in Table 6.3 demonstrates that presence of adult female extended household members appears to be an important predictor of receiving child care help. Respondents who have adult women living with them are significantly more likely to receive child care help from family than are those who do not have adult women present. Although, on the surface, this finding seems contradictory to what one might expect, it may be that these extended household members have children of their own also living with the respondent. If extended female household members have children, then more child care help may be required from outside the household.

Model 2 in Table 6.3 indicates that single respondents with children are significantly less likely to receive child care help from family than are married respondents. However, when economic characteristics are entered into the equation, in Model 3, this relationship is no longer significant. Once socioeconomic status is controlled for, single women are no less likely than married women to receive child care help from family. Socioeconomic status may mediate the relationship between marital status and receipt of child care help from friends. Single mothers are more likely to be economically disadvantaged and are therefore less likely to receive child care help. This relationship is a result of class differences, not of marital status per se. This finding is especially troubling because many female-headed families could benefit greatly from child care help from members of their kin network. In fact, the lack of an extended kin network to assist with child care needs may force some single mothers to work part-time or keep them out of the workforce entirely.

Alternatively, divorced, widowed, or separated women are significantly more likely than married women to receive child care help from friends (Table 6.4). Receipt of child care help from friends for nonmarried women becomes significant in Model 3 when socioeconomic variables are entered. The relationship between marital status and receipt of child care help from friends is being suppressed by socioeconomic status. Social support from friends appears to be an important resource that mitigates against the lack of spousal help regardless of the respondent's socioeconomic status.

It is difficult to discern the exact nature of the relationship between socioeconomic resources, marital status, and receipt of child care among nonmarried women. There may be an interaction effect between socioeconomic resources and marital status that has not been identified in this analysis. Perhaps nonkin networks are more tightly knit than kin networks. Friendships are cultivated by individuals who are usually of similar age and have common interests. In addition, friendships are usually devoid of the tension that characterizes many familial relationships. Perhaps friends are therefore more responsive to respondents' child care needs, regardless of socioeconomic status.

Tables 6.3 and 6.4 reveal that education is positively related to receiving child care help from family and friends, and homeownership and total number of work hours are positively related to receiving child care help from family. As a respondent's socioeconomic status increases, so does her network participation. This finding corroborates earlier results indicating that, contrary to past research, respondents with more socioeconomic resources participate more actively in extended social support networks.

Logistic regression coefficients reveal that receipt of help with child care from family is increased by the availability of siblings within 2 miles and parents within 25 miles. As siblings and parents move farther away, the relationships are no longer significant.

We further see that respondents born in the United States are significantly more likely to receive child care help from family and friends than are respondents born elsewhere. This substantiates earlier findings that demonstrate the importance of examining country of origin before creating general hypotheses about minority group involvement in social support networks. Respondents born outside of the United States may not have the ability to develop extensive network ties, particularly if they have been in the United States only a short time. Future research should examine length of stay in the United States to determine whether individuals who reside in the United States longer have cultivated more extensive network ties.

## Summary and Conclusions

The data reveal several interesting findings. There do seem to be racial differences in the propensity to give and receive child care help; however, they contradict past research findings. African American, Chicana, and Puerto Rican women are not more involved in social support networks than are Anglo women, as hypothesized by the theoretical literature. In fact, whether giving or receiving child care help from family or friends, non-Hispanic White women were more likely than minority women to participate, especially when compared to Black women.

These results suggest three alternative explanations: (a) Past research overestimated minority group involvement in social support networks, (b) the overuse of ethnographic research using nonprobability samples led to inaccurate results that have been generalized inappropriately to all minority groups, or (c) extended networks are no longer as prevalent among minority groups as they were in the past. Although much of the past research did rely on small nonprobability samples and has been overgeneralized, it would be erroneous to reject the research as totally fallacious. The abundance of ethnographic studies depicting familism in particular minority communities indicates that many minority families have been active participants in exchange networks. In addition, there is historical evidence linking ancient extended kinship systems to contemporary African American, Puerto Rican, and Chicano family organization (Del Castillo, 1984; Fitzpatrick, 1981; Herskovits, 1938, 1966). Therefore, the most likely explanation is that the elaborate social support networks characteristic of poor urban minorities in the 1960s and 1970s no longer persist.

There are many socioeconomic factors that may be responsible for the demise of social support networks in minority communities. During the early 1980s, there was a tremendous influx of drugs (particularly crack) in minority neighborhoods. Increasing unemployment and subsequent economic hardships occurred as a result of the deindustrialization of the inner city. Consequently, there was a disturbing rise in violent crime. In addition, the migration of the middle class out of the inner cities and persistent residential segregation have resulted in increasing social isolation of these communities. Given the overwhelming conditions of social dislocation that characterize minority communities, it is not surprising that informal social support networks can no longer flourish (Anderson, 1990; Collins, 1990; Ladner & Gourdine, 1984; Massey & Denton, 1993; Wilson, 1987; Zinn, 1989).

Although Wilson's (1987) discussion of the social isolation of the ghetto poor provides a useful framework for examining the decline of social support networks in minority communities, it should not be uniformly applied to all Latinos. Although dramatic increases in joblessness and long-term poverty identified by Wilson may apply to Puerto Ricans, who primarily reside in deindustrialized central cities, they may not apply to Latinos living in the Sunbelt or in locations that never had a strong industrial base to begin with (Moore, 1989; Moore & Pinderhughes, 1993). In fact, after an initial period of deindustrialization, some Sunbelt cities have experienced reindustrialization with an expansion of low-wage service and manufacturing industries that rely heavily upon immigrant labor (McCarthy & Valdez, 1986; Muller & Epenshade, 1986, as cited in Moore & Pinderhughes, 1993). These diverse forms of economic restructuring require alternative explanations for the loss of social support networks among residents outside the Rustbelt, most of whom are Chicano, Cuban, and South-Central Americans. Future research on social support networks among Latino families should include an analysis of urban renewal and development, government investment, regentrification of Latino communities, and the role of the informal economy, particularly because meager neighborhood resources and overall deprivation often force people to find alternatives to traditional community organization (Logan & Molotch, 1987).

The finding that minority women are not more likely than White women to participate in child care help is especially significant. The practice of giving and receiving help with child care has been identified as a common network behavior frequently associated with low-income minority women. The fact that African American women in particular were consistently less likely than White women to give child care help to or receive help from family and friends is contrary to past research based on both the cultural and structural perspectives. During and after slavery, African American women have often adopted biologically and nonbiologically related children into their extended networks. However, as Collins (1990) argues, this practice has now become difficult for inner-city and poor rural minority groups to maintain because they are plagued with an unprecedented lack of resources and a multitude of social problems. Collins (1990) points out that

> the communal child care networks of the slave era, the extended family arrangements of the rural South, the importance of grandmothers in child care, and even the recreation of Black community structures during the first wave of urbanization appear to be eroding for poor Black women. (p. 64)

Another salient finding with respect to race-ethnicity is that for Latinas, the relationship between ethnicity and child care disappears once migration status is controlled. Past research examining extended living arrangements and informal social support networks has suggested that Puerto Ricans are less involved in these networks because of their lack of cultural values regarding familism. However, the unique back-and-forth migration patterns of Puerto Ricans may prevent them from establishing strong network ties. Because the support network is characterized by exchange reciprocity, migratory Puerto Ricans may have difficulty being accepted as members because participants fear they may return to Puerto Rico and be unable to fulfill their obligation to that network.[3] Further research must be done on more specific indicators of the migration experience. It would be fruitful to examine when respondents migrated to the United States, what generation of immigrants they represent, whether they live in ethnic enclaves or not, and, for Puerto Ricans, the number of times they have migrated back and forth.

The presence of children is an important predictor of women's participation in social support networks. I initially expected that the presence of young children would act as a drain on respondents' resources, inhibiting women's ability to give help with child care but increasing their probability of receiving child care help. However, given the results of the analysis, it is necessary to reconceptualize the effects that young children have on women's network participation.

The presence of young children, particularly those under 5 years of age, facilitates women's involvement in social support networks.

The sharing of child care between women seems to be similar to the exchange networks characteristic of the Flats, identified by Carol Stack (1974). It appears that women provide child care and baby-sitting to their network members with the expectation that when they need help, they will also receive it. Fortunately for women with very young children, the data indicate that they are receiving some support with this often-exhausting responsibility. As children grow to become teenagers, there is less need to rely on the network for help. Surprisingly, the presence of adult extended household members is not an important predictor of giving child care help to family or friends. Therefore, having extra adults present in the home does not necessarily act as a resource that frees respondents to participate more actively in their networks. Given the fact that respondents with adult women present receive child care help from family, it would appear that the addition of adult women in the home is actually a drain on respondents' resources. Based on the research on household structure and single-parent families, it would not be unreasonable to suspect that many of these women residing with respondents are single mothers with children of their own. Perhaps female extended household members have children who reside with them and the respondent requiring child care help from outside the household.

Marital status also appears to be a determinant of giving and receiving child care help. The data suggest that unmarried respondents are less involved in familial networks than their married counterparts. Apparently, the presence of a spouse acts as a resource, providing married women with the freedom to participate in their social support networks.

Conversely, divorced, widowed, and separated respondents are more likely to give child care help to and receive help from friends despite the fact that they do not have spouses present to free up their time. Perhaps divorced respondents are providing child care help to friends and neighbors because they also receive help from those friends and neighbors when they need it. Involvement in support networks among friends may be characterized by lack of resources in some instances, whereas among family, it appears to be characterized by availability of resources. These data suggest that nonmarried respondents rely upon one another to allay the lack of spousal help.

A pattern seems to be emerging in which women who have young children and who are divorced, widowed, or separated are more involved in networks with their friends and neighbors than with their families. These friendship networks may represent a woman-centered experience that is less possible when a respondent has no young children or is attached to a marital partner. Perhaps nonmarried mothers create intimate communities predicated on their shared experiences. These communities may not be open to all women and may comprise a culture in which the exchange of child care bonds them together.

Socioeconomic indicators have the opposite effect on giving and receiving child care help than originally hypothesized. The more education and resources respondents have, the more likely they are to give and receive help. This serendipitous finding requires scholars to reexamine the underlying assumptions of the structural perspective. The structural perspective evolved as a way to interpret the empirical realities of minority family organization. As a result, the underlying tenets of the structural perspective were constrained by the particular socioeconomic conditions that existed at the time of its emergence. Consequently, the structural perspective is situated within a very specific sociohistorical context. As socioeconomic conditions worsen dramatically for minority families, the structural perspective may no longer be pertinent.

This critique of the structural perspective is substantiated by more recent scholarship, which contends that extended social support networks so prevalent among minority communities in the 1970s and early 1980s no longer persist given the current economic and social climate (e.g., see Anderson, 1990; Cochran et al., 1990; Collins, 1990; Ladner & Gourdine, 1984; Wilson, 1987). In fact, scholars argue that national economic shifts and high rates of social dislocation among Blacks and Hispanics have created distinctive forms of racial poverty (Ortiz, 1991; Wilson, 1987; Zinn, 1989). Perhaps these newly emerging patterns of poverty are so overwhelming that individuals have neither the time nor the resources necessary to participate in kin and nonkin networks.

Although the data do not support the structural argument that social support networks represent survival strategies used to alleviate the deplorable effects of poverty, it is evident that economic resources do play a significant role in participation in these networks. Therefore, using an economic framework to understand the dynamics of participation in support networks is useful if we reverse the direction of the expected relationships. The data illustrate that as respondents' income, economic resources, and education increase, involvement in network behavior also increases. Therefore, a reformulation of the structural perspective in which economic deprivation is associated with a decline in familistic behavior may prove fruitful. An examination of poverty as a predictor of lack of involvement in kin and nonkin networks does not imply that cultural norms are irrelevant in the decision to participate. Rather, destitution may prevent women of color from participating in social support networks despite their familistic values.[4] As Wilson (1987) argues, "*Social isolation* does not mean that cultural traits are irrelevant in understanding behavior in highly concentrated poverty areas; rather it highlights the fact that culture is a response to social structural constraints and opportunities" (p. 61).

Therefore, an interesting avenue for further examination would be to examine income differences among each category of racial-ethnic group in four separate analyses. Contrary to the culture of poverty perspective, which argues that extended social support networks represent deviant values among low-income minority families, I suspect that within each racial-ethnic group, as one moves up the socioeconomic ladder, participation in social support networks would increase.

A unique finding of this study is the importance of a respondent's place of birth and the proximity of nuclear family members. Much of the past research on social support networks has not examined issues of migration. This study demonstrates that women born in the United States are more active participants in extended kin and nonkin social support networks than are women born elsewhere. In addition, some of the racial differences initially found between Latinas and non-Hispanic Whites disappeared when place of origin was considered. Women who are more recent immigrants to the United States may have left their kin networks behind. In addition, women who have resided in the United States for only a short time probably have not cultivated strong friendship networks in their new communities. Because of the reciprocal nature of exchange networks, potential members must first gain the trust of the participating members. Consequently, women who were born outside of the United States may be at a disadvantage when it comes to gaining entry into social support networks.

These findings demonstrate the need to examine other elements of migration status, such as length of stay in the United States, generational status, whether respondents live in ethnic enclaves, and back-and-forth migration patterns. Migration status is especially important in examining Puerto Rican involvement in social support networks. Past research has argued that Puerto Ricans are less familistic than other racial-ethnic groups, when in fact their seeming lack of participation may be a consequence of their migration status. Puerto Ricans who frequently move between the island and the mainland may not be perceived by network members as being able to reciprocate help.

Finally, proximity of relatives is an important set of variables that has not been included in past research designs. Perhaps because much of the past research examined small communities or ethnic enclaves, there was an assumption that nuclear family members lived in those communities. However, little research has specifically examined the proximity of family members. This research demonstrates the importance of assessing the availability of relatives. The closer respondents live to their nuclear family members, the more child care help they both give and receive. As family members move farther away, respondents are less likely to give and receive help. The theoretical literature does not address the proximity or availability of family members in discussing participation in social support networks, but clearly this is an important predictor of both giving and receiving child care help. Future research should examine African Americans, Puerto Ricans, and Chicanos separately to determine the proximity of respondents to their nuclear family members.

Past research argues that particular racial-ethnic groups encourage their family members to remain in close proximity. For both Chicano and Puerto Rican families, primary importance is placed on kin relations. Proponents of the cultural perspective have argued that regardless of generational differences in levels of acculturation, strong family relationships are still characteristic of Latinos. They contend that first-, second-, and third-generation Chicanos and Puerto Ricans are equally likely to live close to kin (De Anda, 1984; Keefe et al.,

1979; Rogler & Santana Cooney, 1984). However, this research is inconclusive because it relies on extremely small sample sizes and makes no comparisons between racial-ethnic groups. Therefore, future research should also compare the dynamics of why some groups remain in close proximity to family members and why others move, providing insight into which factors influence mobility away from family members.

The results of this chapter illustrate the importance of examining race, gender, and class in the analysis of informal social support networks. The claim that minority groups are more familistic than non-Hispanic Whites has not been substantiated. It is not enough to argue that one group is more familistic than another; rather, researchers should be identifying the particular elements involved in deciding when and whether to participate in social support networks. In addition, an examination of the class structure and how it affects the lives of minority women is essential. It is evident that there is a powerful connection between race and class; the decision to participate in network behavior is clearly influenced by both.

In preliminary analyses, it was found that women were primarily responsible for child care. Therefore, this chapter focused on the helping behavior of women only. In addition to this gender role differentiation, other interesting differences in gender role behavior were also uncovered. It appears that teenage daughters (unlike teenage sons) are being socialized to help their mothers with child care and other household responsibilities. These findings illustrate that traditional gender norms persist in which women hold primary responsibility for the private sphere. In addition, women with young children and unmarried women seem to be cultivating friendship networks based on shared familial experiences.

Chapter 7 will examine household assistance help given to and received from family and nonfamily support group members for men only.

## Notes

1. The qualitative study (Roschelle, 1997) did reveal familistic values among Puerto Rican women in the sample. Informants expressed the view that extended social support

networks were important to the cultural survival of the community but had become unavailable, particularly among low-income women.

2. During the 1994 California elections, Proposition 187, an anti-immigration initiative intended to deny services to illegal immigrants and their children, passed overwhelmingly. Approximately 30% of California Latinos voted in favor of Proposition 187. The campaign rhetoric, fueled by Governor Pete Wilson, blamed illegal immigrants for the recent recession and lack of employment opportunities in California. This divide-and-conquer strategy has polarized the Latino community and could have disastrous effects on the ability of newer immigrants to cultivate informal social support networks.

3. The results of the qualitative study revealed that cyclical migration patterns do indeed affect the ability of women to participate in kin and nonkin networks. Laura (not her real name) told me,

> Well, people have good intentions but they don't always follow through on them, you know, they tell you one thing and then do another. I had one friend who worked out a child care arrangement with her cousin, and it worked pretty well for about three months, but then the cousin decided to go back to Puerto Rico to find more stable work and my friend was in a real bind. There was no one else available to help her.

Similarly, Elsa said,

> I have always been a hard worker, but it was awful having to move so many times. Every time I started to get close to people—boom—off I went back to Puerto Rico. People just couldn't rely on me because when they needed help I might not be there to give it.

4. Many of the women said that the loss of child care networks was a result of rising rates of unemployment and economic hardship. For example, Elsa told me "I have lived here over 15 years and have a great network of family and friends. However, with the economy the way it is, no one has the time or energy to help each other out anymore." Furthermore, Laura stated, "You know, the economy has gotten so bad around here that people are really struggling. There used to be lots of factory jobs here, but in the last 10 to 15 years, we have seen a lot of them disappear."

# 7

# Helping Out
## *The Role of Men*

This chapter examines whether there are significant racial differences in participation in social support networks among men and whether these differences are a consequence of cultural values, economic factors, or both. As in Chapter 6, help that respondents both give and receive from family and nonfamily will be examined. Based on the initial bivariate results (see Chapter 5), the dependent variable measuring household assistance for men is a newly constructed variable combining home and car repairs with other work around the house.

## Results

### DESCRIPTION OF THE MODELS

Before discussing the results of the logistic regressions, I would like to briefly reiterate the theoretical and practical considerations that determined the order in which the variables were entered into the model. As with the analysis of women, the variable measuring cultural attitudes was dropped from this model. The attitude variable had no significant effect on giving household assistance to or receiving it from any network members, regardless of the order in which it was entered into the equation.[1]

The order in which the variables are entered into the equation is exactly the same as the models set up for women in Chapter 6. Race was entered first so that the effects of control variables could be examined. Respondents' own demographic characteristics/resources were entered second so I could assess how household structure affected the likelihood of participation in the support network. Some household members act as resources enabling respondents to participate more freely, whereas others act as a drain preventing respondents from participating. I was interested in examining the impact of different members of the household on participating in the network.

Socioeconomic resources were entered next because the theoretical literature argues that extended social support networks ameliorate the deleterious effects of poverty. According to this perspective, socioeconomic variables should have more of an effect on participation in social support networks than race or a respondent's own demographic resources.

Finally, the variables representing the respondent's extended family characteristics/resources were entered into the equation. Included in this set of variables are whether the respondent was born in the United States and the proximity of the respondent's nuclear family. Although the theoretical and empirical literature rarely addresses the proximity and availability of familial network members, I was interested in how relationships between variables entered earlier in the model were affected by the introduction of proximity control variables. I especially wanted to see if the structural indicators changed as these control variables were included, indicating that they might not be as central in the likelihood of participation in social support networks as suggested by the literature. The proximity of nuclear family members was not included in the equations examining nonfamily network members because it was irrelevant.

## GIVING HOUSEHOLD ASSISTANCE TO FAMILY AND NONFAMILY

The discussion of the results of the logistic regression equations begins with a presentation of racial differences in giving household assistance to family members (Table 7.1, Model 1) and to nonfamily members (Table 7.2, Model 1). Next, the relationship between a respondent's own demographic resources and giving help with household assistance to family (Table 7.1, Model 2) and to nonfamily (Table 7.2, Model 2) is presented. The relationship between a respondent's own socioeconomic resources and giving household assistance to family (Table 7.1, Model 3) and to nonfamily (Table 7.2, Model 3) will follow. Finally, the relationship between a respondent's extended family characteristics and giving household assistance to family (Table 7.1, Model 4) and to nonfamily (Table 7.2, Model 4) will be presented. The presentation of the multivariate analysis in this manner makes comparisons between giving household assistance to family and giving household assistance to nonfamily possible.

Tables 7.1 and 7.2 present logistic regression coefficients for giving household assistance to network members. Table 7.1 reveals significant racial differences in giving household help to family members. African Americans and Chicanos are less likely to give household assistance to family members than are non-Hispanic Whites. Net of a respondent's own demographic resources (Model 2), Puerto Ricans are also significantly less likely than non-Hispanic Whites to provide household help to family members. Racial differences in giving household help to family members remain for both African Americans and Chicanos, despite the introduction of statistical controls. However, once origin of birth is entered into the equation, Puerto Ricans are no longer less likely than Whites to give household help to family. Past research that attributes lower rates of familism among Puerto Ricans than among other minority groups rarely takes migration status into account and may, in fact, be based on spurious research results. The majority of Puerto Ricans in the United States were born in Puerto Rico (Bean & Tienda, 1987). In addition to nativity, patterns of circular migration characteristic of Puerto Ricans may prevent them from establishing close ties with community members, an essential component of establishing exchange networks.

**TABLE 7.1** Logistic Coefficients for Regression of Giving Household Assistance to Family Members for Men on Selected Independent Variables

| *Independent Variables* | *Model 1* | *Model 2* | *Model 3* | *Model 4* |
|---|---|---|---|---|
| Black | –.33** | –.42** | –.44** | –.57** |
| | (.09) | (.09) | (.10) | (.10) |
| Puerto Rican | –.42 | –.65* | –.66* | –.46 |
| | (.27) | (.28) | (.28) | (.29) |
| Chicano | –.30* | –.54** | –.58** | –.39* |
| | (.13) | (.14) | (.14) | (.15) |
| Children Under 5 | | –.07 | –.07 | –.07 |
| | | (.05) | (.05) | (.06) |
| Children Between 6-12 | | –.17** | –.17** | –.14** |
| | | (.05) | (.05) | (.05) |
| Female Children Between 13-18 | | .02 | .01 | –.01 |
| | | (.07) | (.07) | (.07) |
| Male Children Between 13-18 | | .22** | .21** | .21** |
| | | (.07) | (.07) | (.08) |
| Adult Female 19 and Over | | .25** | .21** | .22** |
| | | (.05) | (.05) | (.06) |
| Adult Male 19 and Over | | .09 | .07 | .15 |
| | | (.05) | (.05) | (.05) |
| Age | | –.03** | –.03** | –.03** |
| | | (.00) | (.00) | (.00) |
| Divorced, Widowed, Separated | | –.39** | –.37** | –.39** |
| | | (.10) | (.10) | (.10) |
| Single | | –.61** | –.56** | –.53** |
| | | (.09) | (.10) | (.11) |
| Education | | | –.02* | .01 |
| | | | (.01) | (.01) |
| Household Income | | | 5.3 | 1.1 |
| | | | (7.8) | (7.9) |
| Missing Income (1 = missing) | | | .12 | .13 |
| | | | (.08) | (.08) |
| Homeownership (1 = yes, 0 = no) | | | .11 | –.01 |
| | | | (.07) | (.08) |
| Work Hours | | | .00 | –.00 |
| | | | (.00) | (.00) |
| Born in the U.S. (1 = yes, 0 = no) | | | | .36** |
| | | | | (.12) |
| Siblings Within 2 Miles | | | | .11** |
| | | | | (.03) |
| Siblings Between 2-25 Miles | | | | .04 |
| | | | | (.02) |

*(continued)*

**TABLE 7.1 Continued**

| *Independent Variables* | *Model 1* | *Model 2* | *Model 3* | *Model 4* |
|---|---|---|---|---|
| Siblings Between 25-300 Miles | | | | .03 |
| | | | | (.02) |
| Siblings More Than 300 Miles | | | | –.02 |
| | | | | (.02) |
| Adult Children Within 2 Miles | | | | .23** |
| | | | | (.06) |
| Adult Children Between 2-25 Miles | | | | .15** |
| | | | | (.04) |
| Adult Children Between 25-300 Miles | | | | –.00 |
| | | | | (.05) |
| Adult Children More Than 300 Miles | | | | –.09 |
| | | | | (.05) |
| Parents Within 2 Miles | | | | .83** |
| | | | | (.11) |
| Parents Between 2-25 Miles | | | | .38** |
| | | | | (.09) |
| Parents Between 25-300 Miles | | | | .02 |
| | | | | (.10) |
| Parents More Than 300 Miles | | | | –.40** |
| | | | | (.10) |
| Constant | –.38** | 1.14** | 1.31** | .22 |
| -2 log-likelihood | 8079.378 | 7712.502 | 7704.208 | 7451.166 |
| Model chi-square | 19.757 | 366.875 | 8.294 | 253.042 |

NOTE: Numbers in parentheses are standard errors.
$^*p \leq .05$; $^{**}p \leq .01$.

Similarly, Table 7.2 illustrates that Puerto Ricans, African Americans, and Chicanos are significantly less likely than non-Hispanic Whites to provide household assistance to nonfamily members. The relationship between race-ethnicity and household assistance increases when a respondent's own demographic resources are included in Step 2. However, this relationship declines and becomes nonsignificant for African American and Chicano respondents once the socioeconomic variables are entered in Model 4. This finding demonstrates the importance of examining class when making statements about minority group participation in extended kin and nonkin networks. The propensity of non-Hispanic White respondents to provide household help to friends is a function of socioeconomic status rather than race-ethnicity per se. These findings indicate that there are racial differences in giving household help to family and nonfamily. It appears that African American respondents and Chicano respondents are less likely than non-Hispanic White respondents to give household help to family despite their extended family living arrangements, economic resources, or the proximity of their nuclear family. Puerto Ricans are also less likely than non-Hispanic Whites to provide household help to family until country of origin is controlled for. This further supports my earlier contention that migration status is an important issue and may be related to the ability to cultivate an extended network. The results of Table 7.1 do not support earlier research indicating that, overall, minority families tend to be more familistic.

The results of Table 7.2 provide some support for the structural argument that participation in social support networks is based on economic need. Once these control variables were entered into the equation, African Americans and Chicanos were no longer less likely than Whites to provide household help to nonfamily members. However, because the relationship did not disappear for Puerto Ricans when socioeconomic controls were introduced, and because more general findings demonstrate that as socioeconomic status increases, so does participation in the network, this result supports the structural perspective only marginally.

Tables 7.1 and 7.2 indicate that men with children between 6 and 12 years of age are less likely to give household assistance to family, and men with children under 5 years of age are less likely to give household assistance to friends, than are men with no young children. The presence of children under 13 years of age does act as a drain on the respondent's resources, preventing him from giving household help to family and nonfamily support group members.

The presence of young children affects men's and women's network participation differently. Young children hinder the ability of men to participate in kin and nonkin networks. Alternatively, the presence of small children facilitates women's participation in friendship networks (see Chapter 6). Although this finding may seem counterintuitive, it actually indicates that women's network participation is inextricably linked to their fundamental role as child care providers.

Not surprisingly, men with teenage sons are significantly more likely to provide household assistance to family members than are men with teenage daughters (Table 7.1). Traditional gender norms encourage

**TABLE 7.2** Logistic Coefficients for Regression of Giving Household Assistance to Nonfamily Members for Men on Selected Independent Variables

| *Independent Variables* | *Model 1* | *Model 2* | *Model 3* | *Model 4* |
|---|---|---|---|---|
| Black | –.18* | –.25** | –.16 | –.16 |
| | (.09) | (.10) | (.10) | (.10) |
| Puerto Rican | –.72* | –.92** | –.82** | –.77* |
| | (.31) | (.31) | (.32) | (.32) |
| Chicano | –.28* | –.39** | –.23* | –.16 |
| | (.14) | (.14) | (.15) | (.15) |
| Children Under 5 | | –.11* | –.11* | .11* |
| | | (.05) | (.06) | (.06) |
| Children Between 6-12 | | –.08 | –.09 | –.09 |
| | | (.05) | (.05) | (.05) |
| Female Children Between 13-18 | | .09 | .06 | .06 |
| | | (.07) | (.07) | (.07) |
| Male Children Between 13-18 | | .07 | .03 | .03 |
| | | (.08) | (.08) | (.08) |
| Adult Female 19 and Over | | –.25** | –.20** | –.20** |
| | | (.06) | (.06) | (.06) |
| Adult Male 19 and Over | | –.18** | –.15** | –.14** |
| | | (.05) | (.05) | (.05) |
| Age | | –.03** | –.03* | –.03** |
| | | (.00) | (.00) | (.00) |
| Divorced, Widowed, Separated | | .15* | .22* | .22* |
| | | (.10) | (.10) | (.10) |
| Single | | .19* | .35** | .34** |
| | | (.09) | (.10) | (.10) |
| Education | | | .03** | .03** |
| | | | (.01) | (.01) |
| Household Income | | | –2.6 | 2.0 |
| | | | (8.2) | (8.3) |
| Missing Income (1 = missing) | | | .07 | –.08 |
| | | | (.08) | (.08) |
| Homeownership (1 = yes, 0 = no) | | | .15* | .14* |
| | | | (.08) | (.08) |
| Work Hours | | | .00** | .00** |
| | | | (.00) | (.00) |
| Born in the U.S. (1 = yes, 0 = no) | | | | .18 |
| | | | | (.11) |
| Constant | –.61** | .83** | –.05 | –.21 |
| -2 log-likelihood | 7754.970 | 7388.777 | 7351.145 | 7348.537 |
| Model chi-square | 13.502 | 366.193 | 37.632 | 37.632 |

NOTE: Numbers in parentheses are standard errors.
$^{*}p \leq .05$; $^{**}p \leq .01$.

men to bond with their sons by building, tinkering, and repairing, which prepares them for their future role in the public sphere. In addition, men include their sons in network participation only when family members are involved. This tendency of men to keep their public and private lives separate is consistent with Zussman's (1987) finding that men relinquish their responsibility for the emotional life of their families in order to participate more fully in the public sphere. Gender norm differences in the types of household work that men and women do are perpetuated by parents, who transmit these norms through socialization of their children.

The impact of adult extended household members on the likelihood of providing household assistance to family members is presented in Table 7.1. The presence of adult women has a positive significant effect on providing household assistance to family members, while the presence of adult males does not have a significant effect on providing household assistance to family members. Once again, it may be argued that gender norms are at work here. When there is an adult woman coresiding in the respondent's household, she may help with child care and housework, allowing men to pursue network membership more freely. However, the presence of adult male extended household members does not act as a resource enabling respondents to pursue outside interests more freely.

Curiously, Table 7.2 reveals the opposite pattern with regard to presence of extended household members and providing household assistance to nonfamily. Respondents with adult females and adult males present are significantly less likely to provide household assistance to nonfamily members than are respondents with no adult extended household members present. This finding seems somewhat odd, because one would expect the presence of extended adult household members to act as a resource enabling respondents to participate in nonkin networks more freely. However, the presence of extended household members may not always be a resource, especially if they are unemployed, have children present, are elderly, or have health problems.

Tables 7.1 and 7.2 reveal that unmarried respondents are significantly less likely to provide household assistance to either family or nonfamily than are married respondents. Respondents who are married have an important resource (their spouse) not available to unmarried respondents and therefore are able to participate in their support network more actively.

The older a respondent is, the less likely he will be to help both family and nonfamily members with household assistance. As individuals age, they may be less inclined to provide help with such physical activities, or friends and family may be less likely to ask for their help.

The introduction of socioeconomic variables in Model 3 of Table 7.1 reveals that there is a significant negative relationship between completed education and giving household help to family. This relationship declines and becomes nonsignificant once the proximity of family members is controlled for. Because the relationship between education and the likelihood of participation is eliminated by the inclusion of proximity measures, it is evident that socioeconomic resources are less central in predicting involvement in social support networks for men than hypothesized by the theoretical literature. More important than education in the decision to participate in familial support networks is the proximity of those network members.

Table 7.2 illustrates that socioeconomic indicators do predict network participation between respondents and nonfamily network members. As a respondent's education increases, the likelihood of his giving household help to nonfamily members increases. In addition, respondents who own homes are significantly more likely to provide their friends with household assistance. Curiously, as a respondent's hours at work increase, so does participation in exchange networks. I would expect that respondents who work a lot of hours would not have as much time to participate in these networks. Perhaps because they spend large amounts of time working, they are able to cultivate salient friendships with people at work, with whom they then spend their free time. It is also possible that men who work extremely long hours need to exchange help more often than do men who work less or not at all. These findings corroborate an earlier trend in the data that respondents with higher socioeconomic status participate more actively in their informal social support networks.

Finally, Model 4 in Table 7.1 demonstrates the importance of extended family characteristics in predicting giving household assistance to relatives. The logistic regression coefficients illustrate that the propensity to give household help decreases the farther away siblings, adult children, and parents live from the respondent. This finding is consistent with earlier results that demonstrate the importance of proximity for predicting child care help for women (see Chapter 6). Clearly, the availability of relatives is an extremely important predictor of respondents' participation in social support networks. As in Chapter 6, I did not examine proximity of relatives when analyzing participation in social support network for nonfamily because it would have been redundant.

Respondents born in the United States are significantly more likely to give household help to family members than are respondents born elsewhere, providing more support for the importance of migration status in the development and cultivation of extended social support networks.

Many of the arguments made in the theoretical literature remain unsubstantiated. Cultural values and economic deprivation do not predict participation in social support networks. In fact, as a respondent's socioeconomic status increases, the likelihood of his providing household assistance to friends also increases. In addition, contrary to much of the past literature, racial-ethnic minority group members are not significantly more likely than Anglos to participate in extended kin and nonkin networks. African Americans and Chicanos give less household help to family than do non-Hispanic Whites, and Puerto Ricans give less household help to friends than do non-Hispanic Whites.

The data illustrate that availability of resources and proximity of family members are more important predictors of participation in social support networks than are cultural values or economic deprivation. Generally, respondents who have resources available to them are more involved in social support network participation. Respondents who are married provide more household assistance to both family and friends than do respondents who are not married. In addition, the presence of female adult extended household members has a positive impact on providing household help to family. Respondents born in the United States also are more likely to participate in support networks with family members. Conversely, the presence of children under 13 years of age acts as a drain on resources and often prevents network participation. Finally, as family members move farther away, respondents' likelihood of participation decreases, demonstrating that most of the household help is being given by family members living relatively close by.

### RECEIVING HOUSEHOLD ASSISTANCE FROM FAMILY AND NONFAMILY

As before, the discussion of the data begins with a presentation of racial differences in receipt of household assistance from family members (Table 7.3, Model 1) and from nonfamily members (Table 7.4, Model 1). Next, the relationship between a respondent's own demographic resources and receipt of help with household assistance from family (Table 7.3, Model 2) and from nonfamily (Table 7.4, Model 2) is presented. The relationship between respondent's own socioeconomic resources and receipt of household assistance help from family (Table 7.3, Model 3) and from nonfamily (Table 7.4, Model 3) will follow. Finally, the relationship between the respondent's extended family characteristics and receipt of household assistance from family (Table 7.3, Model 4) and from nonfamily (Table 7.4, Model 4) will be presented.

Tables 7.3 and 7.4 present the logistic regression coefficients for receipt of household assistance from family and friends. Racial differences in the likelihood of receiving household assistance from family are presented in Table 7.3. The data illustrate that African Americans and Chicanos are significantly less likely than non-Hispanic Whites to receive household help from family. Once extended family characteristics are introduced into the equation, the relationship is no longer significant for Chicanos. Net of all other variables, African American respondents are significantly less likely than White respondents to receive household help from family.

Table 7.4 reveals that only Puerto Ricans are significantly less likely to receive household assistance from friends than are non-Hispanic Whites. This relationship remains despite the introduction of control variables. Even when country of origin was included in the model, the negative significant relationship between receipt of household help from friends and Puerto Ricans remained. Therefore, there seems to be more support for the refutation of past literature arguing that

**TABLE 7.3** Logistic Coefficients for Regression of Receiving Household Assistance From Family Members for Men on Selected Independent Variables

| *Independent Variables* | *Model 1* | *Model 2* | *Model 3* | *Model 4* |
|---|---|---|---|---|
| Black | –.16 | –.27* | –.30** | –.39** |
| | (.10) | (.11) | (.11) | (.11) |
| Puerto Rican | –.16 | –.35 | –.34 | –.20 |
| | (.31) | (.31) | (.32) | (.32) |
| Chicano | –.07 | –.31* | –.36* | –.23 |
| | (.15) | (.15) | (.16) | (.17) |
| Children Under 5 | | .03 | .04 | .05 |
| | | (.06) | (.06) | (.06) |
| Children Between 6-12 | | –.13* | .12* | –.08 |
| | | (.06) | (.06) | (.06) |
| Female Children Between 13-18 | | .11 | .12 | .12 |
| | | (.08) | (.08) | (.08) |
| Male Children Between 13-18 | | –.03 | –.02 | .01 |
| | | (.09) | (.09) | (.09) |
| Adult Female 19 and Over | | .37** | .34** | .31** |
| | | (.05) | (.06) | (.06) |
| Adult Male 19 and Over | | .25** | .24** | .29** |
| | | (.05) | (.05) | (.05) |
| Age | | –.02** | –.02** | –.02** |
| | | (.00) | (.00) | (.00) |
| Divorced, Widowed, Separated | | –.23** | –.15 | –.15 |
| | | (.11) | (.11) | (.12) |
| Single | | –.50** | –.46** | –.45** |
| | | (.11) | (.12) | (.12) |
| Education | | | –.02* | .01 |
| | | | (.01) | (.01) |
| Household Income | | | 1.4* | 1.7* |
| | | | (8.3) | (8.3) |
| Missing Income (1 = missing) | | | .17 | .14 |
| | | | (.09) | (.08) |
| Homeownership (1 = yes, 0 = no) | | | .27** | .19* |
| | | | (.09) | (.09) |
| Work Hours | | | –.01** | –.01** |
| | | | (.00) | (.00) |
| Born in the U.S. (1 = yes, 0 = no) | | | | .11 |
| | | | | (.13) |
| Siblings Within 2 Miles | | | | .08* |
| | | | | (.03) |
| Siblings Between 2-25 Miles | | | | .06* |
| | | | | (.03) |

*(continued)*

**TABLE 7.3 Continued**

| *Independent Variables* | *Model 1* | *Model 2* | *Model 3* | *Model 4* |
|---|---|---|---|---|
| Siblings Between 25-300 Miles | | | | .00 |
| | | | | (.03) |
| Siblings More Than 300 Miles | | | | –.09** |
| | | | | (.03) |
| Adult Children Within 2 Miles | | | | .27** |
| | | | | (.06) |
| Adult Children Between 2-25 Miles | | | | .19** |
| | | | | (.04) |
| Adult Children Between 25-300 Miles | | | | –.04** |
| | | | | (.06) |
| Adult Children More Than 300 Miles | | | | –.06 |
| | | | | (.06) |
| Parents Within 2 Miles | | | | .40** |
| | | | | (.12) |
| Parents Between 2-25 Miles | | | | .11 |
| | | | | (.10) |
| Parents Between 25-300 Miles | | | | –.16 |
| | | | | (.11) |
| Parents More Than 300 Miles | | | | –.28* |
| | | | | (.12) |
| Constant | –1.15** | –.49** | –.05 | –.55 |
| -2 log-likelihood | 6601.657 | 6426.759 | 6399.552 | 6257.724 |
| Model chi-square | 2.714 | 174.898 | 27.207 | 141.828 |

NOTE: Numbers in parentheses are standard errors.
$^{*}p \leq .05$; $^{**}p \leq .01$.

minority families are more involved in extended social support networks than are White families.

Tables 7.3 and 7.4 reveal that presence of children is not an important predictor of receipt of household assistance from either family or friends. In terms of receiving help with home and car repairs and other types of work around the house, the presence of young children does not act as a drain on resources, and the presence of teenage children does not act as a resource. Perhaps the presence of children does not significantly affect receiving help with household work and repairs because this type of work often involves upkeep and repairs and needs to get done regardless of the number of children present in the household.

**TABLE 7.4** Logistic Coefficients for Regression of Receiving Household Assistance From Nonfamily Members for Men on Selected Independent Variables

| *Independent Variables* | *Model 1* | *Model 2* | *Model 3* | *Model 4* |
|---|---|---|---|---|
| Black | −.11 | −.18 | −.08 | −.08 |
| | (.10) | (.11) | (.11) | (.11) |
| Puerto Rican | −.71 | −.88** | −.76* | −.81* |
| | (.38) | (.38) | (.39) | (.39) |
| Chicano | −.13 | −.23 | −.04 | −.10 |
| | (.15) | (.16) | (.16) | (.17) |
| Children Under 5 | | −.02 | −.04 | −.04 |
| | | (.06) | (.06) | (.06) |
| Children Between 6-12 | | −.10 | −.11 | −.11 |
| | | (.06) | (.06) | (.06) |
| Female Children Between 13-18 | | .13 | .12 | .12 |
| | | (.08) | (.08) | (.08) |
| Male Children Between 13-18 | | .06 | .04 | .03 |
| | | (.09) | (.09) | (.09) |
| Adult Female 19 and Over | | −.30** | −.16* | −.16* |
| | | (.07) | (.07) | (.07) |
| Adult Male 19 and Over | | −.10 | −.05 | −.05 |
| | | (.06) | (.06) | (.06) |
| Age | | −.03** | −.02** | −.02** |
| | | (.00) | (.00) | (.00) |
| Divorced, Widowed, Separated | | .27* | .31** | .32** |
| | | (.11) | (.11) | (.11) |
| Single | | .40** | .50** | .50** |
| | | (.10) | (.11) | (.11) |
| Education | | | .06** | .06** |
| | | | (.01) | (.01) |
| Household Income | | | −2.4 | −2.4 |
| | | | (1.2) | (1.2) |
| Missing Income (1 = missing) | | | −.39** | −.39** |
| | | | (.10) | (.09) |
| Homeownership (1 = yes, 0 = no) | | | .09 | .10 |
| | | | (.09) | (.09) |
| Work Hours | | | .00 | .00 |
| | | | (.00) | (.00) |
| Born in the U.S. (1 = yes, 0 = no) | | | | .14 |
| | | | | (.12) |
| Constant | 1.24** | −.20 | −1.1** | −.96 |
| -2 log-likelihood | 6373.709 | 6141.456 | 6096.596 | 6095.290 |
| Model chi-square | 5.729 | 232.253 | 44.860 | 1.306 |

NOTE: Numbers in parentheses are standard errors.
$^{*}p \le .05$; $^{**}p \le .01$.

Table 7.3 illustrates that respondents who coreside with adult men and women are significantly more likely to receive household help from family than are respondents who have no extended household members present. Family network members may recognize the extra household work required for upkeep when there are several adults residing in the respondents' homes and are therefore more likely to provide respondents with household help.

Conversely, Table 7.4 reveals that respondents who live with an adult woman are significantly less likely to receive household help from friends than are respondents with no adult women present. Friends may perceive the presence of a female adult extended household member as a resource (even if she is not) and therefore may be less inclined to help. It would appear from these results that family and nonfamily network members perceive the existence of coresiding adults in the home differently.

Table 7.3 indicates that single men are significantly less likely to receive household assistance from family than are married men. Alternatively, Table 7.4 reveals that divorced, widowed, or separated men and single men are significantly more likely to receive household help from friends than are married men. Apparently, men who are not married are more entrenched in their nonfamily social support network than are married men. Men spend most of their time in the public sphere, especially if they are not married. Perhaps most of their network members include people from their workplace rather than from their family.

The likelihood of receiving household assistance from family and friends decreases the older a respondent gets. As respondents age, so do their friends, making it unlikely that they would help with physical labor, such as building things and making household repairs. Perhaps as men age, they begin to hire people to make the repairs they made in their youth.

The introduction of socioeconomic variables in Model 3 (Tables 7.3 and 7.4) demonstrates that as a respondent's income increases, the log likelihood of his receiving household help from family members increases. In addition, there is also a positive significant relationship between homeownership and receipt of household assistance from family. Table 7.4 reveals that as a respondent's education increases, so does the likelihood of receiving household assistance from nonfamily members. However, as the respondent's number of work hours increases, he is significantly less likely to receive household help from family (Table 7.3).

These findings confirm earlier results that indicate that as respondents' socioeconomic resources increase, so does participation in support networks. Overall, the results demonstrate that, contrary to the structural perspective, respondents do not participate in social support networks out of economic necessity.

Finally, Model 4 in Table 7.3 further illustrates the importance of proximity of family members as a predictor of receiving household assistance from relatives. Logistic regression coefficients reveal that the likelihood of giving household help decreases the farther away siblings, adult children, and parents live from the respondent. In addition, when siblings and parents live more than 300 miles from the respondent, the relationship becomes significantly negative. As with both giving and receiving child care help (Chapter 6) and with giving and receiving household assistance, proximity of relatives continues to be an important predictor of participation in social support networks. This set of variables clearly is an essential component in the analysis of participation in social support networks among family members.

## Summary and Conclusions

The data reveal several interesting findings regarding racial-ethnic differences in the likelihood of receiving household assistance from family and friends. Contrary to past research, African American, Puerto Rican, and Chicano respondents are not more familistic than non-Hispanic White families. In fact, Anglo men were consistently more likely to participate in giving and receiving household assistance than were African American, Puerto Rican, or Chicano men. These results indicate that commonsense generalizations regarding minority group participation in social support networks are not always accurate.

It is particularly important to refrain from making assumptions about familism among racial-ethnic men. Because past research argued that women made up the core of the extended support network (Stack,

1974), there has been little research examining the role of men in these networks (for an exception, see Taylor, 1986). Therefore, it is difficult to say whether or not there has been a reduction in participation in social support networks among racial-ethnic men since the 1970s as a result of increasing social isolation and economic deprivation characteristic of many minority communities. Whereas this argument is plausible in the case of women, it is more difficult to substantiate when discussing the relationship of racial-ethnic men to their support networks. However, in his analysis of urban change in a northeastern community, Elijah Anderson (1990) discovered that young urban Black men no longer relied upon the "old heads" for advice as they had in the past, providing initial support for this hypothesis. Consequently, the only overarching conclusion that can be drawn from this research is that familism is often attributed erroneously to all minority families. Rather than arguing that certain groups are more familistic than others, scholars must begin to examine the different types of network participation engaged in by different groups under different circumstances.

Migration status is an important element in the decision of Puerto Rican men to participate in social support networks. The negative relationship between Puerto Ricans and providing household assistance to family network members disappears once migration status is controlled for. Past research on extended living arrangements and informal social support networks has attributed the lack of involvement among Puerto Ricans to a lack of cultural values favoring familism. Previous scholarship did not examine the role of migration status in developing network ties and therefore may be fallacious. In addition, the focus was primarily on women, so it is especially unfair to assume that Puerto Rican men would not be active participants in their social support networks. Given the circular migration patterns of many Puerto Ricans and the reciprocal nature of helping behavior, it is possible that they have not established strong network ties even among family members. If individuals are constantly moving, they cannot fulfill their obligations to their network. Further research should examine length of stay in the United States, generational status, back-and-forth migration patterns, nativity, and current residence. Ultimately, my research does not support the argument that minority families participate more actively in kin and nonkin social support networks because of cultural values favoring familism or as a mechanism for survival in an economically hostile world.

Another important component in giving and receiving household assistance is a respondent's own demographic resources. The presence of young children in a household may limit men's network participation, whereas the presence of extra adults in the household may enhance men's network participation. The presence of children under 13 years of age does act as a drain on the respondent's resources, preventing him from giving household help to family and nonfamily social support group members. However, having young children in the household does not affect the likelihood of receiving household assistance from network members. This outcome is not surprising: Having young children may limit the amount of time a respondent has to provide household help to others, but it does not affect receipt of help because this type of help is irrelevant to the presence of children. Home and car repairs and other kinds of work around the house do not necessarily involve children and must get done despite their presence in the household.

The relationship between presence of teenage children and giving household help to family and nonfamily uncovers some interesting gender issues. Men with teenage sons provide household assistance to family members. Men involve their sons in repair work, carpentry, building, and working on cars. Daughters are rarely taught these traditionally male activities and are usually socialized into more female-typed activities. The data demonstrate that the socialization process of young men into "men's work" is still pervasive in contemporary American society.

An examination of extended living arrangements provides conflicting accounts of how coresiding with adult men and women facilitates network participation. Some general patterns can be identified that indicate that the decision-making process to participate in kin networks as opposed to nonkin networks is not identical. The presence of adult women has a positive effect on providing household assistance to family members. Therefore, one could argue that when female extended household members are present, they help with child care and housework, allowing men more freedom to provide other family members with household assistance. This research continues to demonstrate the pervasive nature of the gender division of labor in the home and how it affects network participation. Women are primarily responsible for the care and maintenance of the home sphere, which enables men to participate more actively in the public domain.

Conversely, the presence of adult men and women in the home results in the withholding of household assistance from friends. Although one would expect the presence of extended household members to act as a resource providing respondents with more flexibility to involve themselves in outside activities, this is apparently not the case. Perhaps there are different dynamics involved in helping family network members with repairs and household projects as opposed to helping nonfamily network members.

In homes where adult members are present, household help from family is readily available, whereas household help from friends is not forthcoming when adult women are present. This outcome reveals the complexity of extended living arrangements. Friends may perceive the presence of a female adult extended household member as a resource even though household assistance is traditionally male-dominated work. Friends may not know the particularities of why there is an adult woman present and therefore may be less inclined to help. In actuality, some adult extended household members may be a resource to the family, whereas others may be a drain on familial resources. It appears that family and nonfamily network members perceive the existence of coresiding adults in the home differently.

An interesting avenue for further analysis would be to assess the specific circumstances of extended household members, including the number of children they bring with them, whether or not they are working in the paid labor market, their age, and the status of their health. In addition, an examination of network members' attitudes regarding appropriate gender role behavior of extended household members would prove most fascinating.

Marital status is an important predictor of participation in social support networks. Respondents who are divorced, widowed, or separated, or who are single, are less likely to provide household assistance to either family or nonfamily than are married respondents. The presence of a spouse appears to be an important resource for respondents, allowing them to more actively provide help to family and nonfamily network members. Therefore, men who are married can rely on their wives to maintain the household while they provide repair work to family and friends.

Receipt of help and marital status reveal somewhat different findings. Single men do not receive household assistance from their familial network, but they do receive household help from their nonfamily network. These data further demonstrate the propensity of men to involve themselves in social support networks based on their activities in the public domain. Men who are not married appear to be more involved in their nonfamily social support network than do married men. Because men spend a majority of their time in the public sphere, and because unmarried men have fewer family responsibilities, their network is more likely to include people from their workplace rather than from their family.

Socioeconomic status appears to be an important predictor of participation in social support networks, although in the opposite direction hypothesized. The more socioeconomic resources a respondent has, the more likely he is to both give and receive household help. This finding is consistent with a study of the social support networks of parents and their children in the former West Germany, Sweden, Wales, and the United States. Cochran et al. (1990) found that in all four societies, networks were more highly developed among white-collar families than among families in the lower socioeconomic strata. This research, combined with my own, calls into question the notion that participation in support networks is predicated on economic necessity. The data indicate that the more impoverished respondents do not have the time or resources necessary to become as involved in support networks as past literature has suggested.

As with the findings for women (Chapter 6), the data on men do not support the structural perspective that social support networks represent survival strategies to mitigate against the deleterious effects of poverty. On the contrary, this research demonstrates that as a respondent's economic resources increase, so does his network participation. Because economic resources do influence network participation, it would be worthwhile to reconceptualize the structural perspective and examine how economic deprivation limits, rather than enhances, participation in social support networks. Theoretical hypotheses should predict that the abundance of particular socioeconomic resources will facilitate network participation. Future research should examine more directly how and why the accumulation of wealth, education, prestige, and property enhances participation in informal social support networks.

These results suggest that future research should examine income differences among African Americans, Chicanos, and Puerto Ricans separately. Based on the results of this study, it would not be unreasonable to expect that within each racial-ethnic group, as a respondent's socioeconomic status increases, so will his participation in kin and nonkin networks.

Finally, proximity of relatives is an important set of variables not previously examined in the study of informal social support networks. Past research examined ethnic enclaves or small communities and assumed that nuclear family members lived in close proximity to respondents. However, little attention has been paid to this important set of variables. For both men and women (see Chapter 6), the proximity of one's relatives plays a significant role in the propensity to participate in kin networks. The closer a respondent lives to his nuclear family members, the more actively he participates in his network. As nuclear family members move farther away, participation dissipates. Although the theoretical literature does not discuss proximity or availability of family members, it is clearly an important predictor of giving and receiving household help. Future research should examine the proximity of African Americans, Chicanos, and Puerto Ricans to their family members. In addition, why certain people remain in close proximity to their families and others move away should provide even more insight into this important set of variables.

These results demonstrate the importance of examining race, class, and gender in the analysis of informal social support networks. This research has not corroborated the argument that minority families are more familistic than Anglo families. The argument that one particular group is more familistic than another ignores the complex factors involved in deciding whether or not to participate in social support networks. In addition, it is particularly important to understand the interconnection between race and class. Past assumptions about the effects of race and class on the likelihood of participation in social support networks have not been substantiated by this study. Therefore, new hypotheses regarding the impact of social structural constraints on cultural attitudes and the decision to participate in social support networks are long overdue.

This chapter focused on the helping behavior of men because bivariate analyses indicated that men were primarily involved in home and car repairs and other kinds of work around the house. In addition to this traditional gender role behavior, other gender-specific relationships were revealed. It appears that teenage sons are being socialized by their fathers into traditional gender norms. Men bond with their sons by building and repairing things together. Teenage daughters, on the other hand, are not included in this type of household work. In general, there appears to be a distinct separation between men's public lives and their private lives, particularly for unmarried men who are more entrenched in their nonfamily social support networks than their kin networks. Alternatively, because women are primarily responsible for child care and housework, their network participation is defined by their role in the domestic sphere. Chapter 8 will present overall conclusions of the research findings and discuss policy implications.

## Note

1. Because the qualitative study (Roschelle, 1997) focused solely on women, I have no way of ascertaining whether or not Puerto Rican men share familistic values similar to those of Puerto Rican women. Furthermore, I cannot assume that the results of research on women apply equally to men. Therefore, I will not report on the qualitative study in this chapter.

# 8

# No More Kin

The purpose of this research was to explore the nature and extent of informal social support networks and to determine whether there were racial and gender differences in the likelihood of participation in extended support networks. Of particular theoretical interest was whether or not participation in support networks is primarily a response to economic need, cultural norms, or a combination of both. The data indicate that neither cultural norms nor economic resources alone sufficiently account for the propensity of individuals to participate in informal social support networks. Therefore, scholars must integrate social structural and cultural perspectives by examining the effects of race, class, and gender on network participation.

Focusing on race, class, and gender in the investigation of informal social support networks consolidates the structural and cultural perspectives by including components of each in the analysis of network behavior. The inclusion of race in an integrative approach represents the fundamental relationship between cultural norms and race-ethnicity explicated by cultural theorists. An analysis of class reflects the proclivity of structuralists to focus on the connection between socioeconomic resources and network participation. Although gender has not been a central component in past theorizing about minority families, it must be included in an integrative framework because proponents of both the structural and cultural perspectives consistently argue that women are the primary participants in extended social support networks.

There are racial-ethnic differences in the likelihood of participating in social support networks. However, these racial differences are contrary to what was hypothesized by proponents of both the structural and cultural perspectives. The cultural perspective, which says that network participation among minority families represents cultural norms that value extension, was not supported by this research. African Americans, Chicanos, and Puerto Ricans are not more familistic than non-Hispanic White families. In fact, Anglo men and women give to and receive from network members more child care help and household assistance than do African Americans, Chicanos, or Puerto Ricans. These results illustrate that past generalizations about minority group participation in support networks are no longer applicable.

There are several possible explanations for why minority respondents in this study participated less in social support networks than did Anglo respondents. Perhaps proponents of the cultural perspective have overemphasized the extent to which minority groups are characterized by familistic values. Many of the adherents of the cultural perspective accept a priori that minority groups are more familistic than Anglo families (Del Castillo, 1984; Dodson, 1988; McCray, 1980; Nobles, 1974). Social scientists may have been apprehensive about challenging the strength resiliency perspective because it arose as an attempt to refute stereotypes that depicted minority family organization as deviant. In addition, minority scholars were translating their own familial experiences into a new theoretical paradigm. For example, Joyce Ladner (1972) has argued that her familial experiences did not correspond to racist depictions of the Black family as matriarchal and disorganized. To refute the stereotypical portrayal of the Black family, Ladner invoked her own personal experiences, invalidating the inaccurate claims of culture of poverty theorists (Frazier, 1939; Moynihan, 1965; Rainwater, 1966). Similarly, other scholars who embraced the strength resiliency perspective have focused exclusively on the positive aspects of their own lives, perhaps overgeneralizing their personal experiences to members of the larger social structure (e.g., see Hill, 1972; McAdoo, 1980; McCray, 1980).

Research guided by the cultural perspective has also been problematic. Most of the studies were based on extremely small, nonprobability samples and often failed to make comparisons between racial and ethnic groups. The few studies that did make racial-ethnic group comparisons compared Blacks to Whites or Latinos to Whites. Finally, respondents in these studies were overwhelmingly from low-income families, preventing any analysis of the effect of class on network participation. Because researchers focused their attention on one segment of the social stratum, variation in network participation based on class is largely absent. Differences in network participation attributed to cultural norms actually may have been a reflection of socioeconomic status. Therefore, past research from the cultural perspective, which argued that minority families participate more actively in social support networks because of norms valuing familism, may have been exaggerated.

The most plausible explanation for the lack of network participation among women of color has to do with the escalation of poverty in low-income communities over the past decade. During the first 3 years of the Reagan administration alone, there were drastic cutbacks in Medicaid, maternal and child health programs, Aid to Families with Dependent Children (AFDC), food stamps, funds for day care, and child nutrition programs (Sidel, 1986). Reductions in social services continued unabated throughout the 1980s. In addition, a segmented labor market in which women are segregated into the lowest-paying jobs in the occupational structure has contributed to women's economic disenfranchisement (Reskin & Hartmann, 1986) and may restrict their ability to reciprocate help.

The structural argument that network participation is a survival strategy used to alleviate the conditions of poverty also was not corroborated by this research. In fact, the data indicate that as a respondent's socioeconomic status increases, so does the likelihood of his or her participation in social support networks. These results indicate that past research portraying minority communities as familistic as a consequence of economic deprivation may no longer be correct.

Proponents of the structural perspective often cite Carol Stack's (1974) ethnographic study of the Flats as the quintessential example of how economic deprivation motivates minority women to participate in extended social support networks. Although her groundbreaking research provides rich descriptive detail about kin and nonkin networks within that particular community, other scholars have overzealously attributed her findings to all low-income minority families. Her contention that network participation is characteristic of poor Black families is not based on a comparison with Blacks from other socioeconomic groups. In addition, she fails to investigate the experiences of women from different racial-ethnic groups. Although the women in the Flats participated extensively in kin and nonkin networks, it is fallacious for social scientists to compare them to Anglo and middle-class women *not* in Stack's study. Finally, Stack's study was conducted in 1974. During the past 20 years, the American economy has undergone tremendous structural transformations resulting in tears in the web of kinship networks portrayed so eloquently by Carol Stack.

Because proponents of the structural perspective argue that support networks are deliberate attempts to buffer poverty, one would expect that all poor women would benefit from participation. Perhaps an ethnographic study of low-income, urban White women would have revealed the use of similar survival strategies employed by the women in Stack's study. The lack of research on participation in extended social support networks among Anglo women presumably reflects the assumption that minority families are qualitatively different from White families. This expectation is not necessarily pejorative, but it does perpetuate images of minority families that may be inaccurate.

Past research from the structural perspective that does examine network participation among different racial-ethnic groups tends to rely on Black-White comparisons. These studies found that the greater propensity of African American women to participate in kin support networks actually reflects the higher incidence of single parenthood among Black women than among White women (Hofferth, 1984; Hogan et al., 1990; Parish et al., 1991). Other research that did find stronger kin ties among Black families than among White families was based on small, unrepresentative samples and failed to control for socioeconomic differences (e.g., see Martin & Martin, 1985).

The underlying assumptions of the structural perspective must be reexamined. Initially, the structural perspective was an attempt to provide plausible explanations for kinship patterns found among low-income minority families. However, as socioeconomic conditions change within minority communities, the theory may no longer be relevant. A cross-cultural analysis of social support networks in Wales, the former West Germany, Sweden, and the United States revealed that in all four societies, networks are more highly developed among white-collar families than among families in the lower socioeconomic strata (Cochran et al., 1990). Consequently, an alternative explanation for the current lack of participation in network behavior among minority families is required.

Some scholars now argue that because of increasing social isolation and severe economic deprivation, extended social support networks traditionally found in minority communities may not be as prevalent as they were in the past (Anderson, 1990; Collins, 1990; Jewell, 1988; Ladner & Gourdine, 1984; Wilson, 1987). Although the women in the Flats were economically disadvantaged, perhaps they had the minimal resources necessary to participate in their exchange networks. One could argue that current economic conditions have become so severe that they prevent minority families from participating in their social support networks because these families no longer have any resources to share.

In addition to racial-ethnic differences in network participation, there are also gender differences. Not surprisingly, women and men participate in different types of network activities. Women are more involved in child care help, and men are more involved in home and car repairs and other types of household tinkering. In addition, there appears to be a distinct separation between men's public lives and their private lives, particularly among unmarried men. For women, this separation is less distinctive because much of their interaction with friends (as opposed to family) is devoted to the maintenance of the private sphere (child care).

This compartmentalization of women and men into different domains is consistent with Zussman's (1987) argument that men deliberately keep work and family separate. In a study of middle-class professional men, Zussman (1987) found that the separation between work and family was considered a virtue. The connection between work and family was limited to an exchange of resources in which husbands provided economic support and wives provided emotional support. In fact, Zussman (1987) argues that men "abdicate full participation in the emotional life of their families to their wives" (p. 345).

Zussman's (1987) research provides insight into why nonmarried men in my study participate more actively in their friendship networks than in their familial networks. Once men are no longer part of a marital dyad, they lose contact with family members because women were responsible for maintaining those ties. Once these women are no longer in their lives, men retreat into their friendship networks, where emotional labor is minimal.

These pervasive gender norms are perpetuated by parents, who socialize their children accordingly. The results of my analysis indicate that men of all racial-ethnic groups bond with their teenage sons by teaching them the skills necessary for participation in the public domain. Alternatively, women of all racial-ethnic groups were found to involve their daughters in traditionally female household work, preparing them for their role as nurturers. This socialization process ensures that teenage girls and boys are being inculcated into the "proper" gender role behavior associated with adulthood in U.S. society. That these stereotypical gender norms transcend racial-ethnic boundaries illustrates how intractable they really are.

My research demonstrates the importance of using an integrative theoretical perspective to examine family structure. The integrative framework focuses on how the simultaneity of gender, race, and class oppression affects minority family organization. Rather than merely explicating elements of race, gender, or class oppression, the objective of this perspective is to develop new theoretical interpretations based on the links among these systems of oppression.

One of the issues raised by proponents of the integrative perspective was whether there would be different processes that accounted for variations in participation in social support networks among different racial-ethnic groups. The data indicate that minority families are diverse, and it is counterproductive to treat them as monolithic structures. Participation in kin and nonkin networks does not occur equally within racial-ethnic groups. Socioeconomic status, country of birth, household structure, marital status, and proximity of relatives affect different racial-ethnic groups differently. These empirical findings support my earlier contention that any examination of the diverse axes of race, gender, and class oppression must be contextual and historically specific.

Another question of interest to adherents of the integrative perspective was whether gender differences in the likelihood of participation in extended social support networks would occur within racial categories or whether they would occur independently of race. Women were responsible for child care, whereas men were involved in less time-consuming household work. As a result, men participated more actively in the public sphere, whereas women were relegated to the private sphere. Although gender differences transcend racial-ethnic boundaries, it is inappropriate to treat women as a universal category. Women's participation in child care help differed by race-ethnicity and was influenced by their demographic characteristics and socioeconomic resources, which are, in turn, linked to their race-ethnicity.

Finally, advocates of the integrative approach are interested in how social class affects participation in extended social support networks. Socioeconomic status has proven to be a very important determinant of network participation. As respondents move up the socioeconomic ladder, they are more likely to participate in both kin and nonkin networks. In fact, class privilege is a more robust determinant of participation in social support networks than is race-ethnicity.

This research attempts to explain how gender, race, and class interact to predict differences in participation in social support networks. Non-Hispanic White respondents, who are free from racial oppression, benefit more from extended social support networks than do their minority group counterparts. This finding is disturbing because it has been argued that participation in extended kin and nonkin networks may buffer minority families from racial oppression. In addition, class privilege provides individuals who are least in need of help with the most extensive networks. Finally, gender differences in network participation substantiate Stack's (1974) claim that because of their role in child care, women make up the core of the extended social support network. Now that I have presented an overview of the primary research results and their implications, I will discuss the contributions of the work to the field of family studies.

## Contributions of the Research and Implications for Future Research

An important contribution of this research is that it is one of the few studies to examine determinants of social support networks using a nationally representative probability sample. Past research has tended to rely on ethnographic research or studies using bivariate analysis. In addition, many of the past studies have examined homogeneous ethnic enclaves that do not allow for comparisons across groups. Analysis of these data allows me to make comparisons among and between racial-ethnic groups. Furthermore, the survey includes an oversampling of Blacks, Chicanos, and Puerto Ricans, which allows me to make generalizations about minority families living in the United States. There has been a tendency in the past to study Latino families as if they were a monolithic group. This research represents one of the first attempts to capture the diversity of Latino family organization by examining Puerto Rican and Chicano families separately.

A unique component of this research is the inclusion of respondents' country of origin and the proximity of nuclear family members. There has been very little attention paid to the impact of migration status on participation in social support networks. This study demonstrates that respondents born in the United States are more active participants in extended kin and nonkin social support networks than are respondents born elsewhere. In addition, some of the ethnic differences initially found between Latinos and Anglos disappeared when country of origin was considered. For instance, once country of origin was controlled, Chicanas were no longer less likely than Anglo women to receive child care help from friends. This finding indicates that Chicanas born in Mexico participate less often in friendship networks than do Chicanas born in the United States. Paradoxically, Chicanas who migrate to the United States, and are therefore most in need of help, are unable to develop extensive friendship networks. The inability of Chicanas to cultivate friendship networks upon arrival in the United States may be a result of their lack of English language proficiency. Although one would expect Chicanas to develop network ties within the Spanish-speaking community, this would be possible only if they migrated to a neighborhood that welcomed new immigrants and did not see them as a drain on resources (see Chapter 6, Note 2), and where Spanish was frequently spoken. Therefore, future research should examine levels of English language proficiency among Latino immigrants, and the availability of Spanish-speaking network members, to determine how language skills affect the development of informal social support networks.

Migration status is especially important in examining Puerto Rican involvement in social support networks. Past research on extended social support networks has attributed the lack of involvement among Puerto Ricans to a deficiency of cultural values favoring familism. However, Puerto Ricans' lack of involvement may be a result of their circular migration patterns, which prevent them from cultivating reliable networks. Participation in support networks is predicated on exchange reciprocity. Therefore, Puerto Ricans who frequently travel between the United States and Puerto Rico may be perceived as being unable to fulfill their obligation to the network, and are therefore denied membership. It is also possible that Puerto Ricans do develop informal social support networks, but that they dissipate as people move between Puerto Rico and the mainland. This contention was supported by the findings of my ethnographic research.

An examination of the frequency of circular migration would reveal whether or not constant movement is, in fact, a hindrance to cultivating extended support networks. Generational status and length of stay in the United States among Latino immigrants might indicate that the longer individuals reside in the United States, the more extensive their networks become. In addition, a comparison of individuals who live in ethnic enclaves with those who do not would be a fruitful avenue of inquiry. Perhaps Latinos who migrate to ethnic communities can establish network ties regardless of their English language skills or how long they have been in the United States.

Not surprisingly, my research revealed that the closer respondents live to their nuclear family members, the more likely they are to participate in kin networks (for an analysis of the ways in which emotional support is exchanged via technology, see Aldous & Klein, 1991; Litwak & Kulis, 1987; Rossi & Rossi, 1990). Although the theoretical literature does not address the proximity of family members in discussing instrumental support, it should be included in future research designs. It would be fruitful to examine African Americans,

Chicanos, and Puerto Ricans separately to determine the proximity of respondents to their nuclear family members. In addition, the reasons that some people remain in close proximity to family members and others move would provide more information on the particular factors that influence mobility away from family members. Perhaps particular racial-ethnic group members choose to live close to relatives as a means of maintaining network ties. Alternatively, economic factors (e.g., employment opportunities) may force individuals to move away from their nuclear family despite the desire to remain in close proximity. The decision to live in a homogeneous racial-ethnic enclave may reflect familistic attitudes, or it may represent de facto residential segregation patterns.

Another contribution of this research was the analysis of household structure as an independent variable. By examining household structure as a predictor of network participation, I was able to determine whether or not coresiding adults provided respondents with more flexibility to participate in their networks. Sometimes, the presence of adult extended household members facilitated network participation, whereas at other times it hindered network participation. For instance, men who live with adult females were able to provide household assistance to their family members. Presumably, coresiding adult women assist men with household chores, enabling the men to participate more actively in their familial networks. Conversely, female respondents who coreside with adult women receive child care help from family network members. Although this finding seems counterintuitive, it illustrates that there are some instances in which the presence of adult women can be a drain on household resources. Given the research on extended living arrangements and female-headed families (Ellwood & Bane, 1985; Hill, 1990; Scheirer, 1983), it is reasonable to suspect that these coresiding adult women have children of their own, which may overburden an already strained household. More research is needed that investigates the distinctive conditions that characterize particular households. Identifying the presence and number of children, and the occupational status, age, and health of extended household members, might explain why some individuals contribute resources and others deplete them. I expect that coresiding adults with children will require substantial help from their networks. If extended household members are employed full-time, they should be able to contribute financially to the household, although the amount of household help they contribute may be limited. Conversely, if a coresiding adult is unemployed, he or she might provide child care and housework to members of the household. Elderly household members who are ill might require a lot of assistance, whereas elderly members of the household who are healthy could presumably provide the family with resources.

An examination of network members' attitudes regarding appropriate gender role behavior of extended household members would also provide further insight into this complex set of variables. Results of my research indicate that expectations regarding appropriate behavior might be dictated by persistent attitudes associating women with the private sphere and men with the public sphere. Consequently, I anticipate that women would be expected to help with housework and child care, whereas men would be expected to contribute financially.

Because most of the research on social support networks argues that women make up the core of the network (Adams, 1986b; Stack, 1974), very little research has examined the role of men in these networks (see Taylor, 1988). This research represents an initial attempt to ascertain the nature of men's participation in social support networks. Given the fact that most exchange behavior is associated with the daily running of the household, it is probably not unreasonable to assume that women do make up the crux of the network. In contrast, men's network behavior is intermittent, is often associated with leisure activities, and is not confined to the domestic sphere. Traditional gender norms compelling women to take responsibility for housework, child care, and emotional labor necessitates their continuous participation in kin and nonkin networks. However, more research is necessary to determine exact gender differences in the frequency of network participation as well as gender differences in the specific types of help being given and received. Based on the consistent research findings that women are primarily responsible for child care and housework (Coverman & Sheley, 1986; Hartmann, 1981; Hochschild, 1989), I anticipate that an analysis of gender differences in the frequency and types of help given and received will disclose that women do, in fact, comprise the core of kin and nonkin networks.

## Limitations of the Research

To assess the adequacy of a research project, it is necessary to examine its strengths as well as its limitations. The attitudinal questions included on the National Survey of Families and Households (NSFH) estimated respondents' opinions regarding the exchange of financial support and kin coresidence. Unfortunately, these are not ideal cultural indicators of responsibility to the extended kinship network. The financial questions may have a middle-class bias, because individuals who may be willing to share food, clothing, or shelter but are unable to give money might answer attitudinal questions in accordance with their actual financial situation. In addition, there are many more dimensions of familism than providing financial support or allowing a parent, adult child, or other relative to coreside with a respondent. Attitudinal questions about sharing food, furniture, clothing, transportation, and household labor would reflect more accurately the theoretical literature on the reciprocal nature of the extended kin network. These variables represent the traditional resources exchanged in social support networks and might elucidate differences in familistic attitudes among particular racial-ethnic groups.

Proponents of the cultural perspective argue that an important characteristic of minority families is their willingness to care for children other than their own. These proponents contend that differing historical circumstances (as explored in Chapter 1) have resulted in a predisposition among African Americans, Chicanos, and Puerto Ricans to care for the children of family and friends. Therefore, attitudinal questions relating to child care and the informal adoption of nonbiologically related children would provide much insight into familistic values. Comparing attitudes among African Americans, Whites, Chicanos, and Puerto Ricans would reveal whether or not Whites have profoundly different views from those of minority families about raising other people's children.

Because familism connotes elevating the needs of the family above those of the individual, it is vital to assess how emotionally committed respondents are to their families. Therefore, a series of attitudinal questions about the importance of family and nonfamily members in an individual's life and the importance of living in close proximity to those individuals would be ideal. Rather than vague assumptions about minority groups being "familistic," a comparison of values and attitudes among African Americans, Chicanos, non-Hispanic Whites, and Puerto Ricans would reveal how each group feels about particular dimensions of family life.

In addition to the conceptual limitations of the attitudinal measure, the variable representing cultural attitudes was eliminated from the multivariate analyses because it was not significant. Regardless of the sequence in which the attitude variable was entered into the equation, it remained nonsignificant. Perhaps cultural attitudes do not play a significant role in the decision to participate in social support networks. It is also possible that the variable simply was not a good measure of familistic attitudes. As stated above, a good measure of familism must include attitudinal questions about the exchange of household goods and services, willingness to raise other people's children, and emotional commitment to the family. Because the attitudinal variable was not included in the final models, I was unable to test the cultural perspective directly.[1]

Another limitation of this research is the lack of frequency measures associated with giving and receiving particular types of help. The questions ask whether in the past month a respondent has given or received help with baby-sitting or child care and whether in the past month the respondent has given or received help with home and car repairs and other kinds of work around the house. Unfortunately, I cannot assess how often respondents are participating in these behaviors. Consequently, I was unable to determine whether men or women are more active participants in network behavior. The lack of frequency measures also prevented me from directly testing the hypothesis that because of their role in child care, women constitute the core of the extended social support network (Aschbrenner, 1973; Keefe et al., 1979; McAdoo, 1980; Stack, 1974). However, I did find that women of all racial-ethnic groups are overwhelmingly responsible for child care. Child rearing is a continual activity that is often physically and emotionally exhausting. In contrast, home and car repairs and other work that men do around the house are sporadic endeavors and are often associated with leisure activities. The finding that men and women participate in helping behavior associated with traditional gender norms leads me to speculate that women's network behavior is more frequent and intense.

In addition, the lack of frequency measures prevents me from identifying who relies most heavily on a social support network. Perhaps single mothers require more child care help than do married mothers, or divorced men provide more household assistance to their network members because they have fewer familial responsibilities. Unfortunately, I cannot evaluate the frequency of participation in social support networks because the survey questions are dichotomous.

Furthermore, because I was unable to identify the number of people in each response category, I was unable to determine if network size is a significant factor in the likelihood of participating in exchange networks. It seems reasonable to assume that the potential for giving or receiving help would increase as the size of the social support network increased. Future research should examine how network size affects participation in informal social support networks.

Although this research examines giving and receiving help from network members, because of the nature of the data, I cannot specifically examine the reciprocal nature of the extended social support network. There is no way to identify if the individuals giving help to respondents are the same individuals who are also receiving that help. Therefore, no comparisons between who gives help and who receives help can be made.

The NSFH was constructed as a general social survey in which a multiplicity of family-related research could be conducted by a variety of social scientists. Consequently, the data do not include information on particular network members. The inability to test the hypothesis that kin and nonkin networks are characterized by exchange reciprocity is a major drawback of this research. Proponents of both the structural and cultural perspectives fervently argue that support networks are predicated on the exchange of goods and services. Cultural theorists contend that exchange reciprocity is a reflection of familism inherent in minority families, whereas structural theorists argue that it is an economic necessity. In addition, there is no way to determine whether or not individuals who do not fulfill their obligations to the network are subsequently dropped from that network. As a result, I can neither refute nor support the theoretical supposition that informal social support networks are characterized by reciprocal obligations.

Another limitation of this study is based on my choice to exclude affective indicators of social support. Future analyses should include an examination of the affective dimensions of social support. If racial-ethnic families are providing more emotional support to kin and nonkin network members than are Anglo families, that would further substantiate my contention that economic disenfranchisement has eroded traditional networks in minority communities. If, however, non-Hispanic White families provide more emotional support than racial-ethnic families, many of the assertions made throughout this book will have to be reconsidered.

Finally, because this research was concluded prior to the completion of the second wave of the NSFH, I was unable to examine the data longitudinally. The use of longitudinal data to examine participation in social support networks would be extremely illuminating. As fluctuations in the economy occur, researchers could directly test the premise that racial-ethnic families are less likely to participate in informal social support networks because of economic constraints. Using the third wave of data (not yet collected) would be especially illuminating because it would capture the effects of the welfare reform bill passed in 1996 by the 104th Congress. Because welfare benefits are meted out as block grants to the states, it is likely that more families will become more severely impoverished. A corresponding decline in welfare benefits and network participation would support my assertion that as resources become more scarce, network participation disintegrates because of a lack of resources to exchange.

In addition, the use of longitudinal data would allow researchers to determine direct causal links between marital status, number and ages of children, extended household members, migration status, and network participation. As respondents in the sample divorce, marry, remarry, move, have children, restructure their living arrangements, and so on, researchers can compare their participation in social support networks over time.

## Theoretical Implications

Before discussing the theoretical implications of this research, I would like to reiterate briefly the integrative framework that guided it. Proponents of the integrative perspective argue that research on family organization must examine the impact of cultural as well as structural constraints on family life. Minority families must be examined within the context of their racial-ethnic heritage because racial stratification influences family resources and subsequent patterns of family organization (Zinn, 1990). In addition, it is critical to identify how patriarchy is inextricably linked to class and race inequality. The analysis of race, class, and gender as interacting hierarchies of resources and rewards is necessary for an accurate depiction of minority family structure (Andrade, 1982; Collins, 1990; hooks, 1981; Mirande & Enriquez, 1979; Smith, 1983; Zinn, 1990). A primary goal of this perspective is to develop new theoretical interpretations of the links between gender, race, and class oppression.

To ascertain the links between race, class, and gender oppression, both economic determinants and cultural determinants of participation in extended social support networks were examined. Because the variable measuring attitudes toward extension was dropped from the model, it is difficult to evaluate the importance of cultural values in the likelihood of participation in support networks. Perhaps the attitudinal variable was nonsignificant because attitudes do not predict network participation. Alternatively, the attitudinal indicator may have been an inadequate measure of familistic values. It is also possible that individuals who are familistic may be unable to participate in exchange networks because they do not have the necessary resources.

Despite the inability to measure cultural attitudes directly, one can still theorize about the relationship between race-ethnicity and culture. Proponents of the integrative perspective argue that cultural norms and economic exploitation interact to create alternative family forms. African Americans participate in exchange networks because racial oppression has resulted in high rates of poverty. Confronted with this economic exploitation, Black families rely on an Afrocentric worldview that provides alternative definitions of community and family (Sudarkasa, 1981). Similarly, extended social support networks found in Chicano and Puerto Rican communities also represent the use of ancestral values to mitigate against economic conditions (Del Castillo, 1984; Fitzpatrick, 1981). Because the integrative perspective borrows heavily from the structural approach, there is a tendency to equate economic deprivation with participation in support networks.

However, because the main tenet of the integrative approach is that racial-ethnic families adapt to the social structure by invoking cultural forms whenever possible (Zinn, 1990), theorists can restate the perspective to reflect the lack of participation among impoverished families.

The contention that minority group members participate actively in extended social support networks because of cultural norms valuing familism has not been substantiated. The propensity of Anglo respondents to participate in network behavior more often than minority respondents may indicate that racial-ethnic heritage has no effect on contemporary societal norms. However, the historical evidence depicting the importance of extended kinship systems to minority families has been well documented. Many of the African cultural patterns reflected in language, music, art, household structure, and religion were found among African descendants living in Brazil, the West Indies, and the United States (Herskovits, 1938). Approximations of Aztec residential clan organization based on the calpulli system, in which a parcel of land was shared by independent consanguineal nuclear families, has been documented in contemporary Chicano families residing in the American Southwest (Sena-Rivera, 1979). The deep sense of family obligation characteristic of contemporary Puerto Rican families has been traced to Spanish colonial rule (Fitzpatrick, 1981). Therefore, it is erroneous to argue that contemporary minority families are not influenced by their cultural lineage. An alternative explanation is that the interacting systems of race and class oppression prevent minority families from realizing their familistic identities.

It is possible that minority group members are familistic and want to participate actively in exchange networks but are unable to because they lack the necessary resources. Despite their adherence to cultural norms valuing familism, the constraints of a hostile economic system may prevent minority families from participating in exchange networks. Consequently, minority group members are oppressed both culturally and economically: They are unable to live by the values essential to their cultural survival because they are economically disadvantaged. Given the results of my data analysis (and on the results of the qualitative study), which indicate that individuals with more socioeconomic resources participate more actively in their exchange networks, it is not unreasonable to argue that cultural norms are constrained by class oppression. Proponents of the structural perspective vehemently argue that extended kin and nonkin networks are survival strategies used to mitigate against poverty. However, as this research demonstrates, participation in social support networks cannot be attributed to economic deprivation. Socioeconomic indicators have the opposite effect on network participation than hypothesized by the structural perspective. The more education and resources respondents have, the more likely they are to participate in their social support networks. Consequently, a reformulation of the structural perspective is required.

The structural perspective on minority families evolved as an inductive approach in which empirical observations were used to construct social theory. Because the structural perspective was formulated specifically to explain patterns of minority family organization, it is economically and historically grounded. Perhaps changes in the class structure that have occurred since the inception of the structural perspective render it ineffective. However, because socioeconomic resources do play a significant role in the propensity to participate in kin and nonkin networks, they must continue to be included in social theory.

Economic resources are clearly a salient predictor of participation in extended support networks. Therefore, using an economic framework to understand the dynamics of network participation is useful if we reverse the direction of the expected relationships. A reconceptualization of the structural perspective in which economic deprivation is associated with a decline in participation in social support networks would be worthwhile. Perhaps as individuals move down the socioeconomic ladder, they become too overburdened to participate actively in their networks. Participating in exchange networks may have become a luxury afforded exclusively to people with time and money. Although network participation is certainly not necessary for survival among affluent families, it may enhance the quality of their lives. Perhaps past researchers found thriving networks among minority communities because economic exploitation was less severe than it is now. Rates of poverty and female headedness among minority families have risen dramatically since the late 1970s and early 1980s. The interacting systems of race and class oppression may have become so severe that they supersede cultural norms and values.

More recent research has begun to demonstrate that poverty is no longer associated with high rates of participation in extended social support networks (Cochran et al., 1990), corroborating my speculation that minority families are no longer able to realize their familistic identities.

I would now like to discuss how the interlocking nature of class and race oppression contributes to gender inequality. My data indicate that there is an implacable gender division of labor in contemporary households. This division of labor can also be found in the paid labor market. Despite women's entrance into the labor market in record numbers since the 1960s (Reskin & Hartmann, 1986), they remain almost entirely segregated from their male coworkers (Beller, 1984; Bielby & Baron, 1986). This workplace segregation represents the persistence of traditional gender ideology that excludes women from men's domain, even when both men and women work in the public sphere. The same gender ideology (referred to as patriarchy) that facilitates segregation in the marketplace also perpetuates the division of labor in the home. Women remain primarily responsible for housework and child care despite their participation in the labor market (Hochschild, 1989). Because women have primary responsibility for the domestic sphere, men are free to participate more actively in the public sphere, which simultaneously facilitates capitalist production (Hartmann, 1981; Sokoloff, 1980). This dialectical relationship between capitalism and patriarchy ensures that women will continue to remain the guardians of home and hearth.

Gender inequality based on patriarchy is further exacerbated by race and class inequality. Scholars have demonstrated that there are often conflicts between minority family ideology and structural conditions. It has been argued that African American women have conservative attitudes in which the institutions of marriage and motherhood are highly valued (Hill, 1972; Staples, 1989). However, as a result of racial and economic discrimination, Black women are often compelled to have children out of wedlock rather than marry unemployed males who will be a drain on their already meager resources (Wilson, 1987). The lack of child care availability and the high rates of Black female unemployment further limit marriage as a viable opportunity. Despite the presence of familistic attitudes among women of color, the simultaneity of gender, race, and class oppression prevents them from participating in the extended social support networks that traditionally have been found in their communities.

It should now be apparent that neither the cultural nor the structural perspective fully explains the processes involved in network participation. I have attempted to integrate social structural and cultural components by examining how gender, race, and class affect network participation. The results of my analysis demonstrate the importance of including these three components in any analysis of social support networks. It is evident from this research that there is a powerful connection between gender, race, and class, and that the decision to participate in social support networks is influenced by all three.

Clearly, these three classifications are inextricably linked and represent different levels of historical processes of domination and subordination (Amott & Matthaei, 1991). As feminist scholars continue to develop this epistemological framework, we must continue to examine the particular contexts in which these socially constructed categories interact. The explication of how race, gender, and class interact within the culture-structure nexus and constrain network participation is my contribution to this emerging theoretical orientation.

## Policy Implications

The results of this research have important policy implications. Many of the past assumptions about minority family organization have not been substantiated. Contemporary minority families do not participate more frequently than Anglo families in kin and nonkin social support networks.

Proponents of both cultural and structural perspectives argue that exchange behavior is often predicated on child care obligations. Structural theorists argue that minority women share child care responsibilities as a means of survival in an economically hostile environment. Adherents of the cultural perspective argue that because child rearing has high priority in minority families, it is not unusual for a family member who can provide more help to raise the child of a sibling. African American women have had a long history of caring for other people's children, dating back to slavery. It has been argued that this strong support system among Black women (whether a result of cultural norms or economic deprivation) often provides the backbone for both family and community survival (Hill, 1972; McCray, 1980).

The child care component of the social support network was not found to be as prevalent among African American, Chicana, or Puerto Rican women as expected. If the sharing of child care is no longer routine among minority communities, the survival of their families may be greatly threatened. The lack of available child care has led to a crisis among poor women, particularly minority women. Policymakers can no longer assume that poor women can endure infinite hardships because of the strength of their community networks. The Welfare Reform Act passed by the 204th Congress, which eliminates welfare benefits for unmarried mothers under 18 and discontinues AFDC after 2 years, assumes that poor women will simply rely on extended kinfolk for their survival. This legislation will certainly force more women and children into the depths of poverty and may increase the number of homeless families. Therefore, it is critical to the survival of low-income minority families that federal child care programs be implemented immediately.

Educational reform and the implementation of employment policies are also desperately needed. The transformation of the urban economy has created a mismatch between educational attainment and available employment, particularly for Blacks and Latinos living in inner cities. In addition, the movement of the production economy out of the central cities to corresponding suburbs, to Third World countries, and to the South has exacerbated unemployment rates among minority communities. In 1982, the four largest U.S. cities (New York, Chicago, Philadelphia, Detroit), which accounted for more than one fourth of the nation's central-city poor, lost more than one million manufacturing, wholesale, and retail jobs at the same time that their populations were becoming minority dominant. By 1980, Blacks and Latinos accounted for virtually one half of New York City's population, 57% of Chicago's, 67% of Detroit's, and 43% of Philadelphia's. The dramatic increase in unemployment rates (Wilson, 1987) and the persistence of residential segregation (Massey & Denton, 1993) may have contributed directly to the erosion of exchange networks previously found in these communities.

Educational reform that corresponds to the needs of a changing production economy would better prepare individuals to compete in the job market. Imposing regulations and eliminating tax incentives for companies that move to "offshore" locations would eliminate the continual deindustrialization of the American economy. Providing transportation for inner-city residents to get to jobs in corresponding suburbs would enable them to compete for jobs currently unavailable to them. Rather than altering "pathological" subcultural traits among minority families, policymakers must focus their attention on creating economic opportunities for disenfranchised minority families. In addition to improving the general quality of life, instituting economic reform might also facilitate the return of extended social support networks that once flourished among minority communities.

## Conclusion

In an attempt to refute the negative stereotypes perpetuated by culture of poverty theorists, advocates of the strength resiliency perspective focused solely on positive aspects of minority family life. In addition, as a result of the caustic debate that beset the Moynihan report, liberal scholars refused to examine behavior that could be construed as stigmatizing to racial minorities. Consequently, for several years after the debate had subsided, the growing problems of poverty concentration, unemployment, and social dislocation in the inner-city ghetto were virtually ignored by progressive social scientists (Wilson, 1987).

While progressive scholars ignored inner-city social problems, neoconservative scholars began an intensive discussion about the urban underclass. Neoconservative social scientists argued that the growth of the urban underclass was a direct result of failed liberal social policies. Charles Murray (1984) argued that social welfare programs increased rather than reduced poverty. Increasing rates of unemployment, crime, out-of-wedlock births, female-headed families, and welfare dependency were blamed on the social programs that were intended to reduce these problems (Wilson, 1987). Consequently, neoconservative policymakers argued that the solution to the increasing urban underclass was to cut federal programs that created incentives for people to remain on welfare, have more children, and stop looking for work (Murray, 1984). Given the racialized discourse of the 104th Congress, it is clear that policymakers are once again relying upon the stereotypic assumptions of the culture of poverty approach to formulate social policy. Ironically, the same legislators who expect minority families to rely on their extended kinship networks for survival argue that these networks are, in fact, deviant.

My research is one attempt to examine the impact of social dislocation among minority families from a more progressive viewpoint. The examination of gender, race, and class and their impact on social support networks is a first step in reevaluating the dynamics of contemporary minority family life. It is no longer appropriate for progressive scholars to ignore the pervasive problems suffered by low-income minority families in the United States. Looking only at the positive aspects of minority family organization leads to a functionalist argument in which every aspect of family organization is seen as contributing to the maintenance of the family and society. It is the responsibility of social scientists to use a more comprehensive approach in understanding the problems confronting minority families while simultaneously recognizing the dignity and vitality of these cultures. The image of the "happy poor" surviving in the face of unendurable hardships must finally be eliminated.

## Note

1. The results of the ethnographic study of participation in informal social support networks among Puerto Rican women in upstate New York (Roschelle, 1997) did illustrate the presence of familistic norms in that particular community. However, because the study used a nonprobability sample, the findings cannot be generalized to women outside of that community. In addition, because the data collection was confined to a Puerto Rican ethnic enclave, I cannot make comparisons between racial-ethnic women and non-Hispanic White women.

# Appendix

The data presented in the Appendix examine the same four categories of help among family and non-family members discussed in Chapter 5. These data supported the findings in Chapter 5 and helped determine the final logistic regression models.

**TABLE A1.A** Proportions of Giving Household Help by Racial-Ethnic Groups Based on *t* Tests: Means (Standard deviations)

| *Household Help Item* | *Black* | *White* | *Chicano* | *Puerto Rican* |
|---|---|---|---|---|
| Baby-sitting or child care | | | | |
| 1. Family | .27[d] | .26[d] | .27[d] | .17[a,b,c] |
| | (.44) | (.44) | (.45) | (.37) |
| 2. Nonfamily | .16[b,c,d] | .18[a,c,d] | .10[a,b] | .08[a,b] |
| | (.36) | (.38) | (.31) | (.28) |
| Transportation help | | | | |
| 1. Family | .24[b,d] | .29[a,c,d] | .25[a,d] | .12[a,b,c] |
| | (.43) | (.45) | (.43) | (.32) |
| 2. Nonfamily | .27[b,d] | .35[a,c,d] | .26[b] | .19[a,b] |
| | (.45) | (.48) | (.44) | (.39) |
| Repairs to home or car | | | | |
| 1. Family | .14[b,c] | .22[a,c,d] | .21[a,b,d] | .11[b,c] |
| | (.35) | (.41) | (.40) | (.32) |
| 2. Nonfamily | .14[b] | .18[a,d] | .15 | .09[b] |
| | (.34) | (.38) | (.36) | (.29) |
| Other kinds of work around the house | | | | |
| 1. Family | .26 | .30[d] | .30[d] | .21[b,c] |
| | (.44) | (.45) | (.46) | (.41) |
| 2. Nonfamily | .14[b,c,d] | .17[a,c,d] | .09[a,b] | .08[a,b] |
| | (.35) | (.38) | (.29) | (.27) |

a. Significantly different from Black ≤ .05.
b. Significantly different from White ≤ .05.
c. Significantly different from Chicano ≤ .05.
d. Significantly different from Puerto Rican ≤ .05.

**TABLE A1.B** Proportions of Receiving Household Help by Racial-Ethnic Groups Based on $t$ Tests: Means (Standard Deviations)

| *Household Help Item* | *Black* | *White* | *Chicano* | *Puerto Rican* |
|---|---|---|---|---|
| Baby-sitting or child care | | | | |
| 1. Family | .15 | .14[c] | .18[b,d] | .11[c] |
| | (.36) | (.34) | (.38) | (.31) |
| 2. Nonfamily | .08[b] | .10[a] | .09 | .08 |
| | (.27) | (.30) | (.28) | (.28) |
| Transportation help | | | | |
| 1. Family | .22[b] | .18[a] | .21 | .21 |
| | (.42) | (.39) | (.41) | (.41) |
| 2. Nonfamily | .20 | .21 | .19 | .19 |
| | (.40) | (.40) | (.39) | (.40) |
| Repairs to home or car | | | | |
| 1. Family | .12[b,c] | .15[a,c,d] | .18[a,b,d] | .07[b,c] |
| | (.33) | (.35) | (.38) | (.26) |
| 2. Nonfamily | .12 | .13[d] | .13[d] | .07[b,c] |
| | (.33) | (.34) | (.34) | (.26) |
| Other kinds of work around the house | | | | |
| 1. Family | .21 | .20 | .21 | .19 |
| | (.41) | (.40) | (.41) | (.40) |
| 2. Nonfamily | .11[c] | .12[c] | .08[a,b] | .06 |
| | (.31) | (.33) | (.26) | (.24) |

a. Significantly different from Black ≤ .05.
b. Significantly different from White ≤ .05.
c. Significantly different from Chicano ≤ .05.
d. Significantly different from Puerto Rican ≤ .05.

**TABLE A2.A** Proportions of Giving Household Help by Gender Based on $t$ Tests: Means (Standard Deviations)

| *Household Help Item* | *Men* | *Women* | *Difference Between Means* |
|---|---|---|---|
| Baby-sitting or child care | | | |
| 1. Family | .21 | .30 | –.09** |
| | (.41) | (.46) | |
| 2. Nonfamily | .12 | .22 | –.10** |
| | (.32) | (.42) | |
| Transportation help | | | |
| 1. Family | .27 | .28 | –.01 |
| | (.45) | (.45) | |
| 2. Nonfamily | .35 | .32 | .03** |
| | (.48) | (.47) | |
| Repairs to home or car | | | |
| 1. Family | .28 | .14 | .14** |
| | (.45) | (.35) | |
| 2. Nonfamily | .27 | .09 | .18** |
| | (.45) | (.29) | |
| Other kinds of work around the house | | | |
| 1. Family | .29 | .27 | .02** |
| | (.46) | (.45) | |
| 2. Nonfamily | .20 | .13 | .07** |
| | (.40) | (.34) | |

$^{*}p \le .05$; $^{**}p \le .01$.

**TABLE A2.B** Proportions of Receiving Household Help by Gender Based on *t* Tests: Means (Standard Deviations)

| *Household Help Item* | *Men* | *Women* | *Difference Between Means* |
|---|---|---|---|
| Baby-sitting or child care | | | |
| 1. Family | .11 | .17 | –.06** |
| | (.31) | (.37) | |
| 2. Nonfamily | .08 | .11 | –.03** |
| | (.28) | (.31) | |
| Transportation help | | | |
| 1. Family | .16 | .22 | –.06** |
| | (.36) | (.41) | |
| 2. Nonfamily | .20 | .20 | .00 |
| | (.40) | (.40) | |
| Repairs to home or car | | | |
| 1. Family | .14 | .15 | –.01 |
| | (.34) | (.35) | |
| 2. Nonfamily | .15 | .11 | .04** |
| | (.36) | (.31) | |
| Other kinds of work around the house: | | | |
| 1. Family | .18 | .22 | –.04** |
| | (.38) | (.42) | |
| 2. Nonfamily | .14 | .10 | .04** |
| | (.34) | (.30) | |

$^*p \leq .05$; $^{**}p \leq .01$.

**TABLE A3.A** Proportions of Giving Household Help by Race-Ethnicity and Gender Based on *t* Tests: Means (Standard Deviations)

| | *Black* | | |
|---|---|---|---|
| *Household Help Item* | *Men* | *Women* | *Difference Between Means* |
| Baby-sitting or child care | | | |
| 1. Family | .19<br>(.39) | .33<br>(.47) | –.14** |
| 2. Nonfamily | .11<br>(.31) | .20<br>(.40) | –.09** |
| Transportation help | | | |
| 1. Family | .24<br>(.43) | .24<br>(.43) | .00 |
| 2. Nonfamily | .31<br>(.46) | .24<br>(.43) | .07** |
| Repairs to home or car | | | |
| 1. Family | .21<br>(.41) | .09<br>(.29) | .12** |
| 2. Nonfamily | .24<br>(.43) | .06<br>(.23) | .18** |
| Other kinds of work around the house | | | |
| 1. Family | .26<br>(.44) | .26<br>(.44) | .00 |
| 2. Nonfamily | .18<br>(.38) | .11<br>(.32) | .07** |

$^{*}p \le .05$; $^{**}p \le .01$.

**TABLE A3.B** Proportions of Receiving Household Help by Race-Ethnicity and Gender Based on *t* Tests: Means (Standard Deviations)

| | *Black* | | |
|---|---|---|---|
| *Household Help Item* | *Men* | *Women* | *Difference Between Means* |
| Baby-sitting or child care | | | |
| 1. Family | .10 | .19 | –.09** |
| | (.30) | (.40) | |
| 2. Nonfamily | .06 | .10 | –.04** |
| | (.23) | (.30) | |
| Transportation help | | | |
| 1. Family | .17 | .27 | –.10** |
| | (.37) | (.44) | |
| 2. Nonfamily | .21 | .20 | .01 |
| | (.41) | (.40) | |
| Repairs to home or car | | | |
| 1. Family | .11 | .13 | –.02 |
| | (.32) | (.33) | |
| 2. Nonfamily | .15 | .10 | .05** |
| | (.36) | (.30) | |
| Other kinds of work around the house | | | |
| 1. Family | .16 | .25 | –.09** |
| | (.37) | (.43) | |
| 2. Nonfamily | .12 | .10 | .02 |
| | (.32) | (.30) | |

*$p \le .05$; **$p \le .01$.

**TABLE A4.A** Proportions of Giving Household Help by Race-Ethnicity and Gender Based on *t* Tests: Means (Standard Deviations)

| | *White* | | |
|---|---|---|---|
| *Household Help Item* | *Men* | *Women* | *Difference Between Means* |
| Baby-sitting or child care | | | |
| 1. Family | .22 | .30 | –.08** |
| | (.41) | (.46) | |
| 2. Nonfamily | .13 | .23 | –.10** |
| | (.33) | (.42) | |
| Transportation help | | | |
| 1. Family | .28 | .30 | –.02 |
| | (.45) | (.46) | |
| 2. Nonfamily | .36 | .35 | .01 |
| | (.48) | (.48) | |
| Repairs to home or car | | | |
| 1. Family | .30 | .15 | .15** |
| | (.46) | (.35) | |
| 2. Nonfamily | .30 | .10 | .20** |
| | (.45) | (.30) | |
| Other kinds of work around the house | | | |
| 1. Family | .31 | .27 | .04** |
| | (.46) | (.45) | |
| 2. Nonfamily | .21 | .14 | .07** |
| | (.40) | (.34) | |

*$p \leq .05$; **$p \leq .01$.

**TABLE A4.B** Proportions of Receiving Household Help by Race-Ethnicity and Gender Based on *t* Tests: Means (Standard Deviations)

| | *White* | | |
|---|---|---|---|
| *Household Help Item* | *Men* | *Women* | *Difference Between Means* |
| Baby-sitting or child care | | | |
| 1. Family | .11 | .16 | –.05** |
| | (.31) | (.37) | |
| 2. Nonfamily | .09 | .11 | –.02** |
| | (.28) | (.31) | |
| Transportation help | | | |
| 1. Family | .16 | .21 | –.05** |
| | (.36) | (.41) | |
| 2. Nonfamily | .20 | .21 | –.01 |
| | (.40) | (.41) | |
| Repairs to home or car | | | |
| 1. Family | .14 | .15 | –.01 |
| | (.35) | (.36) | |
| 2. Nonfamily | .15 | .11 | .04** |
| | (.36) | (.31) | |
| Other kinds of work around the house | | | |
| 1. Family | .18 | .22 | –.04** |
| | (.38) | (.41) | |
| 2. Nonfamily | .12 | .10 | .02 |
| | (.32) | (.30) | |

*$p \le .05$; **$p \le .01$.

**TABLE A5.A** Proportions of Giving Household Help by Race-Ethnicity and Gender Based on *t* Tests: Means (Standard Deviations)

| | *Chicano* | | |
|---|---|---|---|
| *Household Help Item* | *Men* | *Women* | *Difference Between Means* |
| Baby-sitting or child care | | | |
| 1. Family | .21 | .34 | –.13** |
| | (.40) | (.48) | |
| 2. Nonfamily | .07 | .14 | –.07* |
| | (.26) | (.34) | |
| Transportation help | | | |
| 1. Family | .21 | .30 | –.09* |
| | (.41) | (.46) | |
| 2. Nonfamily | .31 | .20 | .11** |
| | (.47) | (.40) | |
| Repairs to home or car | | | |
| 1. Family | .27 | .14 | .13** |
| | (.44) | (.35) | |
| 2. Nonfamily | .26 | .04 | .22** |
| | (.44) | (.19) | |
| Other kinds of work around the house | | | |
| 1. Family | .27 | .32 | –.05 |
| | (.45) | (.47) | |
| 2. Nonfamily | .08 | .10 | –.02 |
| | (.28) | (.30) | |

*$p \leq .05$; **$p \leq .01$.

**TABLE A5.B** Proportions of Receiving Household Help by Race-Ethnicity and Gender Based on *t* Tests: Means (Standard Deviations)

| *Household Help Item* | *Chicano* *Men* | *Chicano* *Women* | *Difference Between Means* |
|---|---|---|---|
| Baby-sitting or child care | | | |
| 1. Family | .11 | .25 | –.14** |
| | (.31) | (.43) | |
| 2. Nonfamily | .08 | .10 | –.02 |
| | (.26) | (.30) | |
| Transportation help | | | |
| 1. Family | .14 | .27 | –.13** |
| | (.35) | (.45) | |
| 2. Nonfamily | .20 | .18 | .02 |
| | (.40) | (.38) | |
| Repairs to home or car | | | |
| 1. Family | .18 | .18 | .00 |
| | (.38) | (.39) | |
| 2. Nonfamily | .16 | .09 | .07* |
| | (.37) | (.30) | |
| Other kinds of work around the house | | | |
| 1. Family | .17 | .27 | –.10** |
| | (.37) | (.44) | |
| 2. Nonfamily | .09 | .06 | .03 |
| | (.29) | (.23) | |

$^{*}p \leq .05$; $^{**}p \leq .01$.

**TABLE A6.A** Proportions of Giving Household Help by Race-Ethnicity and Gender Based on *t* Tests: Means (Standard Deviations)

| | *Puerto Rican* | | |
|---|---|---|---|
| *Household Help Item* | *Men* | *Women* | *Difference Between Means* |
| Baby-sitting or child care | | | |
| 1. Family | .07 | .24 | .17** |
| | (.26) | (.43) | |
| 2. Nonfamily | .00 | .15 | –.15** |
| | (.00) | (.36) | |
| Transportation help | | | |
| 1. Family | .09 | .14 | –.05 |
| | (.29) | (.35) | |
| 2. Nonfamily | .21 | .17 | .04 |
| | (.41) | (.38) | |
| Repairs to home or car | | | |
| 1. Family | .20 | .05 | .15** |
| | (.40) | (.22) | |
| 2. Nonfamily | .16 | .04 | .12** |
| | (.37) | (.19) | |
| Other kinds of work around the house | | | |
| 1. Family | .21 | .20 | .01 |
| | (.41) | (.41) | |
| 2. Nonfamily | .10 | .06 | .04 |
| | (.31) | (.23) | |

*$p \leq .05$; **$p \leq .01$.

**TABLE A6.B** Proportions of Receiving Household Help by Race-Ethnicity and Gender Based on *t* Tests: Means (Standard Deviations)

| *Household Help Item* | *Puerto Rican* Men | *Puerto Rican* Women | *Difference Between Means* |
|---|---|---|---|
| Baby-sitting or child care | | | |
| 1. Family | .08<br>(.27) | .13<br>(.34) | –.05** |
| 2. Nonfamily | .05<br>(.21) | .11<br>(.32) | –.06 |
| Transportation help | | | |
| 1. Family | .22<br>(.42) | .20<br>(.40) | .02 |
| 2. Nonfamily | .16<br>(.37) | .22<br>(.42) | –.06 |
| Repairs to home or car | | | |
| 1. Family | .07<br>(.26) | .07<br>(.27) | .00 |
| 2. Nonfamily | .09<br>(.29) | .05<br>(.23) | .04 |
| Other kinds of work around the house | | | |
| 1. Family | .16<br>(.37) | .22<br>(.41) | –.06 |
| 2. Nonfamily | .07<br>(.25) | .06<br>(.23) | .01 |

$^{*}p \leq .05$; $^{**}p \leq .01$.

# References

Acock, A. C., & Demo, D. H. (1994). *Family diversity and well being.* Thousand Oaks, CA: Sage.

Adams, B. (1970). Isolation, function and beyond: American kinship in the 1960s. *Journal of Marriage and the Family, 32,* 575-597.

Adams, B. N. (1968a). Kinship systems and adaptation to modernization. *Studies in Comparative International Development, 4*(3), 47-60.

Adams, B. N. (1968b). *Kinship in an urban setting.* Chicago: Markham.

Adams, B. N. (1995). *The family: A sociological interpretation* (5th ed.). Philadelphia: Harcourt Brace.

Aldous, J., & Klein, D. M. (1991). Sentiment and services: Models of intergenerational relationships in mid-life. *Journal of Marriage and the Family, 53,* 595-608.

Allen, W. (1978). The search for applicable theories of Black family life. *Journal of Marriage and the Family, 40,* 117-129.

Allen, W. (1979). Class culture and family organization: The effects of class and race on family structure in urban America. *Journal of Comparative Family Studies, 10,* 301-313.

Allen, W. (1995). African American family life in societal context: Crisis and hope. *Sociological Forum, 10,* 569-592.

Almaguer, T. (1994). *Racial fault lines: The historical origins of White supremacy in California.* Berkeley: University of California Press.

Alvirez, D., & Bean, F. D. (1976). The Mexican American family. In C. H. Mindel & R. W. Haberstein (Eds.), *Ethnic families in America* (pp. 271-292). New York: Elsevier.

Amato, P. R. (1993). Urban-rural differences in helping friends and family members. *Social Psychology Quarterly, 56,* 249-262.

Amott, T. L., & Matthaei, J. A. (1991). *Race gender & work: A multicultural economic history of women in the United States.* Boston: South End Press.

Andersen, M. L. (1988). Moving our minds: Studying women of color and reconstructing sociology. *Teaching Sociology, 16,* 123-132.

Andersen, M. L., & Collins, P. H. (Eds.). (1992). *Race, class, and gender: An anthology.* Belmont, CA: Wadsworth.

Anderson, E. (1990). *Streetwise: Race, class, and change in an urban community.* Chicago: University of Chicago Press.

Anderson, K. L., & Allen, W. (1984). Correlates of extended household structure. *Phylon, 45,* 144-157.

Andrade, S. J. (1982). Family roles of Hispanic women: Stereotypes, empirical findings, and implications for research. In R. E. Zambrana (Ed.), *Work, family and health: Latina women in transition* (pp. 95-106). New York: Hispanic Research Center, Fordham University.

Angel, R., & Tienda, M. (1982). Determinants of extended household structure: Cultural pattern or economic need? *American Journal of Sociology, 87,* 1360-1383.

Aschbrenner, J. (1973). Extended families among Black Americans. *Journal of Comparative Family Studies, 4,* 257-268.

Aschbrenner, J. (1978). Continuities and variations in Black family structure. In D. B. Shimkin, E. M. Shimkin, & D. A. Frate (Eds.), *The extended family in Black societies* (pp. 181-200). The Hague: Mouton.

Bane, M. J., & Ellwood, D. T. (1984). *Single mothers and their living arrangements.* (Working Paper DHHS-100-82-0038). Washington, DC: Government Printing Office.

Beale, F. (1970). Double jeopardy: To be Black and female. In T. Cade (Ed.), *The Black woman* (pp. 90-110). New York: Signet.

Bean, F. D., & Tienda, M. (1987). *The Hispanic population in the United States.* New York: Russell Sage.

Beller, A. (1984). Trends in occupational segregation by sex and race. In B. F. Reskin (Ed.), *Sex segregation in the workplace: Trends, explanations, remedies* (pp. 338-346). Washington, DC: National Academy Press.

Bermudez, M. E. (1955). *La vida familiar del Mexicano.* Mexico City, Mexico: Robredo.

Bernard, J. (1966). *Marriage and family among Negros.* Englewood Cliffs, NJ: Prentice-Hall.

Bielby, W., & Baron, J. (1986). Men and women at work: Sex segregation and statistical discrimination. *American Journal of Sociology, 91,* 759-799.

Billingsley, A. (1968). *Black families in White America.* Englewood Cliffs, NJ: Prentice-Hall.

Billingsley, A. (1992). *Climbing Jacob's ladder: The enduring legacy of African American families.* New York: Simon & Schuster.

Blassingame, J. W. (1972). *The slave community.* New York: Oxford University Press.

Bonilla Garcia, L. (1959). *La mujer a traves de los siglos.* Madrid: Auguilar.

Bordo, S. (1990). Feminism, postmodernism, and gender skepticism. In L. J. Nicholson (Ed.), *Feminism/postmodernism* (pp. 133-156). New York: Routledge.

Bordo, S. (1993). *Unbearable weight: Feminism, western culture, and the body.* Berkeley: University of California Press.

Cantor, M. H. (1979). The informal support system of New York's inner city elderly: Is ethnicity a factor? In D. E. Gelfand & A. J. Kutzik (Eds.), *Ethnicity and aging: Theory, research and policy* (pp. 153-174). New York: Springer.

Carroll, J. C. (1980). A cultural consistency theory of family violence in Mexican-American and Jewish ethnic groups. In M. A. Straus & G. T. Hotaling (Eds.), *The social causes of husband-wife violence* (pp. 68-85). Minneapolis: University of Minnesota Press.

Cherlin, A. J. (1996). *Public and private families.* New York: McGraw-Hill.

Chow, E. N-L., Wilkinson, D., & Zinn, M. B. (1996). *Common bonds, different voices: Race, class, and gender.* Thousand Oaks, CA: Sage.

Cochran, M., Larner, M., Riley, D., Gunnarson, L., & Henerson, C. R. (1990). *Extending families: The social networks of parents and their children.* Cambridge, UK: Cambridge University Press.

Collins, P. H. (1986). Learning from the outsider within: The sociological significance of Black feminist thought. *Social Problems, 33,* S14-S32.

Collins, P. H. (1990). *Black feminist thought: Knowledge, consciousness, and the politics of empowerment.* Boston: Unwin Hyman.

Comas-Diaz, L. (1987). Feminist therapy with mainland Puerto Rican women. *Psychology of Women Quarterly, 11,* 461-474.

Coontz, S. (1992). *The way we never were: American families and the nostalgia trap.* New York: Basic Books.

Cordasco, F. (1967). The Puerto Rican family and the anthropologist: Oscar Lewis, la vida, and the culture of poverty. *Urban Education, 3,* 32-38.

Coverman, S., & Sheley, J. F. (1986). Change in men's housework and child-care time, 1965-1975. *Journal of Marriage and the Family, 48,* 413-422.

Davis, A. (1981). *Women, race, and class.* New York: Random House.

Davis, J. F. (1991). *Who is Black? One nation's definition.* Pittsburgh: University of Pennsylvania Press.

De Anda, D. (1984). Informal support networks of Hispanic mothers: A comparison across age groups. *Journal of Social Service Review,* 7(3), 89-105.

Del Castillo, R. G. (1984). *La familia: Chicano families in the urban Southwest, 1848-the present.* South Bend, IN: Notre Dame University Press.

Diaz-Guerrero, R. (1975). *Psychology of the Mexican: Culture and personality.* Austin: University of Texas Press.

Dill, B. T. (1983). Race, class and gender: Prospects for an all inclusive sisterhood. *Feminist Studies, 9,* 131-150.

Dodson, J. (1988). Conceptualizations of Black families. In H. P. McAdoo (Ed.), *Black families* (pp. 77-90). Newbury Park, CA: Sage.

Dubey, S. N. (1971). Powerlessness and orientation toward family and children: A study in deviance. *Indian Journal of Social Work, 32,* 35-43.

Eggebeen, D. J. (1992). Family structure and intergenerational exchanges. *Research on Aging, 14,* 427-447.

Eggebeen, D. J., & Hogan, D. P. (1990). *Giving between the generations in American families.* Toronto: Pennsylvania State University, Population Issues Research Center.

Eitzen, D. S., & Zinn, M. B. (1992). Structural transformation and systems of inequality. In M. Andersen & P. H. Collins (Eds.), *Race, class, and gender* (pp. 178-182). Belmont, CA: Wadsworth.

Elkins, S. W. (1959). *Slavery.* Chicago: University of Chicago Press.

Ellwood, D. T., & Bane, M. J. (1985). *The impact of AFDC on family structure and living arrangements.* Report prepared for Harvard University.

Ezekiel, R. S. (1995). *The racist mind: Portraits of American neo-Nazis and Klansman.* New York: Viking Penguin.

Facio, E. (1993). Gender and the lifecourse: A case study of Chicana elderly. In A. de la Torre & B. M. Pesquera (Eds.), *Building with our hands: New directions in Chicana studies* (pp. 217-231). Los Angeles: University of California Press.

Fernandez-Mendez, E. (1972). *Art and mythology of the Taino Indians of the greater West Indies.* San Juan, PR: Ediciones El Cemi.

Fitzpatrick, J. P. (1981). The Puerto Rican family. In C. H. Mindel & R. W. Haberstein (Eds.), *Ethnic families in America: Patterns and variations* (pp. 189-214). New York: Elsevier.

Fox, M. F., & Hess-Biber, S. (1984). *Women at work.* Palo Alto, CA: Mayfield.

Fraser, N., & Nicholson, L. J. (1990). Social criticism without philosophy: An encounter between feminism and postmodernism. In L. J. Nicholson (Ed.), *Feminism/postmodernism* (pp. 19-38). New York: Routledge.

Frazier, E. F. (1932). *The Negro family in Chicago.* Chicago: University of Chicago Press.

Frazier, E. F. (1939). *The Negro family in the United States.* Chicago: University of Chicago Press.

Frazier, E. F. (1949). The Negro family in America. In R. N. Anshen (Ed.), *The family: Its function and destiny* (pp. 142-158). New York: Harper & Row.

Glenn, E. N. (1985). Racial ethnic women's labor: The intersection of race, gender and class oppression. *Review of Radical Political Economics, 17*(3), 86-108.

Glenn, E. N. (1987). Gender and the family. In M. M. Ferree & B. B. Hess (Eds.), *Analyzing gender: A handbook of social science research* (pp. 348-375). Newbury Park, CA: Sage.

Goode, W. J. (1963). *World revolution and family patterns.* New York: Free Press.

Gutman, H. G. (1973). Persistent myths about the Afro-American family. In M. Gordon (Ed.), *The American family in social-historical perspective* (pp. 467-489). New York: St. Martin's.

Gutman, H. G. (1976). *The Black family in slavery and freedom: 1750-1925.* New York: Vintage.

Hareven, T. K. (1978). The dynamics of kin in an industrial community. In J. Demos & S. S. Boocock (Eds.), *Turning points: Historical and sociological essays* (pp. 151-182). Chicago: University of Chicago Press.

Harris, M. (1971). *Culture, man, and nature.* New York: Thomas Y. Crowell.

Hartmann, H. (1981). The family as the locus of gender, class, and political struggle: The case of housework. *Signs, 6,* 366-394.

Hatch, L. R. (1991). Informal support patterns of older African-American and White women. *Research on Aging, 13,* 144-170.

Hawkes, G. R., & Taylor, M. (1975). Power structure in Mexican and Mexican-American farm labor families. *Journal of Marriage and the Family, 37,* 807-811.

Hayden, R. G. (1966). Spanish-Americans of the Southwest: Lifestyle patterns and their implications. *Welfare in Review, 4,* 14-25.

Hays, W. C., & Mindel, C. H. (1973). Extended kinship relations in Black and White families. *Journal of Marriage and the Family, 35,* 51-57.

Heller, C. (1966). *Mexican American youth: Forgotten youth at the crossroads.* New York: Random House.

Herskovits, M. J. (1938). *Dahomey.* New York: J. J. August.

Herskovits, M. J. (1941). *The myth of the Negro past.* Boston: Beacon Press.

Herskovits, M. J. (1966). *The new world Negro.* Bloomington: University of Indiana Press.

Hill, M. S. (1990, May). *Shared housing as a form of economic support for young, unmarried mothers.* Paper presented at the Population Association of America Meetings.

Hill, R. (1972). *The strengths of Black families.* New York: National Urban League.

Hochschild, A. (1989). *The second shift: Working parents and the revolution at home.* New York: Viking Penguin.

Hofferth, S. (1984). Kin networks, race, and family structure. *Journal of Marriage and the Family, 46,* 791-806.

Hogan, D. P., Eggebeen, D. J., & Clogg, C. C. (1993). The structure of intergenerational exchanges in American families. *American Journal of Sociology, 6,* 1428-1458.

Hogan, D. P., Hao, L-X., & Parish, W. L. (1990). Race, kin networks, and assistance to mother-headed families. *Social Forces, 68,* 797-812.

hooks, b. (1981). *Ain't I a woman: Black women and feminism.* Boston: South End Press.

Hoppe, S. K., & Heller, P. L. (1975). Alienation, familism, and the utilization of health services by Mexican-Americans. *Journal of Health and Social Behavior, 16,* 304-314.

Hoyert, D. L. (1991). Financial and household exchanges between generations. *Research on Aging, 13,* 205-225.

Jaffe, A. J., Cullen, R. M., & Boswell, T. D. (1980). *The changing demography of Spanish Americans.* New York: Academic Press.

Jewell, K. S. (1988). *Survival of the Black family: The institutional impact of U.S. social policy.* New York: Praeger.

Kasarda, J. D. (1983). Caught in a web of change. *Society, 21,* 41-47.

Kasarda, J. D. (1985). Urban change and minority opportunities. In P. E. Peterson (Ed.), *The new urban reality* (pp. 33-67). Washington, DC: The Brookings Institution.

Keefe, S. E., Padilla, A. M., & Carlos, M. L. (1979). The Mexican-American extended family as an emotional support system. *Human Organization, 38,* 144-152.

Ladner, J. (1972). *Tomorrow's tomorrow: The Black woman.* Garden City, NY: Doubleday.

Ladner, J., & Gourdine, R. M. (1984). Intergenerational teenage motherhood: Some preliminary findings. *Sage: A Scholarly Journal on Black Women, 1*(2), 22-24.

Landale, N. S., & Tolnay, S. E. (1991). Group differences in economic marriage opportunity and the timing of marriage: Blacks and Whites in the rural South, 1910. *American Sociological Review, 56,* 33-45.

Laslett, P. (1977, Summer). Characteristics of the Western family considered over time. *Journal of Family History, 2,* 89-115.

Lee, G. R. (1980). Kinship in the seventies: A decade review of research and theory. *Journal of Marriage and the Family, 42,* 923-934.

Lewis, D. (1977). A response to inequality: Black women, racism, and sexism. *Signs, 3,* 339-361.

Lewis, O. (1959). *Five families: Mexican case studies in the culture of poverty.* New York: Basic Books.

Lewis, O. (1966). *La vida: A Puerto Rican family in the culture of poverty—San Juan, New York.* New York: Random House.

Lieberson, S. (1980). *A piece of the pie: Black and White immigrants since 1880.* Berkeley: University of California Press.

Liebow, E. (1967). *Tally's corner: A study of Negro streetcorner men.* Boston: Little, Brown.

Litwak, E. (1960a). Occupational mobility and extended family cohesion. *American Sociological Review, 25,* 9-21.

Litwak, E. (1960b). Geographic mobility and extended family cohesion. *American Sociological Review, 25,* 385-394.

Litwak, E., & Kulis, S. (1987). Technology, proximity, and measures of kin support. *Journal of Marriage and the Family, 49*, 649-661.

Logan, J. R., & Molotch, H. L. (1987). *Urban fortunes: The political economy of place.* Berkeley: University of California Press.

Logan, J. R., & Spitze, G. (1996). *Family ties: Enduring relations between parents and their grown children.* Philadelphia: Temple University Press.

Madigan, T. J., & Hogan, D. P. (1990). *Kin access and residential mobility among young mothers.* Pennsylvania: Population Issues Research Center, Pennsylvania State University, University Park, PA.

Madsen, W. (1964). *The Mexican-Americans of South Texas.* New York: Holt, Rinehart & Winston.

Marks, N. F., & McLanahan, S. S. (1993). Gender, family structure, and social support among parents. *Journal of Marriage and the Family, 55*, 481-493.

Martin, E. P., & Martin, J. M. (1978). *The Black extended family.* Chicago: University of Chicago Press.

Massey, D. S., & Denton, N. A. (1993). *American apartheid: Segregation and the making of the urban underclass.* Cambridge, MA: Harvard University Press.

Mathis, A. (1978). Contrasting approaches to the study of Black families. *Journal of Marriage and the Family, 40*, 667-676.

McAdoo, H. (1978). Factors related to stability in upwardly mobile Black families. *Journal of Marriage and the Family, 40*, 761-778.

McAdoo, H. P. (1980). Black mothers and the extended family support network. In L. Rodgers-Rose (Ed.), *The Black woman* (pp. 125-144). Beverly Hills, CA: Sage.

McCray, C. A. (1980). The Black woman and family roles. In L. Rodgers-Rose (Ed.), *The Black woman* (pp. 67-87). Beverly Hills, CA: Sage.

Mirande, A. (1977). The Chicano family: A reanalysis of conflicting views. *Journal of Marriage and the Family, 39*, 747-756.

Mirande, A. (1985). *The Chicano experience: An alternative perspective.* South Bend, IN: University of Notre Dame Press.

Mirande, A., & Enriquez, E. (1979). *La Chicana: The Mexican American woman.* Chicago: University of Chicago Press.

Montiel, M. (1970). The social science myth of the Mexican American family. *El Grito: A Journal of Mexican American Thought, 3*(4), 56-63.

Moore, J. (1989). Is there a Hispanic underclass? *Social Science Quarterly, 70*, 265-283.

Moore, J., & Pinderhughes, R. (1993). Introduction. In J. Moore & R. Pinderhughes (Eds.), *In the barrios: Latinos and the underclass debate* (pp. xi-xxxviii). New York: Russell Sage.

Moynihan, D. P. (1965). *The Negro family: A case for national action.* Washington, DC: Government Printing Office.

Murillo, N. (1971). The Mexican American family. In N. N. Wagner & M. J. Haug (Eds.), *Chicanos: Social and psychological perspectives* (pp. 97-108). St. Louis, MO: C. V. Mosby.

Murray, C. (1984). *Losing ground: American social policy, 1950-1980.* New York: Basic Books.

Mutran, E. (1985). Intergenerational family support among Blacks and Whites: Response to culture or to socioeconomic differences. *Journal of Gerontology, 40*, 382-389.

Nobles, W. W. (1974). Africanity: Its role in Black families. *The Black Scholar, 5*(9), 10-17.

Nobles, W. W. (1978). Toward an empirical and theoretical framework for defining Black families. *Journal of Marriage and the Family, 40,* 679-690.

Ortiz, V. (1991). Latinos and industrial change in New York and Los Angeles. In E. Melendez, C. Rodriguez, & J. B. Figueroa (Eds.), *Hispanics in the labor force: Issues and policies* (pp. 119-132). New York: Plenum.

Padilla, F. (1987). *Puerto Rican Chicago.* South Bend, IN: University of Notre Dame Press.

Parish, W. L., Hao, L-X., & Hogan, D. P. (1991). Family support networks and the welfare and work experiences of young American mothers. *Journal of Marriage and the Family, 53,* 203-215.

Parsons, T. (1943). The kinship system of the contemporary United States. *American Anthropologist, 45,* 22-38.

Penalosa, F. (1968). Mexican American family roles. *Journal of Marriage and the Family, 30,* 680-689.

Rainwater, L. (1965). Crucible of identity: The Negro lower-class family. In T. Parsons & K. B. Clark (Eds.), *The Negro American* (pp. 160-204). Boston: Beacon Press.

Rainwater, L. (1966). Crucible of identity: The Negro lower-class family. *Daedalus, 95,* 172-216.

Rainwater, L. (1970). *Behind ghetto walls.* Chicago: Aldine.

Raley, R. K. (1995). Black White differences in kin contact and exchange among never married adults. *Journal of Family Issues, 6,* 77-103.

Reskin, B. F., & Hartmann, H. (1986). *Women's work, men's work: Sex segregation on the job.* Washington, DC: National Academy Press.

Rodman, H. (1971). *Lower class families.* New York: Oxford University Press.

Rogler, L. H., & Santana Cooney, R. (1984). *Puerto Rican families in New York City: Intergenerational processes.* Maplewood, NJ: Maplefront Press.

Romano, O. (1968). The anthropology and sociology of Mexican Americans: The distortion of Mexican American history. *El Grito: A Journal of Mexican American Thought, 2,* 13-26.

Roschelle, A. R. (1997). Declining networks of care: Ethnicity, migration, and poverty in a Puerto Rican community. *Race, Gender, and Class in the World Cultures,* 4(2), 1-19.

Rossi, A. S., & Rossi, P. (1990). *Of human bonding: Parent-child relations across the life course.* New York: Aldine de Gruyter.

Rothenberg, P. (1995). *Race, class, and gender in the United States: An integrated study.* New York: St. Martin's.

Rubel, A. J. (1966). *Across the tracks: Mexican Americans in a Texas city.* Austin: University of Texas Press.

Rudoff, A. (1971). The incarcerated Mexican-American delinquent. *Journal of Criminal Law, Criminology, and Police Science, 62,* 224-238.

Samora, J. (1971). *Los mojados: The wetback story.* South Bend, IN: University of Notre Dame Press.

Santana Cooney, R., & Colon, A. (1980). Work and family: The recent struggle of Puerto Rican females. In C. Rodriguez, V. S. Korrol, & J. O. Alers (Eds.), *The Puerto Rican struggle: Essays on survival in the U.S.* (pp. 58-73). Maplewood, NJ: Waterfront Press.

Santana Cooney, R., & Min, K. (1981). Demographic characteristics affecting living arrangements among young currently unmarried Puerto Rican, non-Spanish Black, and non-Spanish White mothers. *Ethnicity, 8,* 107-120.

Scanzoni, J. (1971). *The Black family in modern society.* Boston: Allyn and Bacon.

Scheirer, M. A. (1983). Household structure among welfare families: Correlates and consequences. *Journal of Marriage and the Family, 45,* 761-771.

Sena-Rivera, J. (1979). Extended kinship in the United States: Competing models and the case of la familia Chicana. *Journal of Marriage and the Family, 41,* 121-129.

Sidel, R. (1986). *Women and children last: The plight of poor women in affluent America.* New York: Penguin.

Simms, M., & Malveaux, J. (1986). *Slipping through the cracks: The status of Black women.* New Brunswick, NJ: Transaction Books.

Smith, B. (1983). Introduction. In B. Smith (Ed.), *Home girls: A Black feminist anthology* (pp. xix-xxvi). New York: Kitchen Table Press.

Smith, S. A., & Tienda, M. (1988). The doubly disadvantaged: Women of color in the U.S. labor force. In A. H. Stromberg & S. Harkess (Eds.), *Women working* (pp. 61-80). Palo Alto, CA: Mayfield.

Sokolof, N. J. (1980). *Between money and love: The dialectics of women's home and market labor.* New York: Praeger.

Spitze, G., & Ward, R. (1995). Household labor in intergenerational households. *Journal of Marriage and the Family, 57,* 355-361.

Stack, C. (1974). *All our kin: Strategies for survival in a Black community.* New York: Harper & Row.

Staples, R. (1973). *The Black woman in America.* Chicago: Nelson-Hall.

Staples, R. (1981). The myth of Black matriarchy. In F. Steady (Ed.), *The Black woman cross culturally* (pp. 335-348). Cambridge, MA: Schenkman.

Staples, R. (1988). The Black American family. In C. H. Mindel, R. Habenstein, & R. Wrigth, Jr. (Eds.), *Ethnic families in America: Patterns and variations* (pp. 303-324). Englewood Cliffs, NJ: Prentice-Hall.

Staples, R. (1989). Changes in Black family structure: The conflict between family ideology and structural conditions. In B. J. Risman & P. Schwartz (Eds.), *Gender in intimate relationships: A macrostructural approach* (pp. 235-244). Belmont, CA: Wadsworth.

Staples, R., & Johnson, L. B. (1993). *Black families at the crossroads: Challenges and prospects.* San Francisco: Jossey-Bass.

Staples, R., & Mirande, A. (1980). Racial and cultural variations among American families: A decennial review of the literature of minority families. *Journal of Marriage and the Family, 42*(4), 157-173.

Stimpson, C. R. (1980). The new scholarship about women: The state of the art. *Annals of Scholarship: Metastudies of the Humanities and Social Sciences, 2,* 2-14.

Sudarkasa, N. (1981). Interpreting the African heritage in Afro-American family organization. In H. P. McAdoo (Ed.), *Black families* (pp. 37-53). Beverly Hills, CA: Sage.

Sussman, M. B. (1965). Relationships of adult children with their parents in the United States. In E. Shanas & G. F. Streib (Eds.), *Social structure and the family: Generational relations* (pp. 62-92). Englewood Cliffs, NJ: Prentice-Hall.

Sussman, M. B., & Burchinal, L. (1962). Kin family network: Unheralded structure in current conceptualizations of family functioning. *Marriage and Family Living, 24,* 231-246.

Sweet, J., Bumpass, L., & Call, V. (1988). *The design and content of the National Survey of Families and Households* (NSFH Working Paper No. 1). Madison: University of Wisconsin, Center for Demography and Ecology.

Taylor, R. J. (1985). The extended family as a source of support to elderly Blacks. *The Gerontologist, 25,* 488-495.

Taylor, R. J. (1986). Receipt of support from family among Black Americans demographic and familial differences. *Journal of Marriage and the Family, 48,* 67-77.

Tienda, M., & Angel, R. (1982). Headship and household composition among Blacks, Hispanics, and other Whites. *Social Forces, 61,* 508-530.

Tolnay, S. E. (1983, Winter). Fertility of southern Black farmers in 1900: Evidence and speculation. *Journal of Family History,* pp. 314-332.

Torres-Matrullo, C. (1976). Acculturation and psychopathology among Puerto Rican women in mainland United States. *American Journal of Orthopsychiatry, 46,* 710-719.

Treiman, D. J., & Hartmann, H. (1981). *Women, work, and wages: Equal pay for jobs of equal value.* Washington, DC: National Academy Press.

U.S. Bureau of the Census. (1985). Characteristics of the population below the poverty level, 1983. *Current Population Reports* (Series P-60, No. 147). Washington, DC: Government Printing Office.

U.S. National Center for Health Statistics. (1990). *Morbidity and mortality weekly report 42(20).* Washington, DC: Government Printing Office.

Wagner, R. M., & Schaffer, D. M. (1980). Social networks and survival strategies: An exploratory study of Mexican American, Black, and Anglo female family heads in San Jose, California. In M. Melville (Ed.), *Twice a minority: Mexican American women* (pp. 173-190). St. Louis, MO: C. V. Mosby.

Walker, H. (1988). Black-White differences in marriage and family patterns. In S. M. Dornbush & M. H. Stroeber (Eds.), *Feminism children and the new families* (pp. 87-112). New York: Guilford.

Weber, M. (1994). Objectivity in social science. In W. Heydebrand (Ed.), *Max Weber: Sociological writings* (pp. 248-259). New York: Continuum.

White, L. K., & Peterson, D. (1995). The retreat from marriage: Its effects on unmarried children's exchange with parents. *Journal of Marriage and the Family, 57,* 428-434.

White, L. K., & Riedmann, A. (1992). Ties among adult siblings. *Social Forces, 71,* 85-102.

Williams, N. (1990). *The Mexican American family: Tradition and change.* New York: General Hall.

Wilson, W. J. (1987). *The truly disadvantaged: The inner city, the underclass, and public policy.* Chicago: University of Chicago Press.

Wilson, W. J. (1991). Studying inner-city social dislocations: The challenge of public agenda research, 1990 Presidential Address. *American Sociological Review, 56,* 1-14.

Ybarra, L. (1983). Empirical and theoretical developments in the study of Chicano families. In A. Valdez & A. Camarillo (Eds.), *The state of Chicano research on family, labor, and migration: Proceedings of the First Stanford Symposium on Chicano Research and Public Policy* (pp. 91-110). Stanford, CA: Stanford Center for Chicano Research.

Young, V. (1970). Family and childhood in a southern Negro community. *American Anthropologist, 72,* 269-288.

Zavella, P. (1987). *Women's work & Chicano families: Cannery workers of the Santa Clara valley.* New York: Cornell University Press.

Zinn, M. B. (1979). Chicano family research: Conceptual distortions and alternative directions. *Journal of Ethnic Studies,* 7(3), 58-71.

Zinn, M. B. (1982a). Review essay: Mexican American women in the social sciences. *Signs, 8,* 259-272.

Zinn, M. B. (1982b). Urban kinship and Midwest Chicano families: Evidence in support of revision. *De Colores: Journal of Chicano Expression and Thought,* 6(1,2), 85-98.

Zinn, M. B. (1987). Structural transformation and minority families. In L. Beneria & C. R. Stimpson (Eds.), *Women, households, and the economy* (pp. 155-171). New Brunswick, NJ: Rutgers University Press.

Zinn, M. B. (1989). Family, race, and poverty in the eighties. *Signs, 14,* 856-874.

Zinn, M. B. (1990). Family, feminism, and race in America. *Gender & Society, 4,* 68-82.

Zinn, M. B., & Dill, B. T. (1994). *Women of color in U.S. society.* Philadelphia: Temple University Press.

Zussman, R. (1987). Work and family in the new middle class. In N. Gerstel & H. E. Gross (Eds.), *Families and work* (pp. 338-346). Philadelphia: Temple University Press.

# Index

# About the Author

**Anne R. Roschelle** is Assistant Professor of Sociology and Director of the Women's Studies Program at the University of San Francisco. She received her Ph.D. in sociology from the State University of New York at Albany. The analytical framework of her research and teaching focuses on the intersection of race, class, and gender. She has conducted workshops on integrating race, class, and gender into the curriculum and is on the Editorial Board of the journal *Race, Gender, & Class in the World Cultures.* Her current research involves qualitative analysis of homeless and formerly homeless families in the San Francisco Bay Area.